THE

COMMONWEALTH

OF LEARNING

Henry Steele Commager

1817

HARPER & ROW, PUBLISHERS
NEW YORK, EVANSTON,
AND LONDON

THE COMMONWEALTH OF LEARNING
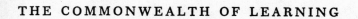

To Calvin Plimpton
With Affection

CONTENTS

PART III. *Aspects of Academic Freedom*

FOREWORD

The twenty-some essays on American education which now reappear in this book are, for the most part, the product of the past ten or twelve years. Though the educational scene has changed rapidly, even convulsively, in these years, I find—perhaps too readily—that much of what I have argued and advocated over the past decade is still relevant, and some of it prophetic. These essays explore a variety of subjects, from children's literature and the McGuffey Readers to the nature of the American University, and of academic freedom; if they do not have a unity of theme they do have, I trust, the harmony of a reasonably consistent point of view.

The selection and much of the editing of these essays has been done by my son, Professor Steele Commager, of Columbia University; I am deeply grateful both for his willingness to undertake this chore and for the skill and acumen he has brought to its performance. Most of the essays which appeared originally as articles have been reprinted pretty much in their original form; those which emerged as lectures have been subjected to that literary revision which is almost invariably called for in translating the spoken to the written word. Inevitably in a collection of this kind, written over a span of years and addressed to diverse audiences, there are repetitions of ideas, and occasionally of phrases. I have tried to eliminate verbal repetitions where that was possible, but I could not—nor indeed would I—avoid recurrence to central themes and fundamental ideas in my thinking about education.

I am grateful to the editors of the *Saturday Review, The New York Times Magazine,* and other journals, for their willingness to let me reprint material which first appeared in their publications.

HENRY STEELE COMMAGER

Amherst, 1968

PART I

The School

THE AMERICAN
HIGH SCHOOL

1

It is not chance that the prodigious issue of racial equality should have come to a boil in a case called *Brown* v. *Board of Education* and that it should have boiled over, as it were, in Little Rock High School. Even the most ardent critic of the Supreme Court would not take issue with the *obiter dicta* of the Brown case:

> Today education is perhaps the most important function of the state and local governments. Compulsory school attendance laws and the great expenditures for education both demonstrate our recognition of the importance of education in our democratic society. It is required in the performance of our most basic public responsibilities. . . . It is the very foundation of good citizenship. Today it is a principal instrument in awakening the child to cultural values, in preparing him for later professional training, and in helping him to adjust normally to his environment. In these days it is doubtful that any child may reasonably be expected to succeed in life if he is denied the opportunity of an education. [347 U.S. at 493.]

This argument, with its brief but comprehensive references to the relation of education to citizenship, culture, special skills, and social adjustment, is an echo of a long series of statements, proclamations, and arguments that began in the 1630's and have re-

The School Review, Spring, 1958.

echoed down the corridors of our history. It takes us back to the justification of the School Act of 1642, "that learning which may be profitable to the commonwealth," and the Act of 1647, "that learning may not be buried in the graves of our fathers in the church and commonwealth," and the commitment to education, not for narrow religious, but for broad commonwealth, purposes throughout the history of the Bay Colony. It found expression, particularly, in the Revolutionary generation: no body of nation makers were ever so conscious of the role that education should play as were the American Founding Fathers.

The characteristic features of the American educational system emerged early and were in large part the product, or the accident, of circumstances and of environment. By the time the high school made its appearance on the educational landscape, the pattern was pretty well fixed: pluralism, or local rather than centralized control of education; secularism, or separation from religious control; a general or liberal rather than a vocational education; and an education of the general populace rather than of the elite.

If we can, formally, date elementary education from the Massachusetts Act of 1642, we can date the high school from the Massachusetts Law of 1827, although both laws were ineffective for a long time. Thus the formal advent of the high school came late in our educational system. In fact, it came a good deal later than these dates would indicate, for not until 1864 did New York State require the maintenance of high schools, and as late as 1890 there were only 2,526 public high schools in the entire nation (this in a population of 63,000,000).

Yet recent as is the high school on the American educational scene, it is, by comparison with the scene abroad, almost a venerable institution. To be sure, there had been schools called "high" in England as early as the fourteenth century (in Exeter, for example, in 1313), and our own earliest high schools took their name from the high schools of Edinburgh and Glasgow. These were not high schools in our meaning of the word, merely the principal schools, and not until well into the twentieth century did any European country provide an effective system of free public secondary education for all who desired it. Thus, at the beginning of this century, only 109,000 pupils attended the secondary schools of Britain, and not until 1907 was provision made for secondary education for those unable to pay the ordinary fees. Only since the Second World War has Britain begun to provide for its fourteen- to eighteen-year-olds as adequately as the United States did sixty or seventy years ago. And what is true of Britain is true of all Continental countries, except possibly Holland, Switzerland, and the Scandinavian nations.

The American high school, then, was the pioneer—the pioneer not only in time but in program as well—and, if older European nations do not borrow heavily from our experience, many of the new nations outside Europe do. In the comprehensive high school, the amalgamation of preparation for college and for work, the openness of the curriculum and of the whole academic course (the easy, almost unconscious merging into college), the emphasis on doing in the processes of learning, on student government and student activities and in coeducation—in all these the American high school has been a pioneer.

It is the most hackneyed of observations that schools are a function of society, but we should keep in mind that, as American society differed profoundly from European in the eighteenth and the early nineteenth centuries, the functions we imposed upon schools differed from those which older societies imposed upon their schools. The story is familiar, how, especially in the nineteenth century, we required our schools to train citizens competent to govern themselves (a requirement not urgent in the Old World), to absorb and Americanize millions of newcomers from the Old World and elsewhere, to encourage and strengthen national unity, and to teach the habits and practices of democracy and equality and religious tolerance.

Looking back on the American experience in the perspective of a century or so (about the time we have been at the job of comprehensive education), we cannot but be impressed that we have managed so well in so short a time. If we look only to the educational achievement, we see that we have provided more education to a larger portion of society than has any other country in history; we have built a magnificent physical plant and equipped it with educational apparatus, including gymnasiums and school libraries; we have supplied more than one million teachers—and who will deny that they are better prepared for their jobs than were the teachers of a half century or a century ago? If emphasis seems to be laid too heavily on quantity, may we not add that, in the crisis of World War II and its aftermath, the products of the American school system compared favorably with the products of German or French school systems both in competence and in judgment?

As schools are commonly blamed for the failings or inadequacies of society, perhaps it is not unfair to give them some credit for the larger successes and achievements. After all, the products of the American educational system succeeded in a great many things which involve intelligence and judgment. They established a nation and held it together, expanding thirteen to fifty states with less difficulty than England had with Ireland alone in the same period. They made democracy work reasonably well and did not gratify the expectations of those who were so sure that a majority would inevitably exercise tyranny over minorities. They elected mediocre Presidents, but never a wicked or a dangerous one. They never yielded to a military dictator. They settled all their problems, but one, by compromise and concession instead of by violence (and perhaps that one, slavery, could not be solved by compromise). They adjusted themselves speedily to their responsibilities as a world power. These are not accomplishments that can be confidently traced to the educational system, but it would be absurd to deny that the schools contributed to them.

Not only do our schools deserve some credit for these accomplishments; they deserve some credit for the things they have avoided. Much of our history is, in a sense, an achievement in avoidance—nationalism without *Nationalismus*, world power without imperialism,* majority rule without majority tyranny, capitalism without class warfare, and so on.

The schools, too, have somehow managed to avoid many of the dangers that might have worked irreparable harm to our social or intellectual fabric. They began in New England as exponents of a particular religion but avoided religious fanaticism or too intimate

* It is no longer certain that we can claim immunity from imperialism.

a dependence on the church even in the Colonial period. Since that time, public schools have had no religious dependence, and even private schools have been open to children of all faiths. Yet as late as the 1870's a Catholic could not attend Oxford or Cambridge University, and Leslie Stephen severed his connection with Cambridge because he could not subscribe to the Thirty-nine Articles.

Though required to take all comers, mass education has not meant a watering-down of the intellectual content of learning or a serious vulgarization of culture. If the American high school does not do as good a job in formal education as the English public school, the French *lycée*, and the German *Gymnasium*, it is part of an educational process which eventually goes as high here as does any other in the world.

Though the tasks that have confronted Americans—and that have appealed for educational support—have been intensely practical, there has not been an overemphasis on vocational education, a rejection of humanism, or even an abandonment of education as was threatened by some of the enthusiasts of the Revolutionary period.

Though few societies have displayed greater differences and divisions than the American, our schools have not accentuated, but, except in the South, have mitigated, these differences educationally. Except for racial segregation in the South—a very large exception to be sure—we have not distinguished in our high schools between the many who are called and the few who are chosen, as is still the practice in almost all European countries.

Though upon the schools has been placed heavy responsibility for encouraging national unity and inculcating pride in the history and traditions of the nation, the schools have not been instruments of nationalism or of chauvinism, nor have they, except in the pre-war South, allowed themselves to become instruments of the state.

Keep in mind that the school has never been a merely passive agent in the process of serving the needs of our society. Indeed, as a result of the peculiar circumstances of American life, schools have played a somewhat more active role here than elsewhere in setting standards and creating social patterns: first, because almost from the beginnings of our national history education has been a secular religion; second, because the schools furnished perhaps the largest and the most familiar framework of experience to a heterogeneous and fluctuating population, and the tendency was strong to adjust to the school; and, third, because in the nineteenth and much of the twentieth century the school, by giving each generation of young a better education than their parents had enjoyed, set standards for the parents and persuaded the adult world to yield to those standards and adjust to those demands. In most societies of the Old World (as in more primitive societies), each generation tends to have about the same educational experience as did their parents: the children of those who have not gone to secondary school do not themselves go to secondary schools; the children of those who have not gone to a university do not ordinarily go to a university. But in American society it has almost always been the other way around. Here, in the game of "schoolmanship," the young know all the ploys and have their elders at a disadvantage. This is one of the explanations of that habit which Europeans find so difficult to understand—the grownups' habit of yielding to the standards, demands, and expectations of their children and conforming to the notions brought home from school.

Now our entire educational system, but especially our high schools, has entered, or is in process of entering, a new era—an era which demands new things of the school and requires new things from the school. It is useless to intone the old litanies. The schools are called upon to play a role closer, perhaps, to that imagined for the academies and colleges in the eighteenth century than to that which they did play in the nineteenth. What are the considerations and conditions which require a rethinking of the functions of our schools?

First, our schools are, in a sense, the victims of their own success. If they are not precisely buried beneath the ruins of their own triumph, they are conditioned and committed by their achievements. Many of what we may call the nonacademic functions of the schools in the nineteenth and early twentieth centuries have been performed. Thus the school no longer bears the heavy responsibilities in the nonacademic realm that it did in the nineteenth century. It now shares with many other agencies responsibility for nonacademic educational activities, and is in a better position to devote its attention to what we may call academic functions than ever before. Schools do not need to educate parents through their children, as they once did; and the parents themselves not only are more sophisticated but have more leisure time for their own responsibilities and duties than they had in the nineteenth century. Most important, scores of other agencies are now doing what the school did in the nineteenth century: the press, radio, television, movies, organizations like the Boy Scouts and Girl Scouts, the churches in their enlarged social functions, and others.

Indeed, insofar as schools are agents of social development as well as instruments of society, they have a duty to resist, rather than to yield to, many community pressures. Because schools are a function of society, a great many educators think it the primary duty of the schools—and especially the high school, which here occupies a crucial position—to "adapt" the young to the society in which they are to live. Needless to say, if each generation of young is merely fitted to the existing order of things, we shall end up with a Byzantine, not a Western, civilization. A dynamic society cannot stay dynamic if the existing order fixes the standards to which all must conform and into which all must be fitted.

Schools are a part of society, but should not be a mirror of society. They should offer not a repetition of experience but a challenge to, and an extension of, experience. At their best, they are not a tranquilizer but a conscience for society. Yet at a time when schools are in a stronger position to emancipate themselves from community pressures and the necessity of challenge and experimentation is perhaps more urgent than ever before, our schools seem to make a fetish of adaptation and conformity. When almost every agency proclaims the merits of "private enterprise," the schools, all too often, weakly yield to pressures from filiopietistic or business organizations and beat the academic drum for private enterprise. When almost everybody reads *Reader's Digest* and *Life* and *Look* and *Newsweek* anyway, and the young can be trusted to see them outside the schoolroom, students are fobbed off with these same magazines in the school library, rather than being exposed to less popular and less readily available magazines which they may otherwise never come to know. When the discussion of current affairs commands the daily press, the radio and television, and most conversation at home, schools, instead of diverting the young to a contemplation of less immediate affairs, the history of Greece and Rome, let us say, or of the Renaissance, concentrate on current affairs. At a time when society is perhaps overly concerned with material things—business and industry, roads and automobiles—when things are in the saddle and ride mankind, the schools, too, emphasize the practical and the material rather than the intellectual or the aesthetic.

At a time when almost all the institutions of society are in a conspiracy to suppress individuality and heterodoxy and eccentricity and to produce organization men and women, the schools, too, put the hobbyhorse away in the basement and organize group games, emphasize at every point (but nowhere more than in the high school) the virtues of conformity and adaptability in order to produce organization boys and girls. When society hangs breathless on the prowess of famous athletes, schools, too, celebrate competitive sports. When the climate of nationalism is pervasive and almost stifling and a hundred agencies proclaim, day and night, the superiority of everything American to everything non-American, the schools, instead of encouraging the young to challenge shibboleths and develop broader and more spiritual loyalties, join in the parade of ostentatious patriotism. When it is regarded as good manners, almost everywhere, to avoid controversy and blur differences of opinion, schools, instead of preparing the young for a world of controversy, discourage sharp differences of opinion and meaningful discussion, in order to achieve general agreement and contentment.

In this connection it is appropriate to observe that, whatever difficulties schools may have in getting enough money for their needs, they no longer have the elementary task of winning or enlisting community support to their very existence that they had in the nineteenth century and need not make convulsive efforts to win that support. Everybody takes for granted, now, the necessity of free public education through the high school and even the university; everybody takes for granted the desirability of adequate classrooms, libraries, laboratories, playing fields, and well-trained teachers. Yet in one notorious realm our schools are still engaged in enlisting community interest and support on an elementary level and with crude techniques. I refer, of course, to the emphasis on competitive athletics. Clearly sports have other functions than that of exciting community interest—to teach fair play, provide physical training to all, furnish a healthy outlet for the competitive spirit, and provide areas in which success and prestige are independent of wealth or family. But these purposes are rather frustrated by our current emphasis on sports than advanced by it. A system where a handful of boys devote most of their energies to football, while five thousand students sit in stands and watch them, is not designed to provide sound bodies to go with sound minds. A system where victory counts for more than the game is not conducive to encouraging stands of fair play (and those standards have gone steadily down in the last quarter century). Neither wealth nor family insures prestige in our schools today, and the alternative of the playing field is by no means as important as it was. As for the safety valve of competition, our need is rather to restore competition in the classroom and to discourage it on the playing field and elsewhere.

Just as we have not fully assimilated the fact that schools now have community support and that they do not need to use the playing fields as they did a generation ago, so we have not assimilated the fact that the problem of what we may roughly call Americanization has likewise been solved except for the Negro. In the nineteenth and early twentieth century—up to 1914, in fact—when our schools were confronted with the children of immigrants and of freedmen having no knowledge of American history or institutions, and when the problem of creating a harmonious society out of heterogeneous racial and religious elements was a pressing one, the schools were properly required to take on large responsibilities here. That particular problem is no longer acute. Yet just at a time when there are scores of other media to inculcate a knowledge of and pride in America, and when the greatest need is to understand

other countries and other cultures, high schools everywhere concentrate heavily on the teaching of American history, civics, and
literature. All too often, emphasis on the study of things American
has wrong motives and wrong objectives. The motives are chauvinistic; the objectives, parochial. The young do not need more nationalism, but less. They do not need less study of Greece and
Rome, Britain, Canada and South America, and France, but more.
They do not need to be confirmed in their instinctive belief that
fifty years of American literature is worth a cycle of English or
French, nor do they need to have their enthusiasm for something
called vaguely "the American system" whipped up artificially.
There is no reason to suppose that the compulsory study of American history at various levels in the elementary school and again in
the high school necessarily makes good citizens. We might all remember that the great men who won our independence and laid
the foundations for our Republic—Washington, Jefferson, Adams,
Hamilton, Madison, Mason, and others—were trained on the histories of Greece, Rome, and Britain.

Educators seem not to have adjusted themselves to the significance of the most elementary educational statistics. In 1890, when
our population was 63 million, our college population was 122,000.
Since then, the population has increased almost threefold, the college and university population, 26 times!* Add to this the fact that
perhaps 25 or 30 million Americans participate in some adult-edu-
cation programs, and the conclusion is inescapable that the high
school is no longer our educational terminus. A single generation
has seen a revolution: the college today occupies the place which
the high school occupied in 1912.

In a general way, we all know what is happening, but we still
use the high schools as if they were, in a sense, our last chance. An
ever-increasing number of our young people will have three or four
years in which to learn many of the things that high schools now try
to inculcate. They are not under such heavy pressure as they were
to learn manners and social dancing, typewriting and driving, to

* These statistics are already out of date. As of 1967 total population has
increased more than threefold, and college and university population forty-
five times!

enjoy competitive sports and adult social life, to learn the other nonacademic subjects to which schools gave, and give, their attention. Some of these things they can be expected to learn in college. Some should be taught in the elementary school; or by the many other agencies now engaged in assuring that the young are well adjusted. Now that most adults enjoy a thirty-five- or forty-hour week and that labor-saving devices have shortened the hours devoted to housework, perhaps even parents can resume their traditional tasks of teaching their young some of the things they should know! It is a paradox that, just when technology has made it possible for parents to spend far more of their time in training their children than ever before, they should foist so much responsibility on schools. There is more justification for using the crucial high-school years for training the mind than there was in the nineteenth or early twentieth century and less justification for not doing so.

There is an additional argument here for concentration on academic activities, and even on rather traditional academic interests. On the one hand, modern technology and automation have simplified the purely mechanical tasks of industry to the point where any reasonably intelligent young man or woman can learn what he needs to know in a few months. On the other hand, the demands of the professions are so large and elaborate that, more and more, the professional schools prefer that the young learn special skills in college or in the professional school rather than in the high school. Industry, business, college, and professional schools unite in urging the desirability of thorough training in elementary skills in the high schools of today and tomorrow, and the key word here is "thorough."

Finally, it is possible that abandonment of many of the extracurricular activities of the high school and greater concentration on academic activities might hasten one badly needed change: the reduction by one year, or more, of the time ordinarily devoted to preparation for college or for industry or business.

It was (characteristically) an American, John Fiske, who hit upon the important social law of the prolongation of infancy as one of the human habits that explains not only civilization but morality. Americans have, perhaps, carried the practice to excess. A rich nation can doubtless afford, financially, the prolongation of child-hood and youth well into the twenties, but a sensible people will not permit the growing waste of years and of talents involved in our current educational practices.

It is in one sense an illusion that life is growing longer. It is, to be sure, growing longer at one end (for those who survive), but there is little evidence that the span of years available for work or for public service has lengthened appreciably since the eighteenth century. Men live longer but retire or are put on the shelf in their fifties or sixties. On the other hand, instead of plunging into their profession or into public service at twenty, they are not ready until they are thirty. The doctor, the lawyer, the school administrator, the psychiatrist, the scholar, the statesman are rarely able to get under way until they are thirtyish. And all of us are familiar with the growing habit of turning preparation for a career into a career and of regarding a writer, a scholar, or a statesman who is only forty as something of an infant prodigy.

We are, in a sense, prisoners of the nineteenth-century habit of thinking of education in terms of twelve years. But there is nothing sacred about twelve years, whether divided into eight and four or into six and three and three. Nor, for that matter, is there anything sacred about the additional four years we customarily devote to the university. Other societies have not allowed themselves to be-come bemused by this chronological arrangement and have not suffered for their independence. There is every reason now for speeding up the educational process and getting young men and women into productive careers as rapidly as possible. Military serv-ice exacts one or two years of the lives of many of our young men; the demands of professional training are ever more time-consum-ing; the nation desperately needs the talents and the energy of the young; the costs that society has to pay for maintaining them in school are immense, and they themselves, in revolt against the prolongation of infancy, are marrying and rearing families in their early twenties. How much longer can we go on accepting four years as the norm for secondary education?

As the high school is released, or releases itself, from responsibil-ity for many of the extraneous duties placed upon it in the nineteenth century, it can devote more time to academic duties. As teachers are better trained, students better prepared, and new techniques for speeding up the teaching and learning processes developed, the high schools may be expected to do in three years, perhaps less, what they now do in four.

I suspect that, if they did, many students who now go on to college would enter with more enthusiasm for learning than they now have and that many young persons who find it necessary to go to work at eighteen would be able to enjoy one or two years of college work—and perhaps find the experience so delightful that they would somehow manage to stay on.* General conclusions cannot be drawn from special cases, but it is at least interesting that Jefferson graduated from William and Mary at nineteen, Gouverneur Morris from King's College at sixteen, and Jay at nineteen, Hancock and Samuel Adams and Emerson from Harvard at eighteen and Charles W. Eliot at nineteen, while the first president of the University of Chicago, William Rainey Harper, graduated from Muskingum College at sixteen and received his Ph.D. from Yale when he was nineteen!

Educators, then, should emancipate themselves from the notion that they are to reflect, rather than to guide, the interests of society; that they must cater to community prejudices as well as to community interests; that they are somehow bound by the educational mechanics of the past. They should emancipate themselves, too, from one fear whose roots go back into the Old World—the fear of becoming financially involved with the national government.†

For reasons familiar to all of us, our schools were, from the beginning, controlled by district, town, and state rather than by the nation. This was, and is, all to the good, for local control made it impossible for any government or any party to use the schools of

---

* The spectacular development of the community college in the past decade confirms this prediction.

† So rapidly does opinion change in America that these observations are already dated, but I have left them in just to dramatize the swiftness with which opinion can change. In the forties and fifties I was frequently warned that to discuss the propriety of federal aid to education would so antagonize local opinion as to nullify whatever I might otherwise say. I remember especially being warned in Indianapolis that it would be fatal to my usefulness even to bring up the possibility of federal aid to public education in that state.

the nation as a political instrument. We have assumed that local and state, or private, control cannot be retained if the national government helps foot the bill. This assumption is both illogical and pernicious. It is illogical because it flies in the face of our experience with national support to state universities and to agricultural experiment stations, as well as to a series of scholarly, scientific, and artistic enterprises, such as the Library of Congress, the National Gallery, the U.S. Geological Survey, the Smithsonian Institution, and others—all of them largely dependent on federal money but happily free from federal control of their substantive activities.

It is pernicious because it inevitably condemns large groups of our children—those who reside in poor states—to an education inferior to that enjoyed by children in rich states. Nor is this a matter that concerns the states alone. The vote of a badly educated young man or woman counts just as much as the vote of a well-educated young man or woman; both alike vote for congressmen and for President and therefore decide national questions of concern to everyone.

Fear of political interference in education is deep-seated and understandable. But so far as the record shows, the national government has not been more guilty than have local or state governments of interference with intellectual freedom; it has been less guilty. The task of educators is not to bewail the inadequacy of local funds and fight the threat of federal appropriations, which may carry with them improper controls, but to find whatever money is necessary to do the job of education as it should be done and educate legislators and administrators, local and national alike, to the perils of improper interference.

One final suggestion. In the generation after 1830 a large number of American educators—notably Horace Mann, Henry Barnard, Calvin Stowe—streamed over to Germany and France to study educational practices there and came home to apply the lessons that they had learned to conditions in this country, particularly to elementary education. Again, in the period from 1880 to 1900, American educators turned to Europe, this time to study higher education, and again they brought back much of value—

and some things of little value. Today we have much to learn about secondary education, especially from Britain, the Scandinavian countries, Switzerland, and Holland—countries with democratic education systems closer to ours than are the systems of Germany or France, and with social institutions much like ours. Perhaps some future Mann or Barnard, some future Eliot or Gilman, will bring to secondary education, as these did to the elementary and the advanced levels, the benefit of relevant European experience.

Writing in the 1830's when Horace Mann and Henry Barnard, Thaddeus Stevens and John D. Pierce, Mary Lyon and Catherine Beecher were just beginning their great work, and the high school was still an experiment, Alexis de Tocqueville said: "In that land the great experiment was to be made by civilized man, of the attempt to construct society upon a new basis, and it was there, for the first time, that theories hitherto unknown, or deemed impracticable, were to exhibit a spectacle for which the world had not been prepared by the history of the past."

And at almost the same time Horace Mann, commenting on the "Olde Deluder Satan Law" of the Bay Colony, observed: "As a matter of *fact* it had no precedent in world history, and as a *theory* it could have been refuted and silenced by a more formidable array of argument and experience than was ever marshaled against any other institution of human origin. But time has ratified its soundness."

We, too, can say that time has ratified the soundness of the American experiment in mass education, even to our own time, and that nations whose leaders a century ago had only contempt for that experiment imitate it today. The experiment was successful because the men and the women who launched it and guided it consulted their hopes and not their fears. It was successful because they and their successors gambled on the intelligence and the virtue of the people. It was successful because, in the light of conditions which obtained in the nineteenth century, they were bold, generous, and imaginative.

As the high school enters a new era—an era in which most of its graduates will go on to advanced education, and in which its

products will be citizens of the most influential of world powers—
we should make sure that it is not too timid to challenge its own
society, that it is not too conservative to break with its own habits,
that it is not too wanting in faith to have confidence in the integrity
of its own government.

HOW FAR SHOULD
SCHOOLING GO?

2

One of the things that has struck all of us, again and again, in recent years, is the way in which the obvious and the inevitable seem to take us by surprise. We have known for years that our population was moving to the cities and that our cities were not properly organized or governed to cope with the new population and its problems, but we have heretofore done nothing about it. We have known for years that the toll of our automobiles is as high as that of a major war—something like fifty thousand lives a year —and that this recurrent catastrophe is caused by factors that are avoidable, but we have as yet done nothing about it. We have known for years that China would someday have the atomic bomb, but when that day arrived we acted as if it had all been the best-kept secret in history and as if we had to readjust our thinking all at once.

We have known for years, too, that the baby-boom that set in shortly after World War II would surely reach the schools and the colleges, but we permitted ourselves to drift along and be taken by

Address at Conference on Two More Years of Schooling, San Juan, November, 1964. Reprinted in *Universal Higher Education*, edited by Earl McGrath, McGraw-Hill, Inc., 1966, used with permission of the publisher.

surprise with each new demand upon our educational enterprise, until now, twenty years after the war, we find ourselves unprepared to cope with even the material problems of education.

It is reassuring, then, that the groups and skills represented here should be taking thought for what is pretty clearly ahead in the next decade—the extension of schooling for almost everyone for an additional two years.

Let us consider the historical background and the implications of this prospect.

I

Let us begin this inquiry with the observation that the eighteenth century took two things for granted about human nature: first, it was corrupt; and second, it was universal. Man was everywhere corrupt and depraved, a creature of interests and passions, ambition and greed, selfishness and envy; man was everywhere irrational. This had always been true—history proved that—and it would always be true, for human nature did not change. That was the second great principle to which almost everyone subscribed: human nature was the same everywhere and had always been the same. It was for this reason that the philosophers and the historians were so ready to draw their illustrations from Persia or Greece, the South Sea Islands or the forests of Canada, Italy, France, or England—it was all one. There was no reason to suppose that nature would change and no reason to suppose that man would change. These were the fixed elements with which the philosophers started, and it was unsafe ever to get very far away from them.

Yet all was not desperate, not by any means, for the doctrine that man was everywhere the same, and everywhere ruled by immutable laws of nature, had its encouraging aspect. Man was a child of nature, but he was also a child of reason, for reason was part of nature. Progress was possible—the eighteenth century had really invented that concept as we know it—but it was possible only within the accepted pattern, for clearly nothing could break the pattern of nature or even of history. Progress was to be achieved by conforming to nature and nature's laws—a familiar phrase even in the New World. Reason could discover these laws, and persuade man to conform to them. The prospect, to be sure, was not entirely encouraging (that was Voltaire's conclusion in *Candide*), for although the philosophers and scientists could discover the laws, rulers were singularly unprepared to conform to them.

This was, in substantial measure, the philosophy which Europeans brought with them to the New World, and which, as Americans, they were presumed to subscribe to in the eighteenth century. It was not a philosophy which encouraged the belief that the American experience would differ in any marked degree from the European, or that America's fate would be more benign than that of other nations. It was still the same universe, controlled by the same laws. The great chain of being obtained in the New World as in the Old, and man's place in it was of course the same. Human nature, too, remained stubbornly the same. That was what John Adams argued in his magisterial *Defence of the Constitutions;* that was what Hamilton made clear in *The Federalist Papers;* that was what a legion of statesmen asserted in their discussions of the new state and national constitutions. There might, to be sure, be some room for maneuver, but not enough to provide any basis for hope for revolutionary change.

Sometime in the eighteenth century a new theory emerged—one which we can, with some propriety, designate "American," perhaps the *first* American principle. We can call it, for convenience, the theory of environmentalism, or of change, or even of progress. It was this: man was not really either depraved or virtuous, but a creature of circumstances—a point of view which found support in the philosophy of "the Great Mr. Locke," and which seemed, besides, the common sense of the matter. Depravity, corruption, crime, vice, superstition, ignorance, folly—all these were products not of nature but of history, that is they were man-made, not God-made. Granted that in the Old World man appeared corrupt and ignorant, was that not because for centuries he had been weighed down by the tyranny of rulers, the might of soldiers, the superstition of priests; because for centuries he had been ground down in poverty, misery, and ignorance? Was it not because in the Old World man had never really been vouchsafed a chance to use those talents with which God and nature had endowed him?

But in the New World all this might be changed. For it was *really* a New World—it took a long time for that to sink in. Here, for perhaps the first time in modern history, man could escape the tyranny of the past, the tyranny of power, superstition, poverty, and ignorance. Here, for perhaps the first time, he could stand on his own feet, a free man exercising all his God-given faculties. Here there would be no tyranny of state, for he was the state; no tyranny of church, for he made the church; no tyranny of the military and of war, for there was no military, and the New World was to be free of those wars so long the curse of the Old. And there would be no tyranny of poverty, either, for no people in history had ever enjoyed such abundance—room enough, as Jefferson said, for our descendants to the thousandth and thousandth generation, and all enjoying the rich bounty of nature. All this promised to take care of a good part of the problem of depravity.

It did not, however, take care of the problems of ignorance and of folly. Those problems were to be taken care of by education. No wonder education so quickly became the American religion; no wonder all the Founding Fathers were educators—Franklin, Washington, John Adams, John Dickinson, Noah Webster, Richard Rush, and, above all, Thomas Jefferson. Education was to be the instrument of change—change of nature (science was to make that possible) and of human nature. Education was to be what religion had been in a less secular age—the chief instrument for the regeneration of the human race.

It is superfluous to elaborate on the interest, and the passion for education which animated the generation of the Founding Fathers. All remember how John Adams wrote provisions for education, and for the support of Harvard College, into his Constitution; all recall how Franklin and Dickinson and Benjamin Rush founded learned societies and colleges and libraries in that Pennsylvania which was the eighteenth-century utopia; all are familiar with the story of Jefferson's educational interests. How appropriate that the greatest of American democrats should also be the greatest of

American educators! And how touching was that provision written
into the Northwest Ordinance: "Religion, morality, and knowledge
being necessary to good government and the happiness of mankind, schools and the means of education shall forever be encouraged." Less familiar perhaps are some of the rapt poetic tributes to
the role of education in the New World: Joel Barlow's *Vision of
Columbus,* for example:

> In no blest land has science rear'd her fame
> And fixed so firm her wide extended reign;
> Each rustic here that turns the furrow'd soil,
> The maid, the youth, that ply mechanic toil,
> In freedom nurs'd, in useful arts inured,
> Know their just claims and see their rights secured.

There is that other Connecticut wit, Timothy Dwight:

> How bless'd this heaven distinguished land,
> Where schools in every hamlet stand:
> Far spread the beams of learning bright,
> And every child enjoys the light,
> At school, beneath a faithful guide,
> In teaching skill'd, of morals tried. . . .
> For on this microscopic plan
> If form'd the wise, the useful man,
> Let him a taste for books inspire,
> While you to nurse the young desire
> A social library procure
> And open knowledge to the poor.

How interesting that almost everyone, in Europe and America
alike, agreed that the American people were the most generally
enlightened on the globe, that here in these little American settle-
ments a larger proportion of the people were educated, read their
Bible, almanacs, and newspapers, than elsewhere on the globe.
How remarkable that this uprooted and transplanted people,
scattered along a far-flung frontier, should have created nine colleges before independence, and seven during the years of war and
postwar confusion. How extraordinary that Jefferson's principle
that self-government depended on an educated electorate should
have been vindicated with such unprecedented promptness: the
constituency was enlightened, and self-government worked. How

impressive the level of public discussion of great political questions such as independence, or the state and federal constitutions, in town meetings, state conventions, the Constitutional Convention, and the press. Imagine publishing *The Federalist Papers* in our newspapers today.

II

Obviously an education which was required to fit into some preexisting scheme of things, continue tradition, support the *status quo,* and to regenerate man and remake society would have to be new and different. From the beginning American education was rooted in Old World experience; how could it be otherwise? But from the beginning, too, it departed from that experience, and the divergence grew sharper with the passing years. To this day Americans expect their schools to do a very different job from that which Old World schools perform; indeed, they expect schools to do almost everything, which is one reason that they are continually disappointed in them.

In a broad sense the schools were to be the chief instruments for change in the New World, change in man and change in society. They were to be the chief instruments for the growth of democracy, equality, and freedom, and of morality as well. In many quarters they are still regarded in this light; that is one reason it seems to be assumed that if there are no prayers in school, prayer is at an end, that if God is banished from the school, then God is leaving us.

American schools were, and are, required to do a hundred and one things not expected of European schools: this is an old story, and a current one. Imagine a French *lycée* teaching driver training; imagine a German *Gymnasium* teaching social dancing; imagine a Swedish high school teaching basketball, or cheerleadership!

The contrast between Old World and New grows sharper the higher we go on the educational ladder. So much was expected of the colleges and universities that they came in time not to be merely an American version of a familiar European institution, but a new kind of institution: a multiversity, not a university (I know I am using the terms wrongly but so did Clark Kerr*), an institution whose business it is to supply all the needs of society and to provide training in all the skills which society thinks it needs, from mastery of atomic physics to mastery of hotel operations, from knowledge of Greek literature to knowledge of advertising copy, from training for medicine or law to training for athletic directorships. How appropriate it was that one of the greatest of American educational statesmen, Andrew D. White, should undertake to create a university where any person could study any subject. To the European, with his traditional standards of what constituted the domain of the university, much of this was absurd; to the American, impatient with traditional restrictions, the American policies were the common sense of the matter. Is it not irrelevant to add that European universities today (like European schools) are adapting themselves, increasingly, to the American model rather than the other way around.

What Americans recognized, almost by instinct, and what Europe is only slowly coming to recognize, is the immense range and variety of abilities necessary for the efficient functioning of modern society, and the potential role of schools and universities in providing these abilities. During most of the eighteenth and nineteenth centuries Europeans persisted in using their schools for the re-creation of traditional skills and the perpetuation of inherited values. In the nineteenth century the Germans added research but even this was to be confined to orthodox subjects. The university was, in very fact, the citadel of tradition, its function to preserve the past and to train the young along familiar lines. Americans, most of whom (after 1640) came from groups unfamiliar with classical academic patterns, and whose society and economy demanded very different patterns, had no misgivings about using their schools and universities to do the things they wanted done, no misgivings and no embarrassments. How illuminating that almost from the beginning American colleges were more concerned to attract a wide cross-section of society than to preserve religious orthodoxy,

* *"University"* does not mean an institution devoted to a single subject or profession, but one open to all; in this context the term "multiversity" is a misleading play on words.

and that even Colonial colleges, like the College of New Jersey (Princeton) and Rhode Island (Brown), provided in their charters for representation from various religious denominations. Contrast this to Oxford and Cambridge University, where dissenters were rigorously excluded from the student body and faculty until the last quarter of the nineteenth century. How illuminating, too, that so many of the early American educators, like Franklin and Benjamin Rush, should have opposed the classical pattern of education and championed, even at this stage, education for commerce and business, while Oxford and Cambridge did not give up their Latin requirements until the 1950's.

There is, to be sure, a sobering qualification to our celebration of New World education. It is this: the Old World had, after all, any number of institutions to do the various tasks and supply the various skills required by its society, and did not have to rely wholly on schools and universities. It could allow the academy to continue in its ancient ways, and mostly did so, until the middle of the nineteenth century or later; it could permit the four faculties largely to monopolize university education; ignore much of modern science and almost all of modern technology; indulge the extravagance of academic resources concentrated, or wasted, on a very small segment of a social elite. After all, the court, the aristocracy, the church, the army and navy, the temples and inns of court, the museums, libraries, technical institutes, the highly structured society, and—in other areas—the merchant guilds, the great companies (who founded their own schools), the apprenticeship system, even—in ways not wholly duplicated in America—the family, with its traditions of authority and its close-knit social and business interrelationships—all these stood ready to prepare each new generation for its familiar functions and duties. If there was no education, excepting the everlasting discipline of drudgery, for farmers and laborers, there was general agreement that these classes had nothing to contribute and had no place in the educational scheme of things.

The situation in the New World was the opposite of this in almost every respect. Here there were few of those familiar institutions prepared to carry on the social arrangements of the past, and scarcely even communities, in the Old World sense of the term. Inevitably the schools were called on to do almost all the things that a score of institutions did abroad, and we have been calling on them for these services ever since. And here, too, in this new society, there were a great many more things to be done, in a rather simple way, practical and material things, as well as intellectual, scientific, and even moral things. Once again much of the burden for seeing that they were done was put on the schools and, a bit later, on colleges and universities. And here, finally, were no class distinctions, none that mattered anyway, except those of color, and the whole of the white population was supposed to be involved and absorbed in the educational enterprise.

All this is familiar. In America the school was called on to teach the elementary things which every European school would take for granted—a single language, for example. It was called on to teach those social habits and practices taught mostly by family and society in the Old World. It was called on to create or foment a sense of nationalism; that was familiar enough, in an overt way, in countries like France and Germany in the nineteenth century, but the American task was at once broader and more delicate. It was called on to teach morals, a subject which the Church and the family took care of in Europe. In many communities, particularly those with a substantial immigrant population, it was called on to teach, vicariously, the parents.

For these reasons, and others, American schools at almost every level early developed into general-purpose institutions. It is interesting that the term "general education" should have caught the fancy of Americans, and interesting, too, that it should harbor some of the ambiguities that Americans read into the word "university." Schools, and universities too, were called on to prepare the young for everything in general: for the professions, industry, farming, business, nursing, the stock market, marriage, citizenship, society, even for *life*. No other educational system on the globe is required to be quite this eclectic or this ambitious. The wonder is not that American schools so often fail, but that they so often succeed in these miscellaneous aims.

This eclectic program had important by-products. One of them, very much in the American grain, was that it did in fact raise the general level of education, and even of culture, if we may use that ambiguous word, with most unexpected consequences. Unexpected? That most perspicacious of observers, Tocqueville, in *Democracy in America*, foresaw what would happen, and rejoiced in it.

When I survey this countless multitude of beings, shaped in each other's likeness, amid whom nothing rises and nothing falls, the sight of such universal uniformity saddens and chills me, and I am tempted to regret that state of society which has ceased to be. When the world was full of men of great importance and extreme insignificance, of great wealth and extreme poverty, of great learning and extreme ignorance, I turned aside from the latter to fix my observation on the former alone, who gratified my sympathies. But I admit that this gratification arose from my own weakness; it is because I am unable to see at once all that is around me that I am allowed thus to select and separate the objects of my predilection from among so many others. Such is not the case with that Almighty and Eternal Being whose gaze necessarily includes the whole of created things and who surveys distinctly, though all at once, mankind and man.

We may naturally believe that it is not the singular prosperity of the few, but the greater well-being of all that is most pleasing in the sight of the Creator and Preserver of men. What appears to me to be man's decline is, to His eye, advancement; what afflicts me is acceptable to Him. A state of equality is perhaps less elevated, but it is more just: and its justice constitutes its greatness and its beauty. I would strive, then, to raise myself to this point of the divine contemplation and thence to view and to judge the concerns of men.*

Even now, more than a century after Tocqueville wrote, this point of view is not everywhere adopted, or taken for granted, and there are still those who fail to see either justice or beauty in the American attempt to lift the general level of culture by universal education, just as there will be those who will fail to see either justice or beauty in the proposals to expand education beyond its present boundaries and to extend it to millions still denied or deprived of its potentialities.

Another product, or by-product, of universal education was that

---

* Alexis de Tocqueville, *Democracy in America* (New York: Vintage Books, Random House, Inc., 1961), vol. II, chap. VII, pp. 350–351.

it did help discover talent among the "mute inglorious Miltons," and did encourage the most varied kinds of creativity.

To this day many Europeans, and, particularly, many English, cling to the notion that education—certainly "higher education" —should indeed be limited to a natural aristocracy, and that a natural aristocracy is, almost by definition, small. There are persuasive practical reasons why the English are reluctant to expand higher education, but behind and controlling these is the widespread conviction that there are not many young people who are capable of taking advantage of it. They are persuaded that their elitist educational system has worked well, and, though less confidently, that it will continue to work well; they look with grave misgivings on the American experiments in mass education and admonish each other to avoid the error of American ways. This is not the place to deal with the English view, but it is relevant to note that the United States was the first country to challenge it. The American theory is that gold is where you find it—in short, that talent is evenly distributed throughout the whole population, and that it is, on the whole, generously distributed. The American position is that talent is not something given, and fixed, but something that can be discovered, encouraged, and developed.

Of all educational philosophers it was the American Lester Ward who argued most persuasively this principle of the ubiquity and universality of talent, and the role of education and of the state in discovering and encouraging such talent. He was characteristically American in his own universality and his ambition. A poor boy who grew up on the Illinois and Iowa frontier, he had little formal education, and most of that bad, but it did not occur to him that this mischance should exclude him from the ranks of the learned, and he became in time perhaps the most deeply and variously learned man in America—botanist, geologist, paleontologist, and founder and leader of American sociology. He was at the same time one of the most original and profound of our educational philosophers, and takes rank here with such giants as Jefferson, Horace Mann, Jane Addams, and John Dewey. His philosophy, set forth first in *Dynamic Sociology* (1883), more elaborately in *The Psychic Factors of Civilization* a decade later, and then in

Applied Sociology (1906) is by now orthodox enough, at least in the United States. All progress, Ward insisted, comes through art, not nature—here we are back with the Founding Fathers and their rejection of fixed laws. Nature is wasteful, slow, and indifferent; man is economical: he speeds up the natural processes, and is himself inextricably involved in the process. Man has survived, and created civilization, by triumphing over nature. Indeed, civilization *is* the triumph of art over nature; it is, precisely, artificial. All civilization comes from the deliberate intervention by man in the processes of nature. Now what directs this intervention, and what assurance is there that it will be benevolent rather than malign? The answer is simple and unambiguous. Government directs the intervention—it is indeed organized intervention—and government is therefore the most important of man's instruments for creating civilization. And as for the assurance that intervention will be benevolent, that must come from education. The function of education is to achieve and prosper civilization. It is a function of any society, for on it depends survival and progress.

What this meant, as Ward never ceased to point out, was that society could not afford to waste any of its intellectual or psychic talents. Heretofore it had always done so, and one reason that progress had not advanced more rapidly was this waste. Ward was convinced, and on scientific grounds, that talent was to be found everywhere, and everywhere, too, in equal abundance—among the poor as among the rich, among Negroes as among whites, among the "perishing and dangerous classes" as among the respectable. Certainly it was to be found as richly among women as among men, indeed rather more among women than men; Ward's law of gynecocracy, or the natural superiority of the female over the male sex, took care of that! Ward rejected *in toto,* then, an elitist philosophy of education, as he rejected *in toto* the notion that government should play a merely passive role in civilization.

These are the principles on which most Americans acted, almost instinctively, from the beginning, and on which they still act, though with less confidence than in the past. A new society, one without the historic institutions of older societies, needs to find varied and disparate talents to do the most miscellaneous jobs.

That means that it must look everywhere for talent. The responsibility is social, that is to say governmental. If the talent can be
found, and utilized, there is some ground for hope that it may
suffice to prosper civilization; if it cannot, the prospect is bleak.

Of course, the country paid a price for this enterprise of educating almost everybody in almost everything, for using the educational establishment for broad social purposes, for rejecting Old
World concepts of culture and of an intellectual elite.

What specifically were some of the costs of this approach to
education? First, it meant that almost all education was to be the
same, and the tendency was (there were exceptions) to level down
rather than to level up. Second, this often meant low standards or
no perceptible standards in secondary or higher education. There
is no better illustration of this than the legal requirement which
still obtains in a good many states—Ohio and Missouri, for example
—that institutions of "higher" learning admit any graduate of a
state high school. Third, it meant that "formal" education was less
important than informal. The business of the high school and even
of college was almost incidentally to train the mind. It was, very
much, to "adapt" the young to their society, or to provide common
social experiences, or to train for jobs, or to serve as a marriage
mart. We may think this is a thing of the past, but only this year
[1965] a *New York Times* survey discovered that over 50 percent
of students planning to go on to college placed the social advantages of education first in the hierarchy of values to be derived
from college, and a substantial number placed the academic last.
Fourth, it encouraged the notion that schools exist in large part for
the benefit of the parents, and of the immediate community, rather
than for the benefit of the students. Thus at almost every level
schools were expected to adapt the young to their society; the
prospect of confronting young people with ideas alien to society
has commonly filled parents with alarm. Society has acquired the
habit of "using" the schools to teach whatever society happens to
be interested in: to teach "values," or citizenship, or the dangers of
Communism, to teach science when the Russians are ahead, and
private enterprise when the welfare staters threaten us, and Christianity when the Supreme Court will not. Fifth, the notion that

education is a quantitative experience, consists of so many years, or so many courses, rather than of an ascertainable body of skills or of knowledge, persists, and this, too, has made its way into "higher" education. Only American colleges are organized around courses, attendance, majors and minors, grades, and other quantitative factors rather than around tests of professional competence.

All this is explicable in the light of the past.

But all of it really belongs to the past.

III

We are all prisoners of that past, perhaps more so collectively than individually, and perhaps more in the realm of ideas than in the realm of the practical. It is easier to change the social attitudes of an individual student, for example, than of a fraternity, and while every professor rejoices in radical thoughts about the curriculum, the faculty, collectively, almost always has sober second thoughts. American education, at all levels, is still conditioned by the body of beliefs and practices which emerged at independence to meet the special needs of this special society and to adapt to the special circumstances of the New World. Both those needs and those circumstances have changed, profoundly. Educational principles and practices have not changed to meet the new circumstances. A new nation was growing, higgledy-piggledy, a nation made up of the most diverse elements, called on to conquer immense new territories, to create a new body politic and a new society, raise standards of living, vindicate democracy and equality and religious freedom—that nation could not be too exacting or too scrupulous in the means it used. It took what was at hand, used what it had, wastefully and even recklessly, in education as in other natural resources. It used the schools, used them for purposes not really educational. Yet on the whole all this worked, and because it worked we have tended to go on pretty much the same way, using the schools for whatever comes to hand, using them wastefully and recklessly.

It is in the light of this history that we are called on to consider the proposal of an additional two years of schooling for all. This proposal comes at a time when everything seems to point to the necessity of additional training to equip the young for the kind of society and economy in which they will live. It comes, too, at a time when the demands on the time and energies of the young are heavier than in the past, and when there is, therefore, strong pressure for saving time and for condensing rather than expanding what has been the normal educational experience.

But if we are to add two years to the present academic offering, or requirement, to what should we devote those years? Should we consider the two years as essentially an extension of high school, or as preparatory to senior college, or should we devote the two years to new forms of education, vocational, for example? In short, should the additional years be assimilated to secondary or to higher education or to something quite new?

The American instinct is for a quantitative solution to most problems, even educational problems. We tend to add on school years, as we have in the past, without giving much thought to the nature of the experience.

If it is merely two more years of schooling that we need, we can get it for a substantial part of our students, in the twelve years that we now consign to elementary and high school. The majority of junior and senior high schools fritter away two or three of the six years which they devote to education. Graduates of European schools—English, French, German, Swiss, Scandinavian—learn by the age of eighteen what few of our students learn until they reach the third year of college.*

What is the explanation of this?

We sometimes overlook the obvious and ascribe to tradition, or to a high standard of selectivity, or perhaps even to talent, what has a much simpler explanation. One reason, perhaps the chief reason, why the graduate of the English public school, the French *lycée*, the German *Gymnasium,* is well ahead of his American

---

* This does not apply to the products of our exceptional schools, the Bronx High School of Science, for example, or the New Trier school; nor am I considering what might be called nonacademic education—the kind of thing which American youngsters learn (sometimes) on the playing fields or in student government, or student newspapers or orchestras, but it does apply pretty generally.

cousin is that, by the age of eighteen he has had two or three more years of actual schooling. The European high school student customarily attends school until five o'clock each day, five and one-half days a week, and for ten or ten and one-half months a year. Add all that up and you quickly get your two years.

There are doubtless other considerations that should be kept in mind. European schools concentrate on the intellectual and academic job far more than do most American schools. On the whole, European secondary schools teach a privileged group—those from middle- and upper-class families with some cultural background; competition for entrance into the university is sharper abroad than here.

These things, rather than native ability, account for the relative backwardness of American secondary education. Account for it— and determine it.

There are, of course, extenuations and even justifications for the American practices and malpractices. These are for the most part rooted in history and we are the prisoners of history. But this history is no longer valid. The school day, week, and year were originally adapted to the needs of a rural society where children were expected to go home and do the chores and help put in and get out the crops; they are no longer expected to do this, but the school year has not changed perceptibly. The habit of prolonging youth was originally rooted in a revolt against Old World habits of child labor and an indulgence in a pleasanter image of childhood than was possible abroad: it is no longer necessary to indulge or pamper the young. Relatively easy standards of education were rooted in the interesting fact that in America alone it could be taken for granted that each new generation was better educated and smarter than the last. This meant that the young set their own standards, which could be counted on to be somewhat higher than those of the past, but never too exacting. This is no longer true. The habit of putting social interests first and academic interests second was rooted in those historical functions of the school which we have already considered: the schools are no longer the sole or the chief agencies for fulfilling these functions, and can now devote themselves to academic and intellectual pursuits.

We can, if we will, incorporate the equivalent of two additional years of schooling into the present twelve years of school, not for all students perhaps, but for a large proportion of them. We should avoid the temptation to make these two additional years which we are now planning merely an extension of high school, academically or socially. To do this would continue that waste of resources and of talents in which we have so long indulged ourselves, and this just at a time when everything urges us to speed up our educational processes. It would be not only academically but psychologically pernicious, confining men and women of nineteen or twenty to high-school activities.

It is probable that the additional two years should be not only a different but a separate educational experience. Two-year colleges, or academies—perhaps we will have to have a new name for them —should be assimilated to higher rather than to secondary education, as their students should be part of the adult rather than the adolescent world. In the making is the use of the two-year colleges for a great variety of educational purposes. Some may provide what the Danish folk high schools so magnificently provided in the nineteenth century, education both cultural and technical. Some will doubtless be college preparatory, as are so many of the community colleges in the California state system, and if they can and do function well in this arena they may relieve the universities of the burden of teaching elementary subjects and permit them to begin where almost all British and European universities begin—with what is generally our third year of college. This, in turn, may enable some of our universities to build on the state colleges, and devote themselves exclusively to graduate and professional work. Still others of the two-year colleges will, let us hope, fill one of the notorious gaps in our educational enterprise by training the young to technical and semiprofessional careers. Like the county colleges and the technical colleges of England, they can supply us with nurses, electricians, automobile mechanics, accountants, skilled farmers, small-town and school librarians, playground and recreation directors, teachers of art and music in the schools and in adult education programs—for the thousand different vocations and semiprofessions that are now so badly served.

IV

The extension of schooling to the age of twenty is consistent
with the American tradition, and with American faith in the sovereign effect of education in our kind of society. Because we are,
inevitably, creatures of the past, our tendency is to use each additional year of schooling as a mere quantitative extension of previous years, and to fit our schools into existing and familiar patterns.
That habit was not unjustified in the nineteenth century, but the
justification for it has disappeared. We are confronted with a demand for more radical reforms. We are required to reconsider the
functioning of our whole educational enterprise from, roughly, the
age of twelve on; to look at it not so much in historical context as
in the context of current and future requirements. Just as the problems of Western Europe are coming to be more and more like ours,
so our situation is coming to be more and more like that of Western Europe. While they are developing a classless society and recognizing the necessity of an immense extension and expansion of
their educational enterprise at all levels, we are coming to realize
that we have a highly complex and sophisticated society, with
many agencies for carrying on the large educational enterprise,
and that we can at last afford to concentrate the formal resources
of our schools on the academic and intellectual task, in order to
prepare the next generation for a world far more exacting than the
world of the nineteenth century.

Here are some of the implications of a program of fourteen years
of education for all: (1) A tightening up and speeding up of
education in grades seven to twelve. Every community should be
expected to have some schools, or some divisions of comprehensive
schools, which do substantially what the better schools of Western
Europe have so long been doing. (2) An increasing concentration
on the academic job, which will require that the many other agencies in the community now looking for useful work will undertake
some of the nonacademic jobs which have in the past been foisted
off on the schools. Let the American Legion and the Rotary Club
or insurance companies take on driver training; let the women's

clubs teach social dancing; let the students run their own games and sports—perhaps all dads' clubs should be abolished, and all those pernicious community organizations dedicated to inspiring big-time football and basketball for the young. (3) The other side of this is that the two years which are to be added onto our current educational enterprise should provide a new educational experience, and should be used for other than high-school purposes. The new colleges should emulate neither the high school nor the university but find their own character. What a pity if those who control them should suppose it necessary to copy the high schools in their athletic programs, or the colleges in their fraternity and sorority organizations. (4) This calls for experimentation. We have already a good body of experience, American and European, to fall back on. In all likelihood we will now need statewide, and perhaps even national, planning to assure that we do get a variety of experiments. Such planning should not make for uniformity; quite the contrary. Uniformity comes voluntarily in our country—Tocqueville saw that back in the 1830's—as communities ape one another. Only centralized planning can assure that experimentation so essential to the prosperity of this new enterprise.

There is no doubt that the national government will find itself involved in this enterprise, both on the academic and the financial levels. The pattern here may well be the familiar one of our agricultural experiment stations, first launched in 1887. There are now some fifty of these, largely supported by federal funds, working on a broad variety of agricultural experiments and programs under both state and national supervision. Another pattern is in process of being worked out by the Health, Education and Welfare Department—support of the most miscellaneous kinds of scientific investigation in colleges and universities, and proposed experimentation in the teaching of language, history, geography, and economics. We can learn something, too, from British and European experience: from the teacher training and technical colleges of Britain, from the trade and technological schools of Germany, from the folk high schools, now vastly changed, of Denmark. The principle of universal education is rooted in history, but the application of that principle, in the past, was vastly experimental, and the application of that principle, for the future, should be no less bold and imaginative than in the past.

Daniel Burnham, the master planner of the world's Columbian Exposition, and of the plans for Chicago and for Washington, used to say, "Make no little plans." If we are to extend universal education by two years, let us be sure that we make no little plans. Let us not permit the potentialities of this immense forward leap to go by default.

FROM NORMAL SCHOOL
TO UNIVERSITY: CHANGING
TASKS OF TEACHER EDUCATION

3

Teacher training had its origins in Europe, chiefly in Germany; it developed there, and in Switzerland and France, in the late eighteenth century. The special school for such training, the *école normale*, antedated Horace Mann's experiment at Lexington, Massachusetts, by half a century. What is most interesting is the way in which American teacher training departed from those models, immensely admired by Mann and Barnard, and imperturbably went its own way. Two things that persist into our own day strike us at once. First, that where in Europe teacher training was assigned almost exclusively to special *écoles normales*, in the United States it was early attached to colleges and universities and that the attachment, no matter with how many quarrels, has not only persisted but also become much closer with the passing years. And, second, this has meant that normal-school habits, attitudes, standards carried on up into the university. In Europe, on the contrary, special teacher training was not a university subject. From the first it was designed almost entirely for the elementary school. After all, until the twentieth century, only upper-middle- and upper-class

Yearbook of the American Association of Colleges for Teacher Education, 1966.

children—with an occasional genius from the lower or working classes—went past the elementary grades. When the poor did go on from there it was commonly to such special schools as the Danish folk high school or to other kinds of adult education, rather than to the *lycée* or the *Gymnasium* or the public school. This meant that the work of the normal school was based largely on needs which emerged from teaching the very young; it was doubtless inevitable that emphasis should be not on what we have amiably come to call "content courses," as if the others had no content, but on techniques of teaching. Teaching in the higher schools, on the other hand, was a serious job; for those who attended these schools were going on to the university or the technical institutes or—as in England—to take their place in the foreign service or the civil service, or—if they had gone to the proper schools—the army or the navy. These schools, therefore, required very high standards of teaching—standards as high as those required by the university. They were staffed almost entirely by the products of the universities, and the teaching was not unlike that in the universities. They could take for granted an elitist student body and take for granted, too, that the young men—only recently have girls been admitted—would devote their full time to their studies. There was no requirement that they go home and do "chores" and—except in England—no nonsense about interschool sports or student activities. There was no need for special teacher preparation; preparation in scholarship was presumed to be sufficient, just as in the United States it was, and still is, presumed to be sufficient for college teaching. The standards in France, Germany, Sweden were very much the standards of our colleges: in Sweden, to this day, high-school teachers are supposed to have the equivalent of a Ph.D. degree.

What this meant was that in most of Europe the universities imposed their standards on teaching at the secondary level. In America, it has been the other way around. There was no elitist group, and it was assumed that a great many students would go on to the high school and the academy. Most of them did increasingly. Almost imperceptibly, the normal schools imposed their standards on many of the colleges. To be sure, these have long abandoned the name "normal school" for "teachers' college," and are now in process of abandoning "teachers' college" for "university." This change, interesting in itself, is also interesting as a symbol, for it suggests how successfully the normal schools of an earlier day have carried their standards, interests, and attitudes into the colleges and universities.

It is this historical experience which accounts in large part for the strains and tensions that have clustered about teacher training in America in this century. Teacher education here has paralleled all other forms of education in that—in contrast to the Old World's —it is expansionist, ambitious, equalitarian, functional, and miscellaneous. Just as we asked our schools generally to take on a vast body of nonacademic duties and responsibilities, so we have expected teacher-training schools to take on far wider duties than those customarily imposed upon them abroad. Teacher-training institutions are expected to prepare for almost every level of teaching, in almost every kind of institution; they are expected to teach both technical, or professional, and subject-matter courses. Because they are called upon to turn out teachers in most subjects—even in typewriting and in football coaching—and at almost every level, they are of necessity forced to settle for fairly low standards. Because they have been maneuvered by circumstances into close association with universities, they have been forced to strive for equality with them, even if this has meant bringing some of these down to their level. More commonly, seeing themselves invaded and their functions usurped by the colleges and universities, they have entered the university arena and usurped some of the functions of these institutions.

Over the years, then, most of the energies and resources of teacher training have gone into the enormous enterprise of training enough teachers to keep up with the implacable demands of our schools by providing teachers for secondary schools, providing administrators—and surely no other school system is so elaborately administered, if only because in other countries administration is central—and even venturing into the teaching of "subjects" at more advanced levels. Who can doubt that on the whole they performed the first, most important, task well—that they managed to do what it was not thought possible to do? They provided teachers who in turn gave enough education to vast masses of children, native born and immigrant, so that they were able to understand the nature and assume the responsibilities of self-government. As for the teaching of subject matter—which traditionally belonged to the universities rather than to teacher-training institutions—we need no longer inquire; for the controversy has been ended to all intents and purposes by the old familiar principle: if you can't lick them, join them. Teacher-training colleges have joined, or have absorbed, or have transformed themselves into, colleges and universities, and thereby have made their own teaching of subjects at least respectable.

From the beginning, American schools were expected, even required, to take on many of the functions performed in the Old World by other institutions: the court, the church, the military, the academy, the guilds, and even the family, which functioned more efficiently as an educational force in a stable and settled society like the European than in one condemned by nature herself to mobility and disintegration. In a sense, schools are still called upon to perform more, and more miscellaneous, tasks here than in the Old World. Although the objectives are fundamentally the same as in the past, it is a new and different set of problems that confronts us, and we must resolutely address ourselves to them.

Almost two centuries after Thomas Jefferson and Noah Webster, a century and a quarter after the pioneering work of Horace Mann and Henry Barnard, more than half a century after Jane Addams and Lester Ward and John Dewey, we find ourselves confronted by problems as complex and intransigent as any which these great educators faced. Once again we see millions of children deprived of equality in education: millions who do not go on to high school, or who drop out once they are there; millions who are not in fact given an education sufficient to enable them to hold jobs or to perform their duties as citizens. We see that, in a nation dedicated to equalitarianism, the standards of schools are shockingly disparate and that the gap between slums and suburbs is greater now than it was a century ago. We see that while the South has quite deliberately condemned the Negro to social, political, and eco-

nomic inferiority, almost unconsciously the North has condemned
him to educational inferiority—an inferiority which all but guarantees that it will be a social and economic and cultural one as
well. Nor is this merely a racial matter. Hundreds of thousands of
white children of our urban slums, of the impoverished areas of
the country—Appalachia, the Deep South, mining country and
share-cropper country—are likewise fobbed off with an education
so inadequate that it condemns its victims to economic and cultural
inferiority.

It is a striking commentary on American optimism, complacency, and self-deception that only now, in the past fifteen or twenty
years, have we discovered that the true emancipation of the Negro
has hardly begun; only now, in the past decade, have we discovered poverty. These are two of the truly significant discoveries of
our time, more important by far, in their immediate implications,
than any of the discoveries in outer space on which we lavish
tens of billions of dollars. We, as a people, have discovered the
Negro and poverty; but only gradually and reluctantly are we as
educators discovering them. Compared to the new tasks and responsibilities that open up before us and clamor for attention, most
of the issues of teacher training which we have been talking and
quarreling about in the past seem almost petty. We have done
those things which we should not have done, and we have left
undone those things we should have done.

The major task confronting teacher education is to prepare
teachers—or Peace Corps workers or what you will—to deal with
these vast and shocking problems of the uneducated and the mis-
educated: victims of color, victims of racism, victims of poverty
and neglect, victims of urban growth and urban blight, victims of
the breakdown of our social fabric and of the family fabric.

What this means for teacher training is clear enough.

First, we shall have to accept greater flexibility and greater experimentation in our schools—accept and prepare for, through
teacher training. We will need to tailor our schools to particular
constituencies far more than is now customary. Because we
deluded ourselves that we had achieved a common social standard
and because we thought almost exclusively in terms of traditional

middle-class white Americans, we allowed ourselves to be bemused by the standard curriculum, the standard textbook, standard entrance examinations to colleges, standard tests of competence and talent. Clearly the requirements for teaching the disadvantaged Negro child, or any child in our great city slums, are quite different from those for teaching the child of the middle-class WASP homes. President Conant has brought home to all of us the gulf that yawns between the schools of slums and of suburbs.

Second, we will need to begin school not at the age of six but, for many children whose home environment is hostile to intellectual or social development, at the age of three or four. These are, alas, numbered by the million. Schools will be increasingly called upon to supply the Negro, the Puerto Rican and the Mexican child and the denizens of the slums with elementary things which the rest of us take for granted—the capacity for ordinary conversation, for example, ordinary habits of social intercourse, so simple a thing as learning to play, or learning to eat sitting down. They will be called upon to provide more ways of physical training, health supervision, and even psychiatric care than has heretofore been thought possible. Would we not all be better off if all the money now poured into—indeed wasted on—spectator sports, coaches and stadia and team equipment and travel, were used for the simplest and most elementary needs of the undernourished and the unskilled?

As we slowly give up the notion of colleges and universities acting *in loco parentis,* the primary and even the secondary schools will have to accept the responsibility for this role for those millions of children who have no parents, or but one parent, or whose parents are off at work, or incompetent to perform the duties of parenthood. How sobering were those figures from New York in 1965: of New York City mothers receiving state aid for dependent children, one-third were unmarried, and another third had been deserted by their husbands, and that of 14,300 children born to mothers on the relief rolls that year, two-thirds were born out of wedlock.

We will have to accept and prepare for a relaxation, even a change, of traditional standards in a great many schools and communities. Granted that in the long run we want to bring all of our schools up to the same high standard; but the present and more urgent task is a different one. It is all very well for schools of Westchester County or the North Shore of Chicago or Montgomery County in Maryland to prepare their students for admission to Harvard and Chicago, Wesleyan and Carleton, but this is not the task that confronts the schools of Harlem or of Englewood, of Alabama or Appalachia. We shall have to recognize new standards having more to do with miscellaneous talents of the young—vocational talents, or artistic, perhaps—and less with their ability to pass college entrance examinations.

Doubtless a program of this nature will call for a new era of discrimination. Large segments of our population have suffered from gross and unremitting discrimination for almost a century; we are going to be called upon to compensate for this by counter-discrimination. We have, after all, but limited resources of talent and intellectual energy and—if we propose to conquer the moon and Vietnam at the same time—of money as well. We already are cutting back on some of our educational and our poverty programs in order to have enough money to pay for outer space and for jungle warfare. We all know that it is more important to explore inner space than outer space and that there are jungles in most of our great cities that need conquering; we know this, but give priority elsewhere.

We may have to spend more on slums and less on suburbs; more on Negroes, Puerto Ricans, Mexicans, and other minorities who have been discriminated against, not always willfully, and less on whites. We may have to spend less, too, on what we think of as formal education and more on informal. In a sense, we are confronted with the kind of problem that confronted the United States in Europe immediately after the end of World War II—a situation where rescue and rehabilitation took precedence over reform. Our response to a shattered, bankrupt, and demoralized Europe was generous and imaginative; our response to the discovery of the perishing and dangerous classes of our own society, of urban decay, the pollution and destruction of natural resources, delinquency and illiteracy, discrimination and neglect will have to be no less generous and imaginative.

Just as in elementary education many of our school people are fighting the battles of the past and are less aware of the challenges of the present than we might expect, so in the realm of secondary education many of our schools seem not to have caught up with reality. There is, to be sure, not one reality but—in a country as large as ours—many. There is the reality of slums and the reality of suburbs, the reality of the dropouts and the reality of the advanced-placement students. There is the reality of schools obsessed with competitive athletics and the reality of schools where standards of health, physical and mental, are lower than in almost any comparable schools in Europe.

What I have said applies, needless to say, with equal force to the secondary schools. If the job we all recognize were done properly in the lower grades, perhaps it would disappear in the high schools; and these institutions could apply themselves more effectively to what we know as the "academic" or "college preparatory" job.

There can be little question that the most impressive development of the past half century or so in secondary education has been quantitative. I hardly need cite you the familiar figures (something of a statistical jungle, I may say, parenthetically). In 1900 there were some 1.9 million students in secondary schools—more than twice as many in nonpublic as in public, by the way; of these 5 percent, less than 100,000, graduated that year. That year, too, the college population numbered less than one quarter million. Today the secondary-school population numbers some 15 million, with 2.3 million graduates; the college and university population is not far from 5 million, though much depends on what and how you count. The significance of these figures is, one would have supposed, inescapable; yet it is by no means clear that it has not in fact escaped many of us. It means that the college is what the high school was only a generation ago; that the whole level of educational expectancy has moved dramatically up; and that for a very large percentage of young people high school is no longer terminal. We can go even further; as we contemplate the figures for graduate and research work and consider the situation in leading colleges, we can say that for a substantial body of students *college* is no longer terminal. Nor may we for a moment doubt that this trend will grow even faster than the population grows or that an ever larger percentage of young people will move on from high school to college, and from college to graduate and professional work.

What this means, or should mean, is that a substantial number of the high schools in the country are in effect college preparatory and that they should adjust their curriculum, their standards, their teaching, and their activities to this elementary fact. They do not have to teach everything, but they must be prepared to teach whatever they do teach very well indeed. They no longer have time for the nonessentials that in the past frittered away so much of the time of students and the energies of teachers and administrators—nor do the students.

What is happening is that in the more prosperous and fortunate school districts of the country—and we are so large that that embraces a substantial part of the school population—our high schools are growing increasingly like the French *lycées*, the German *Gymnasiums*, the English public schools, the high schools of Denmark and Sweden and Holland. Students, parents, and college admissions officers are imposing upon them ever higher standards. This means that teacher-training institutions will have to impose upon secondary-school teachers even higher standards. In Britain and much of the Continent, as we have seen, secondary education was assimilated to higher education and to the standards of teaching set by the university. I doubt we will come to that within the near future, but I do not doubt that the teaching in good high schools will increasingly approximate the teaching of freshmen in many of our bigger universities; let us hope it will be even better teaching!

If we move up the academic ladder in teacher training, we come to—what? Is it too great an exaggeration to say that we come to a void? The most interesting and promising educational development of the immediate future is not to be found in the more traditional areas of elementary and secondary education or even in higher education, but in between. It is in devising and creating institutions and techniques which can provide such education as is needed for the vast displaced adult population of the country—

those millions of young people who are not able or ready to go on to what we have heretofore called "higher" education, and those older people who find themselves, thanks to affluence and the technological revolution, with unprecedented leisure and no way to fill it except to look at the TV screen.

To provide for the first, we are now in process of creating community colleges; this enterprise is, I believe, the most rapidly growing of any on the educational scene. To provide for the second we have hitherto relied on something vaguely and optimistically called adult education. These two enterprises have this in common: that we do not know their province, their function, or their character. Perhaps the only thing that is clear is that they must have a very miscellaneous character to deal with very miscellaneous problems and provide for very miscellaneous constituents. Let us hope that educators will not attempt to impose a pattern upon them as they have, doubtless of necessity, on the more traditional educational institutions.

It is this vast, amorphous, and almost anonymous enterprise of the community colleges to provide education of one kind or another for young people between the ages of seventeen and twenty-one, and of adult education to take care of the needs of some thirty million adults now already involved in continuing education, which offers the greatest challenge and the greatest opportunity to educational statesmanship of the next generation. So far it has produced no statesmen—no Horace Mann, no Jane Addams, no Lester Ward, no John Dewey—and as yet no James B. Conant to formulate the principles of discussion, to make out the lines of progress and to enlist public support.

Turn finally to higher education. In the last two decades the pattern of higher education, never very clear, has been broken up and re-formed. New demands are made on our colleges and universities by the professions, government, society, and, let us not forget, the students. One of the new areas opened up, one of the new demands, is very much the concern of American universities. That is responsibility for the educational development of the underdeveloped countries of the globe.

Perhaps the most urgent task that confronts the new nations is to work an educational revolution which may enable them to advance by peaceful evolution rather than by violent revolution. They need schools at every level, from the most elementary to the most advanced; they have, most of them, neither the material nor the intellectual resources for providing such schools. The West must provide the resources and much of the guidance; help build the schools and the agricultural and technological colleges, and help train teachers, librarians, and administrators. Here is one of the great challenges to those concerned with the training of teachers: to lift their sights from the traditional concerns of schools in Illinois or Massachusetts and to apply their energies, skills, experience, and imagination to the far vaster enterprise of preparing teachers to go out and function on the world stage.

The problems, the needs, the challenges, and the crises are outstripping the responses to them. Many teachers of education have been content to think of their responsibilities in professional and parochial terms; and their energies have been directed, perhaps inevitably, to the narrow task of training teachers to perform pedagogical functions and administrators to administer these.

It was not thus that Rousseau interpreted the nature of education; nor Pestalozzi, nor Froebel, nor the great Sven Grundtvig. It was not in this way that the architects of the American Republic and American democracy interpreted education; Jefferson, Horace Mann, Henry Barnard, Jane Addams, Lester Ward, John Dewey— no nation has a more distinguished roster. They addressed themselves to the role of education in prospering the Republic and to the contribution of education to the great community of learning. It is to the training of teacher-philosophers who have that vision and that understanding that we must return. What an enviable prospect it is that opens up before us. We are called upon to redeem the unbalance of a hundred years, to rescue the lower fifth of the population from neglect and ignorance and the prospect of failure. We are called upon to provide teachers and scholars who will lift the levels of our high schools to those of the best secondary schools of the Old World, to weld the high school and the college and university into a single continuous academic enterprise. We are summoned to shape the character of the new community colleges, which are destined to play a role in our society no less important than that of the high school, the academy, and the college a century ago. We are required to provide academic leadership in the new and unfamiliar area of adult education; an area which should be continuous with all other educational areas but has not been; an area inhabited by some thirty to forty millions of people. We are required by the new position and authority of our own republic to advance what once was called the republic of learning and to help guide the educational progress of a large part of the people of the world into the new age.

TEACHING HISTORY IN
THE HIGH SCHOOLS

4

We should begin, in all fairness, with the question: why teach history at all? What is the *use* of history?

That sounds like a Philistine question, but it is not. The very fact that it comes up so frequently vindicates, in a sense, its relevance. Who, after all, asks what is the use of mathematics or biology or accounting?

Let us admit at once that in a practical way history has no use. Let us concede that it is not good for anything that can be weighed or measured or counted, that can be used as chemistry or accounting can be used. It will not save us from repeating the errors of the past; it will not solve problems; it will not show us how to win wars or, more important, how to avoid them. It will not provide us with scientific explanations of depressions or with keys to prosperity, with scientific guides to nominations and elections, with scientific controls over great questions of national policy. It will not contribute in any overt way to progress.

But the same can be said, of course, for many other things which society values and which men cherish. What use, after all, is a Beethoven sonata, or a painting by Renoir, or a statue by Milles, or

American Education published by the U.S. Office of Education, June, 1965.

a sonnet by Wordsworth? What use, for that matter, are a great many quite mundane things which society takes for granted and on which it lavishes immense thought and effort: baseball, for example, or a rose garden?

Happily a civilized society does not devote all of its thought and effort to things whose usefulness can be statistically demonstrated. There are other criteria than that of ostentatious usefulness and even other meanings of the term "useful" than those acknowledged by the Thomas Gradgrinds of this world.

History is useful in the sense that art is useful—or music or poetry or flowers; perhaps even in the sense that religion and philosophy are useful. Like history, these do not provide certain answers to questions. If you study philosophy, even if you embrace religion, you are in a sense engaged in a gamble, but it is a gamble which all sensible men accept. It is one of those gambles which William James had in mind in that famous passage:

> Suppose that the world's author put the case to you before creation, saying: "I am going to make a world not certain to be saved, a world the perfection of which shall be conditional merely, the condition being that each several agent does its own level best. I offer you the chance of taking part in such a world. Its safety, you see, is unwarranted. It is a real adventure, with real danger, yet it may win through. . . . Will you join the procession? Will you trust yourself and trust the other agents enough to face the risk?"

All of us, in a sense, accept this gamble. All of us, too, instinctively, accept the gamble submitted to us by the study of things which have no guaranteed use. For without these things life would be poorer and meaner; without them we should be denied those intellectual and moral experiences that give meaning and richness to life itself.

Can we go beyond this? I think we can. If history does not have measurable use, it does have rewards and values: we may even call them pleasures. The first and perhaps the richest pleasure of history is that it adds new dimensions to life itself by enormously extending our perspective and enlarging our experience. It permits us to enter vicariously into the past, to project our vision back over thousands of years, and to enlarge it to embrace all the peoples of the earth.

Through the pages of history we can hear Pericles deliver his funeral oration to the Athenians, trek with the Crusaders to the Holy Land, sail with Columbus past the gates of Hercules, share the life of Goethe at the little Court of Weimar, listen to the Lincoln-Douglas debates in little dusty prairie towns, and stand beside Winston Churchill as he rallies the people of Britain to their finest hour. History can supply us with all of those elements that Henry James thought most essential to the life of the mind: density, variety, intricacy, richness in the pattern of thought, and with them a "sense of the past."

This immense enlargement of experience carries with it a second pleasure or reward, for it means that history provides us with great companions. This consideration is perhaps more familiar to adults who have learned how rare is contemporary greatness than to the young who may imagine that they will live on a stage crowded with heroic characters. Wherever the historian or biographer has been, he has given new depth and range to our associations. We have but to take the books down from the serried shelves to be admitted to the company and the confidence of Voltaire and Rousseau, Johnson and Boswell, Thomas Jefferson and George Washington, William James and Justice Holmes. We can, indeed, come to know these and other great men more intimately than their contemporaries knew them, for we can read their letters, journals, and diaries. All this is not merely one of the pleasures of history; it is one of the indispensable pleasures of life. For the best thing we can do for young people is to keep constantly before their eyes the spectacle of greatness. History presents them with that spectacle, and it makes clear what are the attributes of greatness.

A third and familiar pleasure of history is the experience of identifying the present with the past and thus adding a new dimension to places. It was Thomas Macaulay who observed, "The pleasure of history is analogous in many respects to that produced by foreign travel. The student is transported into a new state of society. . . . His mind is enlarged by contemplating the wide diversities of laws, of morals, and of manners."

But history is far more rewarding than travel, for it enables the reader to travel not only in the dimension of space but in the dimension of time, to know not only contemporary England but

Roman Britain, to wander with a good guide not only through modern Florence but through the Florence of Leonardo and Michelangelo. It enables us to see the present through the eyes of the past, to give a new dimension to whatever place we visit.

Suppose we chose to introduce the young to the little town of Salem. It is a lovely town in its own right, its handsome old white frame houses still standing so staunchly along Chestnut and Federal streets. As we look at it through the eyes of history we conjure up a straggling village, older even than Boston, ever busy with fishing and with theological disputes, and we remember that Roger Williams preached here and Mistress Anne Hutchinson too. We look at Gallows Hill and recall the dark story of Salem witchcraft, which haunted Nathaniel Hawthorne, who grew up here and whose spirit still broods over the town.

We conjure up Salem at the turn of the century, when its proud captains sailed all the waters of the globe, when the flag of Salem was thought to be the flag of an independent nation, and when the spoils of the pepper trade and the China trade glittered in every drawing room. And we people its tree-lined streets with perhaps the most remarkable galaxy of talent and genius that one little American town ever boasted.

There is another and perhaps a deeper value in history, for history is the memory of man, and it is therefore the way by which man knows himself. A people without history is like a man without memory: each generation would have to learn everything anew— make the same discoveries, invent the same tools and techniques, wrestle with the same problems, commit the same errors. And as the individual man can know himself only by knowing his own past, so mankind can know itself only through its past. As that remarkable Oxford philosopher-historian Robin Collingwood has said in answering the question "What is history for?":

My answer is that history is "for" Human self-knowledge.
. . . Knowing yourself means knowing what you can do, and since nobody knows what he can do until he tries, the only clue to what man can do is what man has done. The value of history, then, is that it teaches us what man has done and thus what man is. [*The Idea of History*, Oxford, 1946, p. 10.]

For well over two thousand years the study of history has been the interest, the passion, the delight, the consolation of the richest minds. From the days of Homer and Thucydides down to our own day philosophers and scholars have been zealous to record the deeds of the past and to praise famous men. Almost all of our greatest statesmen from Jefferson to Kennedy have been nursed on the study of history; almost all of our imaginative writers from Washington Irving and Nathaniel Hawthorne to William Faulkner and Robert Frost have immersed themselves in history. No subject except religion has won the allegiance of noble minds for as long a span of time as history has.

If then we are justified in teaching history, what history should we teach? There is, after all, so much of it. The most assiduous scholars cannot master even a small part of it in a lifetime of study—cannot master the whole history of a single one of many nations, of a single one of many eras.

Clearly then we must be highly selective. But we do not have any agreed-on standard for selection. We cannot say that we should teach the most important history or the most interesting history, for both of these terms are subjective. We cannot say that there is any one body of history that everyone must know, for this is palpably untrue. We cannot say, let us teach what we want to teach or teach what interests us most, for we have an obligation to our society and to the next generation.

On the whole, however, we have greatly oversimplified the problem—we in America and schoolmen in every other country as well. For the answer is almost everywhere the same: teach the history of your own country, teach national history. The French take this for granted, the Germans, the Danes, the Mexicans, and so do we in America. With us the teaching of American history is almost a nonstop process: we teach it in elementary school and in the high school; then we teach it again in the college.

The logic of teaching boys and girls national history is persuasive enough. One of the essential ingredients of nationalism is a common past, a common memory, a common heritage of tragedy and of glory—so all the historians of nationalism have asserted. If we are to have a nation we must, then, provide this ingredient.

One of the essential ingredients of unity is a body of common denominators—a common body of references and allusions; common heroes, villains, poets, and storytellers; common symbols; common monuments—a flag, a ballad, a shrine, a song, a legend. And one of the essential ingredients of freedom and self-government—it was Jefferson who insisted on this—is a people trained to liberty through the study of history, trained to self-government through the study of democracy, trained by history to conduct themselves as free-born Americans should.

All of these arguments for the study of national history are persuasive. But they are not conclusive. There is something to be said on the other side as well.

There is, for example, the consideration that we have, if anything, too much emphasis on nationalism and that we need to abate this emphasis, not to increase it. There is the consideration that one of the dangers to good citizenship is precisely parochialism: that a study of other peoples and other eras might make much wiser and better citizens. After all, it is pointed out, the Founding Fathers were not trained on American history—there was none.

There is the consideration that much of American history can be allowed to take care of itself; after all, youngsters are exposed to it ceaselessly—in newspapers and magazines, over the radio and on the television, in story books and picture books, in lectures and addresses, in a thousand allusions. How can anyone grow up in a country and not absorb its history? The school should be a kind of countervailing force, should give children what they will not in all likelihood get in later years: the history of other peoples and other times.

For a large number of students there is still another consideration. Half of those who finish secondary school will go on to college. The percentage will in all likelihood increase, and the day when fourteen years of schooling will be taken for granted or required by law is not far distant. Most youngsters will therefore have a chance to study American history at a more mature age later on. Why not give them something different in high school or, if not something different, at least something more?

But what? There is the difficulty; although there is pretty general agreement on the importance of national history, there is no such agreement on any alternative.

When we consider alternative or supplementary programs, two kinds of history commend themselves. One might be called traditional history—the study of those great epochs of the past or of those great nations that by common consent have contributed most to our own inheritance. Traditionally this has meant Greece and Rome, the Renaissance and the Age of Discovery, and—in the United States at least—the history of England.

Now there is much to be said for introducing young people to one or all of these areas of history. This is one way of introducing them to civilization: this is one way of introducing them to their own inheritance. It is one way of recognizing and paying "our debt" to Greece and Rome, to the Renaissance, to what used to be called the "mother country." There are other arguments as well. It is the classical world and the Renaissance that by common consent are the glorious eras of Western history. It is England—or Britain —which has had far and away the strongest impact of all nations on the world in which we live.

Because these eras of history have seemed fascinating they have attracted the best literature, and if youngsters are to be tempted into the study of history it will be through great literature—the great writers of these epochs, the great historians who have written about these epochs. What better introduction to history than Homer and Herodotus and Thucydides? What better introduction, at a later stage, than Gibbon and Mahaffy and Grote and Zimmern? Or let students immerse themselves in the glorious story of Renaissance Florence; of Venice, that "eldest child of liberty"; of Elizabethan England. These are the books that will open new worlds, that will inflame the imagination.

But there is a second approach to history which clamors for consideration. That is the history of the very old and the very new nations. Here we are—say the champions of this new history—in the midst of a revolution. We have neglected and ignored two-thirds of the human race; we have neglected or ignored the history of Asia and of Africa and even of our neighbors south of the Rio Grande. Let us equip ourselves to understand this great revolution;

let us welcome the scores of new nations on the globe, and the old ones too—like China and India. Let us expose the young to their history and their literature.

No one, surely, can quarrel with this diagnosis. The prescription is another matter entirely. Can it be done, and done well, in the time available to the study of history in the secondary school?

Is it possible for teachers, ill-trained as most of them are, to survey the "world, from China to Peru," in Dr. Johnson's phrase? Is it possible to find teaching materials for so complex a task? Is it possible to do justice—or to avoid injustice—to fifty or a hundred nations in the few months available? If teacher and student engage in a convulsive effort to learn something about China, India, Pakistan, Japan, the Arab world, Israel, the Congo, South Africa, and the twenty states of South America, will they achieve anything more than historical indigestion?

In all fairness we must answer that we do not know. But so far this enterprise has not worked very well. Perhaps the British are more nearly right than some of our educators. The British approach to this problem of understanding scores of peoples and nations is not to study the history or the literature or the government of each. That, they think, is hopeless. It is rather to train those carefully selected young men who are to go out and deal with these countries in what might be called the fundamentals of history, of literature, and of politics.

In the past these fundamentals were simple enough: in history it was Greece and Rome; in literature it was Greek and Latin; in politics it was Aristotle and perhaps John Locke and John Stuart Mill. These histories and these writers provided, so the British thought, microcosms of the world, and students thoroughly immersed in this study would be prepared for any exigency.

During the nineteenth century that method worked pretty well. Perhaps it worked better than the very different American approach to the same problem.

We come then to an even more difficult and controversial question: how should history be taught? There are only a limited number of ways in which to teach history in the elementary and secondary schools, and these are familiar enough. We can choose among them, or we can attempt a kind of amalgam of them.

First, we can undertake to instruct the young in the "facts" of history. Our instinct is to shy away from this method and this objective. This is a sound instinct, for we all recognize that the "facts" of history, far from being hard, are in fact elusive, inconclusive, and subjective. We all know that when we look at them closely they act like the Cheshire Cat—they disappear, all but the grin. Yet we should not repudiate this approach altogether.

Something is to be said for having a knowledge of essential historical facts—facts of chronology, geography, and biography—just as something is to be said for having a firm grasp of the multiplication table or English grammar. No one supposes that knowing the multiplication table will enable the student to understand mathematics, or that knowing some of the rules of grammar will enable him to understand literature. But most of us would agree that without knowing these elementary things he can scarcely hope to understand more sophisticated relationships and ideas.

But it will be said that the "facts" of history are readily available in textbooks or almanacs. So they are. But life goes more easily if they are an instinctive part of what we carry about with us—for example, the geography of streets of our home town, or the value of coins. Perhaps it is not really important to know that Arthur succeeded Garfield in the Presidency, but it simplifies matters if we can take for granted that all do know this.

Second and more important is, of course, understanding. If understanding cannot operate without facts, facts are useless without understanding. We teach history so that our students may understand the past and the present. Increasingly we fob off the young with "problems" which are, as often as not, contrived and artificial.

Increasingly we present history to them as a series of headaches —not the story of the Westward movement but the "problem of the frontier," not the winning of independence but the "problem of imperial organization," not the spectacle of social and humanitarian reform but the "problem of social reform." To ask young people to study the problem of the West without reading Parkman or the problem of the Civil War without reading Freeman's *Lee* or Benét's *John Brown's Body* is, in a sense, like asking them to read the Kinsey report before they have read any love poetry.

Most of the historians who have achieved some kind of immortality have known this almost instinctively and have combined narrative and drama with analysis and interpretation. There are exceptions to be sure: Frederick W. Maitland, Lord Acton, and Ernst Cassirer come to mind. But no one would try to enlist the interest of high-school students with these authors. Every child, however, can read Froissart or Shakespeare (Churchill said that he learned English history from Shakespeare), Macaulay or Parkman; let them do so. The Maitlands and the Cassirers will come later.

What we will probably get is something of a combination of these various approaches to the teaching of history. We will continue to teach some agreed-on "facts," however dubious their philosophical foundations; we will introduce students to "problems," or they will force themselves upon the attention of the students. We will appeal, if we can, to the imagination. These are not and cannot be separate activities; they are as much part of the same process as reading notes, using the fingers, and understanding the score are part of playing the piano.

But there is a chronological arrangement, one rooted perhaps in nature rather than in logic. It is this: first stir and enlist the imagination by telling a story; then concentrate on getting the sequence of "facts"—the chronology, the geography, and the like—under control; then turn to the problems.

It is the imagination and the basis of facts that are most important for the purposes of teaching; the problems will, in a sense, take care of themselves. One of the difficulties of so much of the current emphasis on analysis—we call it the "problem" method—is that students are expected to analyze a complex body of data and draw conclusions from that analysis on the basis of the most meager and inconclusive information.

This approach is supposed to be more "scientific" than narration, for example; but it is not one accepted by scientists. No student is expected to analyze problems in biology or physics or chemistry on the basis of a smattering of data. Solving "problems" on the basis of odds and ends of facts would never do for these scientific disciplines; there is no reason to suppose that it will work in history. Indeed this method of approach may do more harm than good, by inculcating slovenly habits of thinking into the young.

A third method of teaching is to excite interest in the spectacle of history and to stir the imagination. This is the old, the traditional approach to history, and not for children alone but for all those who inquired about the past. The first historians were storytellers—the writers of the Old Testament, Homer, Herodotus, Thucydides, and Plutarch—and so too most of their successors down through the centuries.

Teaching is itself the imaginative communication between the old and the young, the imaginative transmission of knowledge and, it is hoped, of wisdom from generation to generation. Certainly history offers no exception to this general principle. Here, if anywhere, such imaginative communication should be encouraged. For no other subject, it is safe to say, can be relied upon more confidently to catch the imagination of the young. No other offers such continuous drama; no other presents such a spectacle of greatness. If there is any value in history, our first task must surely be to catch the interest of the young, to persuade them to read and to study history, to open up to them the inexhaustibly rich world of the past.

One fair objection to so much of the history teaching of our own time is that as it has grown more "scientific" it has grown less interesting to the average student; as it increases its appeal to scholars, it loses its appeal to those who are not scholars—that is, to the great mass of the people.

Those who plan our curricula and who teach seem sometimes to act as if high school were not only the last chance students would have at any subject but the only chance, the only agency of instruction. But should we not keep in mind that students do not study American history in a vacuum or in isolation? Most of them have studied it before; many of them, it is safe to say, will study it again. All of them are exposed to history in some form or other almost every day. They read history in their newspapers and magazines; they see it on television and on the films; they consider it in discussions of current affairs.

Most of them will be invited to the contemplation of American history the rest of their lives. They do not have to learn everything during these high-school years, nor to solve all the problems. It is enough that they become familiar with the problems and with some of the ways of thinking about them. It is enough that they acquire a taste for the reading and study of history, a taste and a habit, so that they will turn to it again and again in the years ahead, not as a chore nor even as a duty—but as a delight.

ON THE EVILS OF A
FOREIGN EDUCATION

5

"Why send an American youth to Europe for education?" asked Thomas Jefferson in a famous letter to his friend John Banister, Jr., in 1785.

Let us view the disadvantages. . . . To enumerate them all would require a volume. I will select a few. If he goes to England he learns drinking, horse-racing, and boxing. These are the peculiarities of English education.

The following circumstances are common to education in that and other countries of Europe. He acquires a fondness for European luxury and dissipation and a contempt for the simplicity of his own country; he is fascinated with the privileges of the European aristocrats, and sees with abhorrence the lovely equality which the poor enjoys with the rich in his own country. He contracts a partiality for aristocracy or monarchy, he forms foreign friendships which will never be useful to him, and loses the season of life for forming in his own country those friendships which of all others are the most faithful and permanent; he is led by the strongest of human passions into a spirit for female intrigue, destructive of his own and others' happiness . . . and learns to consider fidelity to the marriage bed as an ungentlemanly practice and inconsistent with happiness. . . . He returns to his own country a foreigner, unacquainted with the practices of domestic economy necessary to preserve him from ruin. . . . It appears to me then that an

Saturday Review, February 18, 1967.

American coming to Europe for education loses in his knowledge, in his morals, in his habits, and in his happiness.

Alas, the reckless practice of sending American boys abroad for their education persisted, and, after the Civil War, grew to alarming proportions. In 1873 the Reverend Birdsay Grant Northrop, secretary of the Connecticut State Board of Education, felt compelled to launch a crusade against this spreading evil. Northrop was not familiar with Mr. Jefferson's letter, but he said pretty much what Jefferson had said almost a hundred years earlier, and, eager for support and applause, he sent his diatribe "Should American Youth be Educated Abroad?" to scholars and educators throughout the country. Replies poured in by the score, and later that year the triumphant Northrop put together a selection of them in a booklet which he called simply *Education Abroad*. Professor Stewart Fraser of George Peabody College for Teachers has had the happy idea of rescuing this piece of Americana from undeserved oblivion (Stewart Fraser, ed., *The Evils of a Foreign Education, or Birdsay Northrop on Education Abroad, 1873*. International Center, George Peabody College for Teachers, Nashville, Tennessee, 1966).

Neither Northrop's original essay nor the replies which it inspired are of the slightest value as serious discussions of the merits of the question to which they are addressed; on the contrary, they express the effervescence of an emotional binge. But as an expression of the Victorian mind in America they are documents of the first order. If they tell us nothing about education abroad, they tell us much about education at home. And few books of comparable size in our literature reveal as much about the prejudices, vanities, fears, and obsessions of intelligent Americans of the postwar generation as does this potpourri of academic patriotism.

Here is a formidable throng of educational statesmen: university presidents like Eliot of Harvard, Porter of Yale, McCosh of Princeton, Angell of Michigan, Barnard of Columbia, Folwell of Minnesota, Stearns of Amherst, and Mark Hopkins of Williams, all eager to testify; here, too, a gaggle of state superintendents of schools pushing their way to the witness box. Their testimony is eloquent but worthless: a mishmash of clichés, shibboleths, and prejudice expressed in a mixture of rhetoric and jargon. What they had to say about sending American "boys"—age ten to twenty—abroad for an education can be summed up in a single word: Don't. The reasons they gave for this advice added little to those which Jefferson had dredged up a century earlier, except for the addition of complacency, which Jefferson lacked. The arguments are repetitive, and we can summarize them briefly:

First, there was really nothing to be gained by sending a boy abroad—for the most part that seemed to mean Germany—for an education; American schools were almost as good academically as European and for all other purposes they were incomparably better. Second, sending American boys abroad during the formative years of their lives would inevitably give them false and pernicious notions about government, religion, class, and society, and thus make them unfit for practical success in America. Third, and most insistent, to send American boys abroad was to expose them to moral temptations which were sure to corrupt them, but which they would just as surely escape if they stayed at home. Dr. Northrop— he managed to spread these so thin that they made no less than twenty-two arguments—summed it all up. Foreign education, he wrote, means "the loss of a more practical training," inculcates the duty of "homage to king and emperor," encourages a pernicious cosmopolitanism, and forfeits those "national sentiments, traditions, and loyalties" essential to true Americanism. As for morals, Northrop pointed out, "it is not in France alone that a moral malaria pervades the atmosphere"; alas, everywhere in the Old World "a voluptuous refinement veils the grossest immorality and a thin veneering covers the foulest corruption." Finally, American education is cheaper.

The official and presidential chorus echoed these charges with monotonous sycophancy. The superintendent of schools of Georgia, who had cheerfully passed most of his life in a slave society, argued that no American boy should be permitted to go abroad until his "moral principles" were strong enough to resist the dangerous influences of the Old World. The superintendent of schools of Minnesota declared that the function of American schools was "to stamp loyalty on the hearts of our youth, and to teach that it is a glory to be an upright and intelligent citizen of the United States"; how could these ends be achieved by a foreign education? The Ohio superintendent deplored the "refinement and glamour of European immorality," and the Wisconsin superintendent, who seemingly confused Germany with Turkey or India, asserted that only in America was it possible to find "natural, wholesome, and Christian education."

Nor was it only public officials who indulged in this kind of silliness. The president of Middlebury College was sure that foreign influences constituted "a foolish and hurtful taint," and his opposite number at Burlington went so far as to argue that only boys who stayed in America would be exposed to the benign influence of religion. As for girls, he added fatuously, they didn't really count, and if they succumbed to the lure of mere "accomplishments" such as French, music, or art, why, "let them get a French husband and stay in Europe." The president of Trinity College was alarmed because young men who studied abroad came home "disposed to criticize and compare"; this meant that their "patriotism is somewhat dulled." Professor William S. Tyler of Amherst College agreed that young men who went abroad returned "un-Americanized if not unchristianized," and one W. C. Fowler, otherwise unidentified, was fearful that foreign-trained boys might grow up to be "citizens of the world," which was the worst thing that could happen to them. He was supported in this view by no other than the great Eliot of Harvard—he had studied in Germany—who asserted roundly that "persons described as cosmopolitan are, as a rule, an unhappy, useless, and sterile breed."

Not surprisingly, newspaper editors echoed these fears and played on these prejudices. Thus a Utica editor asserted that the habit of study abroad was "anti-American and dangerous," tending to "subvert free institutions," while a St. Louis journalist, unconsciously invoking Thomas Jefferson, assured his delighted readers that a university education abroad was nothing but "guzzling beer, smoking, howling, and gaming all night," and soared to the ultimate of moral chauvinism with the conclusion that "the Fatherhood of God, the brotherhood of man, and the equality of men before the law were distinctive American ideas" which might be forfeited and lost by residence abroad.

"Track almost any German professor or author upon almost any subject," wrote the journalist J. P. Thompson, "and you are pretty likely to catch him in some illogical deduction, some groundless assumption, some substitution of theory for fact." That is a succinct description of the arguments of almost all those who contributed to this symposium. Their method was rigidly deductive: no hint of evidence was permitted to ruffle the surface of their generalizations, nor are any conclusions subjected to even the most elementary of tests. Thus it did not, apparently, occur to any of these commentators who were so sure that a European education corrupted its victims, to wonder how it happened that millions of Germans, Dutch, English, and Irish who had come to the United States after years of European education had somehow escaped corruption.

Implicit in all this material is a body of assumptions—shared no doubt by the vast majority of Americans—which illuminate the mind of the Brown Decades, assumptions not just about education, but about the meaning and the character of America. Consider some of these: first, that the true function of schools was not to train the mind, excite intellectual curiosity, or inspire new ideas, but to train character, impose conformity, and fit the young for the practical circumstances of American life; second, that American society was unquestionably the norm to which all young people should be adjusted, and that whatever deviated from that norm or induced any discontent with it was misguided; third, that "cosmopolitanism" or "internationalism" was a kind of betrayal of America, for it produced not useful men and women but a breed that was abnormal, sterile, and unhappy; fourth, that it was the business of the schools to inculcate unquestioning loyalty to the American way of life and to impose upon students a conviction that America was superior to the rest of the world in everything that mattered, and that, conversely, what Europe might excel in did not matter. This was particularly clear in the realm of religion and morality, for America was preeminently the country of Christian morality.

These educators represented the best of American thought, and of American leadership, in the postwar generation. Yet it never occurred to them that education is the responsibility of society as a

68]   THE SCHOOL

whole, not merely of schools; that young people (up to the age of twenty) might learn anything that is not formally taught them in the schools except wickedness and vice; that any of the young can be trusted to make up their own minds about what they see at home and abroad, or even that they might have minds to make up. It never occurred to them that America had anything important to learn from other countries—unimportant things like art and music, yes, but these were merely icing on the cake. It never occurred to them that there is any value higher than nationalism, or that the cultivation of political, intellectual, and moral chauvinism can be anything but laudable. Certainly it would be difficult to make a stronger argument against parochialism in education and in favor of cosmopolitanism than that made so unwittingly but so persuasively by the educational establishment of the 1870's.

WHEN MAJORS WROTE
FOR MINORS: CHILDREN'S
LITERATURE IN AMERICA

6

At a time when William Dean Howells was the acknowledged dean of American letters, his friend and colleague of *Atlantic Monthly* days, Horace Scudder, could justly claim to be the dean of children's letters, if there was such an office. He had edited the *Riverside Magazine for Young People;* he had written a long list of children's books, among them the famous Bodley series and even fairy stories; he had introduced Hans Christian Andersen to America—that alone was enough to insure him immortality. Toward the close of his life he put together some of his reflections and conclusions on a subject that he knew more about than almost anyone else: childhood in literature. Other literatures, he pointed out, gave proper attention to children, but not, alas, American. Except for Hawthorne no major American writer had concerned himself with children. This was in 1894; Mark Twain had lived in vain, and Louisa May Alcott.

Curiously enough, Scudder had high praise for English literature on this score, but mostly for the wrong things in it. He had a great deal to say about childhood in Shakespeare and something about it in Wordsworth and De Quincey and Blake, and even Dickens, but nothing to say of those who wrote directly to and for children or wrote about them. Somehow the learned Scudder managed to miss the point: that English and American literatures are throughout concerned with children, that almost every major writer of the nineteenth century wrote for children as well as for adults, and that for over a century the line between juvenile and adult literature was all but invisible.

This is a quality not to be found elsewhere except in Swiss and Scandinavian literature, and even there not to a comparable degree, this constant awareness of the claims of the young, this pervasive interest in and concern for them. It was not always deliberate, to be sure; that makes it all the more significant. It is as if English and American writers never quite decided whether they were writing for the young or for the old, and saw no reason to make a sharp distinction.

Many of what were to become the greatest classics were written, assuredly, without children in mind, and were taken over by children, who cheerfully disregarded what they could not understand and cherished what they could. Thus Defoe, old and cantankerous, did not mean to write for children, but they adopted Robinson Crusoe and own him still; soon Crusoe spread all over the globe; he was celebrated in every language; he suffered one metamorphosis after another, most famously in *Swiss Family Robinson*, but in dozens of others as well.* After two hundred years he is read avidly by children in Montana and Tasmania and Norway, and very little by their parents. Nor did the harsh and embittered Jonathan Swift mean to write for the young, but he could not help himself either. The children took over Gulliver and went with him on his travels; they made him into a kind of fairy-story character.

So with most of the classics of English letters. Surely, Thackeray did not think that *Henry Esmond* was being drawn chiefly for the edification of adolescents; it was, he thought, "a book of cut-throat

---

* The imitations and sequels were so numerous that they came to constitute a special category of literature called Robinsonades. The Germans, with characteristic thoroughness, have compiled a bibliography of these: Hermann Ullrich, *Robinson und Robinsonaden: Bibliographie, Geschichte, Kritik,* Weimar, 1898.

melancholy." Yet generation after generation of boys and girls in England and America have learned about Marlborough and his wars from the exploits of the gallant Esmond. And so, too, with Becky Sharp, admired for her exploits rather than her gallantry, perhaps, but admired none the less. And Scott, for whom was he writing, this great heart of the North? Who read *Ivanhoe* and *Rob Roy* and *Quentin Durward,* year after year (now no longer), who but boys and girls? And who reads the books of the Brontë sisters, *Wuthering Heights* above all, and *Jane Eyre;* or for that matter Jane Austen? Or we can turn to the greatest of them all, Dickens, who did not, in his novels, consciously write for children, but who has become next to Hans Andersen and Mark Twain and Louisa Alcott the most dearly beloved of all children's authors. It is the children who best know Pip, who weep over Little Nell, who rejoice at David's good fortune when he finds refuge with Betsey Trotwood, who delight in Samuel Pickwick and his man Weller.

Already with the Victorians there was a change, or the shadow of a change. Trollope, perhaps the most completely Victorian of them all, ignored children, and the children have reciprocated by ignoring him. Nor will they read the giants of the late Victorian era, Meredith or Hardy or Henry James. Yet the tradition of writing for the young as well as for the old was still strong. It flourished with Stevenson, in *A Child's Garden of Verses, Treasure Island, Kidnapped* and most of the others. It was maintained by the Kipling of the *Jungle Books* and *Kim,* of *Stalky* and *Captains Courageous,* and by the wonderful Conan Doyle of *The White Company* as well as of *The Adventures of Sherlock Holmes.* It assures immortality to De Morgan's *Joseph Vance* and *Alice-for-Short,* novels that, we may hope, are suffering only a temporary eclipse. The pleasant tradition persisted into the Georgian era as well, not with Galsworthy, perhaps, but with the Wells of *Mr. Polly* and *Kipps,* the Bennett of *Clayhanger* and *Denry the Audacious,* with Conrad above all, that prince of storytellers, who had something for every age and every philosophy. It continued well into the new century, with John Buchan, who was the successor to Scott and Stevenson, with the neglected Quiller-Couch, with Hugh Walpole. Then after World War I it came to an abrupt end; what normal child reads Virginia Woolf or D. H. Lawrence, Aldous Huxley or James Joyce?

What an astonishing record it is, a record without parallel in any other major literature, except the American and perhaps the French. Certainly Victor Hugo has been taken over by children, in part at least, and Alexandre Dumas, and some of Balzac and, in a special category, the mystery writer Gaboriau. Certainly there is nothing to compare with it in the classical literature that excited the enthusiasm of the Greek-laden Scudder, or in the literatures of Italy or Spain, Germany or Russia.

In America the tradition persisted and flourished as in England. Call the roll of the American novelists and story writers from Cooper and Simms to the twentieth century: almost all of them wrote for children or wrote books that children have taken over. Cooper did, and until our own time boys and girls rejoiced in the exploits of Leatherstocking and Chingachook. Poe did, though not deliberately, and for a century children have worked out the puzzles and ciphers of his stories of detection, or recited "The Raven" and "The Bells." Simms did, poor Simms who lies all but forgotten in his Charleston grave, and whose novels of Indian and Partisan warfare are forgotten with him. And as for Hawthorne, he was Scudder's prize exhibit. He had started with *Grandfather's Chair*, the kind of recreating of history that we might do well to encourage now, and then, convinced that he had a special talent for this kind of writing, had gone on to the retelling of classical myths: *A Wonder-Book*, which "purged out all the old heathen wickedness," and the *Tanglewood Tales*, in which classical myths were "purified from all moral stains." They were fully equal to Mother Goose, so Hawthorne thought, and he added that he had never done anything else quite as well. It was an exaggeration, but one that generations of children were to bear with cheerfully. In our own time it is children who read *The House of the Seven Gables* and most of the famous stories.

Almost all the major writers of the mid-nineteenth century, and the minor too, thought it proper to serve the needs of children, or wrote books that children took on as their own. Most of the poets of the Golden Age belong to both categories—Whittier, Longfellow, Lowell, Holmes—those poets whose benign countenances stared out at us from the cards in the amiable game of Authors, each with its neat little list of works: if you had "Lowell" you asked for *The Vision of Sir Launfal* or *The Biglow Papers,* and put the two together. A bit later it was the gentle Sidney Lanier who somehow found the energy to prepare *A Boy's King Arthur* and *A Boy's Froissart,* and even *The Boy's Percy;* it was Eugene Field or James Whitcomb Riley, whose best poems are all for children or about them, and best of all the rediscovered Emily Dickinson. We may take all this for granted now, because we are so familiar with it, but try to think of comparable poets of our own day who are read by children? Sandburg would qualify, of course, and Stephen Benét, and Robert Frost. But who else? T. S. Eliot, Ezra Pound, e.e. cummings, Robert Lowell, Karl Shapiro?

Neither of the two mid-century writers who have come to be most highly regarded, Thoreau and Melville, wrote consciously for children, but *Walden* is discovered anew by every youngster, and *Moby Dick* has made its way into the high schools, where it is read much as *Gulliver's Travels* was once read. Emerson was assuredly a philosopher, and addressed himself to the high-minded and the mature, but what boy or girl has failed to read him in high school? It is suggestive that our most famous philosophers—Franklin, Emerson, William James, even John Dewey—are all read chiefly by the young.

It was in the mid-nineteenth century that two women were writing books that were to hold their popularity for a century to come. There was Harriet Beecher Stowe, burning with zeal for freedom, and writing away at *Uncle Tom's Cabin,* which was not designed for children at all; it was designed to stir up the parents. But within a short time the children took it over, and it is they who have read it ever since, children who knew virtue and vice when they saw it, no nonsense about it, and who took Little Eva to their hearts, and Topsy and poor Uncle Tom.*

Along with Mrs. Stowe was young Louisa May Alcott, the spinster who never really understood children, and who wrote per-

---

* Curiously enough Uncle Tom, like Moby Dick and Huck Finn, has now been taken back by the critics and scholars.

haps the most widely read child's book to come out of the New World. Children loved *Little Women* from the beginning, and have never ceased to love it. None of the sequels was quite as good, not *Little Men* or *Eight Cousins* or *Jo's Boys*, good as they were. *Little Women* belongs to itself; it is a classic in the sense that Andersen's *Fairy Tales* is a classic, or *Robinson Crusoe*. They have gone all over the world, these little women of Concord; their story has been translated into every language. They have gone into the hearts of children everywhere, giving them a feeling for America that few other books can give.

But perhaps it is Tom, after all, and his friend Huck who are our best ambassadors. For now comes the greatest of them all, the writer who has disturbed so many critics because he is not more adult, or because he is neurotic, or because he did not achieve his full potentialities, or for other reasons, but who has never disturbed the children, who read him uncritically and joyfully. It is an impressive thing that so many Americans should think that *Huckleberry Finn* is the great American novel. What other people, what non-English people, would ever single out a children's book as the great national novel? Can you imagine the Germans doing it, or the French or the Italians? The English might, to be sure, if they went in for things like the Great English Novel, which they do not. They might nominate *Gulliver* and *Vanity Fair* and *Kidnapped* and *Kim* and *Lord Jim* as candidates. But we make no bones about it. Our Great Novel is, for most of us, *Huckleberry Finn*, and, if not, then it is *Moby Dick*.

And, of course, it was not only Tom and Huck Finn; there were half a dozen other books that have nourished the spirits and delighted the hearts of the boys and girls ever since: *The Prince and the Pauper*, for example, or *A Connecticut Yankee*, with their simple humanitarianism and morality which are perhaps not so simple after all, or the exciting *Life on the Mississippi* that stirs the American imagination like the story of Ulysses or of Roland, so distant does it all seem now, and so romantic.

And who was it who aided and abetted Mark Twain in all this, and wrote an account of him as tender as anything that one writer ever wrote about another? Who but the Dean of American Letters? A formidable title, this, and William Dean Howells was in a way a formidable figure—editor of the great *Atlantic,* and then of *Harper's Easy Chair,* author of thirty or forty novels and as many plays and a dozen books of criticism and another dozen of travel, and sponsor of realism, of modernism, of all sorts of isms. Put him in France or England or Denmark and what would you have? A Hippolyte Taine, perhaps, or an Edmund Gosse, or a Georg Brandes; imagine any of these magisterial critics bothering about children, much less writing books for them. But Howells did. It is not only that children everywhere can read *Silas Lapham* for pleasure, and do. Howells wrote directly for the young, and about them. Is there a more charming picture of boyhood in American literature than *A Boy's Town?*

And so it goes, all through the nineteenth century and well into the twentieth. No need to recall Bret Harte, or the local colorists who were, most of them, children's writers as well. No need to list the historical novelists, Winston Churchill and Mary Johnston and S. Weir Mitchell and the many others. Everyone could read *The Crossing* and *The Crisis;* everyone still can for that matter; everyone could read *Hugh Wynne, Free Quaker,* with those lovely Pyle illustrations, or *To Have and to Hold* or *The Long Roll* and *Cease Fire,* still among the best of the Civil War novels. And no need to celebrate those writers whose audience was never quite clear, even to themselves, and who belong impartially to juvenile literature and to Literature with a capital L.; Frank R. Stockton, for example, or Jack London or Joel Chandler Harris, whose Uncle Remus stories are known the world over.

Meantime, with the encouragement and under the stimulus of the *Youth's Companion* and *St. Nicholas,* the best children's magazines in the world, there developed a large and flourishing group of authors who wrote deliberately for children, until in the end this was the one literary field where Americans could claim preeminence, or at least dispute it with the English. Some of them are forgotten, now, but not all, not the Anglo-American Frances Hodgson Burnett, who gave us *Little Lord Fauntleroy, Sara Crewe,* and *The Secret Garden;* not Howard Pyle, who wrote almost as well as he painted; or Palmer Cox of "Brownie" fame; or Charles Carryl,

whose *Davy and the Goblin* is still something of a classic; or Lucre-
tia Hale, of *Peterkin* fame; or Mary Mapes Dodge herself, whose
true monument is not *Hans Brinker* but *St. Nicholas*. Nor are the
"series" wholly forgotten, those series so dear to the hearts of
American children, the Little Colonel, for example, or the Oz
books, or the five Little Peppers.

What a wealth of stories there is in our literature about the
school and the playing field. The type had been set, once and for
all, by *Tom Brown's Schooldays*, and it is interesting to note that
this was about a private school. Not only the English but American
stories fell into that pattern. Not always, to be sure; the *Youth's
Companion* and *St. Nicholas* are crowded with stories of grade and
high school: Noah Brooks' "Fairport Nine," for instance. But the
indefatigable chronicler of school life, Ralph Henry Barbour, chose
to write about private schools. How odd—and yet how natural it
always seemed. For just as in America we civilianized the military
and secularized the theological and Americanized the Continental,
so we democratized privilege. The Hillsides and Fairtops and
Yardleys and all the other schools of the Barbour books didn't
really seem like private schools. And the hero was always a little
democrat: his mother sometimes took in wash to keep him there,
or so it seemed. And the pattern of these dearly beloved school
stories was always the same. It was always the substitute who
came in in the ninth inning and hit a home run, or who dashed in
with five minutes to play and intercepted a forward pass. It was
always the honorable player who won out over the sneak, and the
poor boy over the rich, and the boy with school spirit over those
who derided school spirit. It is a pattern which Margaret Mead has
elaborately reconstructed in such studies as *And Keep Your Powder
Dry*, and which the Barbour heroes, and readers, knew instinctively.

This enthusiasm for the school and the playground seems a bit
naïve, and perhaps it is. Yet compare, or contrast, the juvenile
literature of France or Germany. There is little school literature
here, for school is a very serious affair, a preparation for life and
for a profession; and only the brightest boys, after all, go on to the
lycée or the *Gymnasium*. And as for the playing fields, why, in
many of the schools of France, Germany, and Italy there are none.

There was one great storehouse of children's literature to which America made no contribution: the fairy tale. This was no doubt the oldest form of literature for entertainment—oral literature in every society centuries before it was reduced to writing. It was not designed for children, but for everyone, and it came in time to be not only folklore but even folk religion. But with the growth of sophistication in society, children took it over, and with Giambattista in the early seventeenth century and Perrault in the early eighteenth and the migration of the *Thousand and One Nights* it became a recognized branch of literature. Romanticism, which discovered both children and nationalism, used the fairy tale to appeal to both, as with the Grimm brothers in Germany, Bishop Grundtvig in Denmark, and Asbjörnsen in Norway. It was not really until the romantic Andrew Lang collected the fairy stories of all nations and published them in those delectable color books that they became the common property of children everywhere—the *Red Fairy Book*, the *Green Fairy Book*, the *Yellow Fairy Book*— how familiar they were, these stories drawn from every country.

Not quite; not from America. Why did not America produce her own fairy stories?

Fairy tales belong to the realm of tradition, not of literature, and, as America was born and grew entirely in the era of the printed page, she had no oral tradition except what she inherited from the Old World. She did not, therefore, produce a traditional or mythological literature, but was content with what she had inherited. It is suggestive that the one major writer who created a kind of American fairy tale, Washington Irving, borrowed his stories almost entirely from Holland and Germany. Yet there was stuff for mythology, and for something like fairy tales in the story of the Indian. In time scholars like Schoolcraft and poets like Longfellow and historians like Francis Parkman were to work this rich vein. Cooper, who did more to familiarize the Indian among Americans of all ages than any other writer, did not exploit the folklore or folk tales but contented himself with what he knew of Indians during the period of white settlement, and so did the Southern Cooper, William Gilmore Simms. Not until much later— our own time, indeed—did imaginative writers like Mary Austin

and Willa Cather and Constance Lindsay Skinner incorporate Indian stories and myths in stories that belonged equally to the world
of adult and juvenile literature. But somehow Indian mythology—
the vast collection of stories embalmed in the reports of the Smithsonian Institution—never really caught the American imagination,
and Americans themselves provided no substitute for these.

The literary concern for children persisted into the new century.
Crane's *Maggie: A Girl of the Streets* was not written for children,
but the *Whilomville Stories* were. Young people could read *The
Octopus* with profit if not with pleasure, and much of Jack London
with pleasure if not always with profit. The new realists were not
too realistic for boys and girls: Hamlin Garland, for example,
whose *Son of the Middle Border* was one of the magic books of its
time; or Owen Wister, who celebrated the cowboy in that *Vir-
ginian* which Theodore Roosevelt thought so improper. Tarking-
ton's *Penrod* and *Seventeen* are all but forgotten but we still read
The Magnificent Ambersons or *Alice Adams*, both of them about
adolescents, and watch them in the films, too. Edgar Lee Masters
was dour enough in *Spoon River*, but he wrote boys' stories as
well; William Allen White is at his best in *The Court of Boyville*,
and the loveliest thing he ever wrote was his *Tribute to Mary*.

What explains this preoccupation with children, their interests
and their world, this readiness to deal with them as equals? The
explanation is not primarily literary, but economic and social and
philosophical. Richly endowed by nature, Americans have always
been in a position to pamper and indulge their children, to release
them from much of the work which was taken for granted in less-
favored countries. America, almost alone among nations, could
afford not only the direct costs of universal education but the
hidden costs of leisure for potential workers.

Closely connected with this ability to indulge children, and to
educate them, was the conviction that children were important in
themselves, and that childhood was its own justification. The English had something of this, and the Scandinavians and perhaps the
Swiss, but it is not a Continental attitude. Americans have never
believed that childhood was merely a preparation for life, that
children should be trained to work at fourteen or to enter a partic-

ular profession at twenty, or to go into the army. They have been content to take childhood on its own terms. Long before John Dewey formulated the principle, they acted on the assumption that childhood was not a preparation for life, but life itself, that it had its own interests that were as valid as the interests of the adult world. In simple and homely ways this attitude persists—and never fails to startle visitors from overseas, who do not understand why American parents so habitually yield their own interests and peace, privacy and convenience, to their young.

If there has always been a philosophical principle behind this, it is not necessarily a conscious or self-conscious one. From the beginning and until very recently, Americans have lived in the future and for the future; for them the best was always yet to be. This was true of individuals—after all, the movement to the New World was a vote of confidence in the future; it was true of society as a whole, which was always making ambitious plans for glittering tomorrows. This is merely another way of saying that, more than most people, Americans live in and for their children. The little country town may be dismal and shabby, but in twenty years, or thirty, it will surely be a great metropolis. The newcomer may make but little impression on his new world, but what is to prevent his children from conquering it, from going to the White House even? As Americans have seen in every barefoot boy a future President or corporation executive, they have lived in their children, worked for them, and indulged them.

That principle of equality which Tocqueville saw as pervasive and persistent affected the position of children and the character of children's literature as well. Even English juvenile literature is class-conscious, but not American. Stories are written for children of all classes—or simply for children. If a Veblen would detect class consciousness in *St. Nicholas,* or a less astute critic in Ralph Henry Barbour or in Martha Finley's Elsie stories, all this was for the most part unconscious, and made little impact on the American psychology. Not only did the principle of equality create an immensely broad and uniform audience; it worked in another direction as well. It worked to blur if not wholly to eliminate the differences between the sexes. Just as Americans early accorded a high position to woman, so they wiped out the differences between stories for boys and stories for girls. Note how even English juvenile literature addresses itself mostly to boys, the self-conscious literature, that is. But there is no preferential treatment in the United States.

The past quarter century has seen a sharp departure from the long tradition of literature written alike for the old and the young, and a partial return to that tradition. At first glance the division between the two schools, juvenile and adult, seems deep. The writers for children—Cornelia Meigs, Dorothy Canfield, Rachel Field, Elizabeth Coatsworth, Esther Forbes, Owen Wister, Elizabeth Enright, John Tunis, Armstrong Perry—belong in one world; Theodore Dreiser, Thomas Wolfe, John Steinbeck, Hemingway, Faulkner, Mailer, and Saul Bellow, in another. Yet the old pressures are still at work, both on the authors and on their books. *The Old Man and the Sea* is now in every high-school anthology, and so, too, "The Bear" and "The Red Pony," whether Hemingway and Faulkner and Steinbeck intended this or not. Furthermore, thanks in part to earlier physical maturity, in part to improved education, the level of sophistication is steadily rising. *The New Yorker* now sets the standards for the high schools, as it once set the standards for the colleges, and magazines like *Seventeen* and *Mademoiselle* run stories and articles that would have been thought radically advanced for the women's magazines of yesterday. If adolescents have not embraced Herzog, they have adopted Holden Caulfield.

Yet, in this competition between worlds, it is the children who have, on the whole, lost: they have adopted the world of adults, rather than the other way around. Though Steinbeck may turn aside to write *The Red Pony*, on the whole the new generation of writers makes few concessions to children. Let them enter our world, they seem to say, or let them be content with their comics and their television. They are not to be put down as curmudgeons because they take this attitude; it is after all the attitude of their society. It is a society which substitutes the comics for *St. Nicholas,* builds expensive homes without nurseries or playrooms or attics, spends billions on highways but nothing on bicycle paths, deplores violence in the young but engages in violence on a scale never before known in history.

It is not enough that we pamper our children with magnificent schools, elaborate playgrounds, summer camps and swimming pools, telephones and television in their own rooms, and all the gadgets that inventors can think of or advertisers sell. All these may starve rather than feed the mind. More and more we are treating our children as a rich man who is incapable of love might treat his wife, trying to fob them off with material things in place of the vital experiences they have a right to. More and more we treat them as beings apart, to be pampered, perhaps, to be indulged, to be well-fed, well-dressed, and well-schooled, but we withhold from them what they have a right to know and to enjoy. We nourish their bodies but starve their imagination.

NOAH WEBSTER:

SCHOOLMASTER TO AMERICA

7

In 1783 the United States achieved independence, and President Ezra Stiles of Yale College prophesied that the new nation, happily free of those provincial dialects that confused social and regional differences in less fortunate countries, would be bound together by a single and uniform language. At that very time a young graduate of Yale, teaching obscurely in Goshen, New York, proclaimed what was to be a cultural and linguistic Declaration of Independence. Noah Webster wanted to call his little book *The American Instructor*, but the dignified President Stiles overruled him and dictated the pretentious title, *A Grammatical Institute of the English Language: Part I*. It was in fact nothing more impressive than a Speller; to generations of Americans it was to be familiarly known as *Webster's Blue-Backed Speller*. It caught on, at once; within a few years it all but monopolized the field; under its benign guidance generations of young Americans learned the same words, the same spellings, the same pronunciations; read the same stories; absorbed the same moral lessons.

It was all part of a larger program—a program for cultural as well as political independence from the Mother Country. "Amer-

Saturday Review, October 18, 1958.

ica," wrote the young pedagogue, "must be independent in literature as she is in politics", and in the Preface of his Speller he elabo-
rated on this notion:

> The author wishes to promote the honor and prosperity of the con-
> federated republics of America. . . . This country must in some future
> time be as distinguished by the superiority of her literary improve-
> ments, as she is already by the liberality of her civil and ecclesiastical
> constitutions. Europe is grown old in folly, corruption and tyranny.
> For America in her infancy to adopt the maxims of the Old World
> would be to stamp the wrinkles of decrepit old age upon the bloom of
> youth, and to plant the seeds of decay in a vigorous constitution.
> American glory begins to dawn at a favourable period. . . .

It was characteristic of Webster that he should associate the
dawn of American glory with the publication of his own book, and
it was prophetic, too, for the connection was there, and it was soon
to be notorious. In 1783 Webster had few qualifications for either
education or philology, but enormous enthusiasm for both. It was a
sound instinct that directed his energies into these fields, and held
them there through a long life of distractions, ambitions, and con-
ceits.

The Speller, and after it the Grammar, the Reader, and the
Dictionaries, assured Webster a place among the Founding Fathers. Over the years he consolidated his position, and extended it.
Indeed, wherever we look there is Noah Webster, dour, angular,
and aggressive, busily fathering institutions and organizations that
we now think of as characteristically American. Even in an age of
Fatherhood, he was fabulously progenitive, and insistent, too, on
his parental prerogatives. He was, clearly, the Father of the American Language, and he was certainly one of the Fathers of American Education. If we turn to that group of statesmen who made
the Constitution, there is Webster, holding aloft his "Sketches of
American Policy," and determined to be numbered among the
Founding Fathers. He presents himself no less insistently as one of
the Fathers of American Political Thought, for in voluminous
pages he told Hamilton how to run parties, lectured Madison on
the Presidency, and instructed Jefferson on the nature of democracy. If we look to journalism, there is Webster, editor of the

American Magazine, of the *Minerva* and the *Herald,* and prepared
to toss off a history of American journalism.

If we consider science there, too, is Webster, edging up to Dr.
Franklin and Dr. Rush and Dr. Rittenhouse, hopefully proffering
his two-volume *History of Epidemics,* and with sheafs of scientific
articles bulging in his coat pockets. He is surely the Father of
Copyright; he has some claim to be the Father of the Census.
What with his school histories, and his edition (or was it his?) of
Winthrop's *Journal,* he is one of the Fathers of American History;
and his many essays on banking, finance, and insurance support
his claim to be a Father of American Economics as well. And finally his singlehanded revision of the Bible—he thought it his greatest work—permits us to call him one of the Fathers of the Church!

Even in an age of versatility, it is an astonishing versatility. And
yet it does not quite ring true. The versatility of a Franklin, a
Jefferson, a Bentley, a Rush, a Rumford is the spontaneous expression of a complex personality and an affluent and extravagant nature. But with Webster versatility seems to be the expression,
rather, of nagging ambition, grim determination, and indefatigable
officiousness, and perhaps of vanity as well. He was determined to
make his mark; he was not going to be left out; and he was confident that whatever he touched he improved.

For all his wide and varied interests, he did not have a richly-
stored mind; for all his vitality he did not have an open mind;
narrow, cold, almost passionless, he was wholly lacking in those
grace notes his great contemporaries added to their scores with
such ease. He read everything, but only to get definitions for
his dictionary; he taught music, but revealed not the slightest interest in the musical giants of his own time; he studied history, but
only to learn that man is vile. He knew the languages of twenty
nations, but was interested in none of these; he visited France only
to deplore its licentiousness; he visited Cambridge, only to remark
on the inferiority of its architecture. He was devout, but curiously
untouched by religious sentiment. Religion was to him a kind of
muscular exercise in moralizing; he was ready to drop his closest
friend, Joel Barlow, because he found his poetry godless; and he
thought the Bible would be improved by expunging the word

"womb." He was zealous for education, but had little faith in the young, and thought voting should be restricted to those over forty-five. His reason for founding Amherst College was chiefly to confound and frustrate Unitarian Harvard. He was a cultural busy-body; in an odd fashion he anticipated Big Bill Thompson's wonderful boast about Chicago: he took up culture, and he made culture hum.

And yet this is an ungrateful view; it is not what Webster was that is important, but what Webster did. And what he did is inescapably clear. He helped free generations of Americans from a sense of inferiority about their language, and gave them instead a sense of the dignity of their speech. He contributed more than any other single person to a uniform American speech, and to the avoidance of those differences in accent and vocabulary that might proclaim differences in background, in class, or in region. His wish was, he said,

> to diffuse an uniformity and purity of language in America, to destroy the provincial prejudices that originate in the trifling differences of dialect and produce reciprocal ridicule, to promote the interest of literature and the harmony of the United States.

More specifically, he labored, in his books and his newspapers and his teaching,

> to extirpate the improprieties and vulgarisms which were necessarily introduced by settlers from various parts of Europe; to reform the abuses and corruption which tincture the conversation of the polite part of Americans; to render the acquisition of the language easy both to American youth and foreigners; and to render the pronounciation of it accurate and uniform by demolishing those odious distinctions of provincial dialects which are the subject of reciprocal ridicule.

All this Webster achieved, first through that Speller which went triumphantly from generation to generation until it came to be as familiar as the Bible, and as essential; through the Readers which for a time commanded the field and yielded only reluctantly to the more popular Peter Parley and McGuffey series; through his famous Dictionary which appeared first, and modestly, in 1806, and then monumentally in 1828, and through all its metamorphoses achieved the distinction of being an institution in itself. It was the

Speller that conquered the land. It established its sovereignty in the East; it went west with the Conestoga wagon, and in the knapsacks of countless itinerant pedagogues; it leaped the mountains and established its empire on the Pacific coast; it even invaded the South, and on the eve of that war he was to do much to bring on, Jefferson Davis wrote "above all other people we are one, and above all books which have united us in the bond of common language, I place the good old Spelling-Book of Noah Webster." The demand was insatiable; it sold by the hundred thousand, it sold by the million, it sold by the tens of millions. No other secular book had ever spread so wide, penetrated so deep, lasted so long.

Neither energy nor ambition nor vanity explains anything by itself, for we want to know why these forces took one channel rather than another: why they contributed to social weal rather than woe; found outlet in public rather than in private activities; expressed themselves in national rather than parochial accents, in liberal rather than conservative terms. The driving force in Webster, the compulsion that explains all particular expressions of his ambitions and his energies, was nationalism.

It was, to be sure, an age of self-conscious nationalism, and Webster was typical rather than original. "We are laboring hard to establish in this country principles more and more national, and free from all foreign ingredients," wrote Alexander Hamilton. We must have an American literature, argued Joel Barlow and Philip Freneau and Timothy Dwight. "The business of education acquired a new complexion by the independence of our country," said Benjamin Rush. "One American work is of more value to the United States than three foreign ones, even of superior merit," wrote Horatio Greenough of painting. "The Churches of America are all assuming a new complexion," wrote Dr. John Livingston; "they now become National Churches in this new Empire." Even arithmetic was to be new, for, "as the United States are now an independent nation," said Nicholas Pike, "it was judged that a system might be calculated more suitable to our Meridian than those heretofore published." This was the climate of opinion in which Webster lived and flourished; this was the doctrine to which he enthusiastically subscribed, the gospel he gladly preached. "Unshackle your minds," he admonished his countrymen. "You have an empire to raise and support by your exertions, and a national character to establish and extend by your wisdom and virtue. Every engine," he added, "should be employed to render the people of this country national, to call their attachments home to their own country, and to inspire them with the pride of national character."

The nations of the Old World were the products of centuries of history; America was created. Old World nations had inherited and absorbed all the essential ingredients of nationalism; America had to manufacture them. The peoples of other countries had been born national, as had their fathers and their forebears; in America they were to be "rendered" national. What were the "engines" to be employed in this enterprise?

One of them, and one of the most important, was language. "A national language," Webster said, "is a bond of national union." And so it was—in France, in Denmark, in England, in Spain; and when ancient peoples organized themselves as independent nations in Germany, in Italy, in Greece, in Bohemia. The new United States was fortunate in having a common (even if an inherited) language; could that language be kept common over an immense territory, and among a people made up of so many and such diverse elements? The question might seem more pertinent to the twentieth than to the early nineteenth century; that it is not is because Webster and his colleagues not only asked it but answered it over a century ago.

The peoples of Old World nations had, indeed, their own language, but their language was neither common nor uniform. Everywhere on the Continent the upper classes spoke French, and disdained the vernacular. Each region had its own dialect and each class its own idiom. So pronounced were the local dialects that Frenchmen from Brittany and the Languedoc could not understand each other, or Germans from the Rhineland and Saxony, or Danes from Copenhagen and Jutland, or, for that matter, Englishmen from East Anglia and Devonshire. And if, almost everywhere, speech proclaimed region, it betrayed class, and continued to do so down into our own century; just a few years ago George Orwell

could say that every Englishman was branded on the tongue at
birth. In the Old World these linguistic vagaries were not seriously
divisive (not yet, anyhow) because the classes who confessed them
had little influence and because there were so many other forces—
religion, for example, or history, or the monarchy—binding men
together.

But if nationalism was to work in the United States—and in
1800 that was still very much an open question—it would have to
get along without the monarchy, the church, the military, and the
many other institutions that provided common denominators
abroad, and work with more democratic ingredients and build on
more popular support. It would have to frustrate those class and
religious and racial divisions which were potentially so dangerous;
it would have to overcome differences not merely of accent but of
language itself. The United States, dedicated to the unprecedented
experiment of republicanism in a vast territory; a heterogeneous
population, and a classless society, could not afford differences of
accent or of language.

A great many Americans of the eighteenth century saw this, but
none more clearly than Webster. He labored not only for a common language, but for an *American* language. Like Franklin and
Jefferson he rejected the authority of the hated Dr. Johnson, and of
Dr. Robert Lowth as well; indeed, he rejected all English authority
that seemed to conflict with common sense or common usage. He
knew that language was a living thing, and was confident that
Americans had the same capacity to enlarge it and adapt it as the
English, and that their contribution was not only respectable but
desirable. "New circumstances," he said, "new modes of life, new
laws, new ideas of various kinds" would bring about "considerable
differences between the American and the English language."
Those differences would be, for the most part, improvements, for
"the English language has been greatly improved in Britain within
a century, but its highest perfection with every other branch of
human knowledge is perhaps reserved for the land of light and
freedom." With what was in his day considerable boldness Webster admitted to his Spellers and Readers, and eventually to his
Dictionaries, words regarded in the Mother Country as obsolete or

as barbarisms. He accepted new grammatical constructions. He adopted a simplified spelling—much more simplified, indeed, than public opinion would stand, then or later. And he defined words in American rather than in English terms; this was one of his most significant contributions. In all of this he found authority in popular usage.

For how was the uniformity of the American language to be achieved? Could it be imposed from above? So John Adams thought, and he had early recommended the creation of an American Academy which should fix the standards of good usage. Webster himself was instrumental in establishing a Philological Society whose chief function seems to have been to endorse his own books; certainly it did nothing else memorable. The academy was never born; the society withered and died; but they were not necessary. Webster's books did their work. He found his authority in part in what he thought the less corrupt usage of Elizabethan England, but more clearly in popular (mostly New England) usage. "The *general practice* of a nation is the rule of propriety," he wrote, "and this practice should at least be consulted in so important a matter, as that of making laws for speaking." It was the "general practice" that he tried to incorporate in his Spellers, Grammars, Readers, and Dictionaries, but these, in turn, became authorities. They were, however, authorities with a difference—authorities that (like our governments) drew their power from below, and that were embraced, spontaneously, by the people themselves. Webster was therefore not only a standard and a symbol, but a spontaneous standard and a popular symbol. When, in 1830, he went to Washington to push through a new (and more profitable) copyright law, he was welcomed with reverence by Congressmen, almost all of whom had been brought up on his books.

A nation needs not only a common language; it needs, even more, a common past, and a sense of that past. Every European statemaker of modern times has recognized this. Thus, Bishop Grundtvig in Denmark devoted his volcanic energies to the editing of ancient Danish ballads, the writing of national histories and national songs, the resurrection of the national past. Thus, in Germany Schlegel and Stein and Savigny and the brothers Grimm recreated the German past in order to create a German future. Thus, in his struggle for the unification of Italy, Mazzini was always conscious that "the most important inspiration for nationalism is the awareness of past glories and past sufferings." The philosophers and historians of nationalism, too, recognized the primacy of tradition. Thus, Ernst Renan emphasized for France "the common memories, glories, afflictions, and regrets"; thus, in England, John Stuart Mill concluded that the most important single ingredient in nationalism was "the possession of a national history and community of recollections." And our contemporary, Sir Ernest Barker, has put the matter succinctly: "A nation is not the physical fact of one blood but the mental fact of one tradition."

All true enough, but what was the new United States to do? How does a country without a past—without, in any event, a common past—provide itself with a usable past, or with a substitute for it? How does a country without history, traditions, legends, or symbols create them? And how does it find substitutes for those institutions and symbols which customarily served to unify Old World peoples: the monarchy, the aristocracy, the Church, the army, the university, and others?

Yet all the American past lacked was antiquity, and antiquity, like tradition, could be manufactured. Americans were perhaps the first people to prove what so many of the newer peoples of the twentieth century are now proving, that the past can be telescoped, and the processes of tradition making and symbol making enormously accelerated. Undaunted by their youth, Americans set about resolutely to create what was missing; with immense energy they provided themselves with a common history, a common memory, a set of symbols and of legends. Almost everyone joined in this enterprise: statesmen, soldiers, poets, historians, journalists, explorers, artists, scholars, and teachers.

Webster, it will be noted, fitted into most of these categories, but particularly the last one. It was characteristic—it was almost prophetic—that in America the teacher should play a larger role in the creation of nationalism than almost anywhere else: this because the United States was the first nation to inaugurate anything remotely like universal free education. In other countries governments deliberately used the schools to indoctrinate the young with particular versions of nationalism and patriotism. In the United States, government never performed this dangerous role, but private individuals did, for the most part quite innocently. Noah Webster was perhaps the first to realize the limitless potentialities of education for the encouragement of nationalism, and of the schoolbook as the vehicle. He purposed, from the beginning, to use the schools as engines of nationalism. That purpose he carried out most fully in his Readers, and, eventually, in a bewildering miscellany of histories of one kind or another: the historical introduction he provided to Jedidiah Morse's immensely popular *Geography;* the *Elements of Useful Knowledge*—one volume devoted to American history; the "Federal Catechism" attached to his *Little Reader's Assistant,* and others.

Webster was first in the field with moral and patriotic readers, and set the style for subsequent ventures, notably those of the McGuffey brothers. His Reader (elaborately called *An American Selection of Lessons in Reading and Speaking: Calculated to Improve the minds and refine the taste of Youth*) was Part III of the Grammatical Institute, but came to have an independent life of its own. From the beginning its purpose was patriotic as well as educational—in Webster's mind these things were never separate. On the title page Webster placed the absurd admonition by Mirabeau: "Begin with the infant in his cradle; let the first word he lisps be Washington." Later Webster was to rephrase this pious injunction with more elaborate humorlessness: "Every child in America should be acquainted with his own country. As soon as he opens his lips he should rehearse the history of his own country, he should lisp the praise of liberty, and of those illustrious heroes and statesmen who have wrought a revolution in her favor." The Reader included addresses by Warren and Hancock on the Boston massacre; the Declaration of Independence; Washington's Farewell to his army and his Circular Letter to the States; poems from the practiced hands of Barlow, Trumbull, and Freneau; and an extract —later withdrawn—from Tom Paine. The filiopietistic purpose was clear, but Webster drove it home: "In the choice of these pieces, I have not been inattentive to the political interests of

America. Several of these masterly addresses of Congress . . . contain such *noble, just, and independent sentiments* that I cannot help wishing to transfuse them into the breasts of the rising generation."

Even the Dictionary was exploited for patriotic purposes. It was an *American* dictionary, and its American character was less ostentatious in spelling and grammar and vocabulary than in definitions and illustrations. "The chief glory of a nation," wrote Webster, "is its authors," and it was "with pride and satisfaction" that he cited Washington and Franklin, Adams and Kent, Barlow and Irving, along with Bacon and Milton, Addison and Pope. "I may go further," he boasted somewhat indiscriminately, "and affirm that our country has produced some of the best models of composition . . . President Smith (of Princeton); the authors of the Federalist; Chancellor Kent; the prose of Mr. Barlow, of Dr. William Channing, of Washington Irving . . . in purity, in elegance, and in technical precision, is equalled only by that of the best British authors, and surpassed by that of no English compositions of a similar kind."

Webster's patriotism, to be sure, was ardent but particular. In the beginning broad and generous, embracing the whole of the Union, and all classes of society, it grew increasingly narrow and sectional and ungenerous. He had begun as a disciple of Franklin, an admirer of Jefferson; he ended as an honorary member of the Essex Junto and a crony to the despicable Timothy Pickering. He had begun as a champion of nationalism, republicanism, and democracy; the French Revolution persuaded him to abjure democracy; Jefferson inspired doubts about republicanism; and the Hartford Convention was—for a time at least—the measure of his political nationalism. However, if he never became reconciled to democracy, he did become reconciled to the new form nationalism assumed after 1812.

But we must not expect consistency, or demand it. Webster was, for all his devotion to learning, a creature not of reason but of sentiment. "The eyes of the world are upon me," he wrote hopefully in 1788. We no longer see him, but we speak him and hear him. Surely that is an immortality even beyond his imagining.

THE MCGUFFEYS
AND THEIR READERS

8

When in 1891 William Venable wrote his classic *Beginnings of Literary Culture in the Ohio Valley*, he found room for William Holmes McGuffey and his schoolbooks in a footnote. Within a generation such distinguished public figures as Hamlin Garland, Herbert Quick, and Mark Sullivan were to hail the McGuffey Readers as major influences not only in American education but in American morals and culture as well. Still another generation and the McGuffey Readers became the darling of conservatives, who found in them the very symbol and citadel of traditionalism, and used them to counter and repel all that they thought pernicious in "progressive" education.

In a perverse way the conservatives were right: the Readers were conservative, even pedagogically. William McGuffey—their chief producer—showed no awareness in his Readers, or in his college and university teaching, of those progressive educational ideas which had their origins in Germany, penetrated into France and England, and spread to New England, where Bronson Alcott's Temple School anticipated by more than half a century the benign teachings of Jane Addams and John Dewey. Nor was there even an

Saturday Review, June 16, 1962.

awareness of those new but entirely respectable ideas that Horace
Mann was expounding in his series of annual reports to the legislature of Massachusetts. The McGuffey Readers were improvements on the Webster Readers and Spellers and on Lindley Mur-
ray's widely popular series of Readers, but they differed from these
in degree rather than in kind.

One thing the McGuffey Readers shared with schoolbooks everywhere, and indeed with most literature and art of their day—
the notion that education itself was primarily moral, and only sec-
ondarily intellectual. It had long been taken for granted in England, even in the grammar schools and the universities—it was in
this perhaps that English education differed most strikingly from
the Continental—that the primary business of schools was to train
character. The Puritans, far more interested in education than most
of their contemporaries, added to all this a special emphasis on
religious training: if Puritan schools were not designed to produce
Christian gentlemen, they were certainly designed to produce
Christians. This attitude was explicit in the school laws of the Bay
Colony: that it was "one chiefe project of ye ould deluder, Satan to
keepe men from the knowledge of ye Scriptures . . ." was the
preliminary justification for the famous Act of 1647 requiring every
town to provide elementary education for its children. The generation of the Founding Fathers looked to education to train character—schools, Benjamin Rush thought, should be "engines for
Republicanism." So, too, the Northwest Ordinance stated that as
"religion, morality and knowledge" were "necessary to good government and the happiness of mankind, schools and the means of
education should forever be encouraged." Clearly the schools were
expected to inculcate these qualities, and probably in that order.
McGuffey's generation took this principle for granted, and carried
it into the Ohio country and beyond. Even the great educational
reformers of the thirties and forties did not reject or seriously
modify this concept: Horace Mann himself thought education
primarily moral, and insisted that intellectual training must always
take second place after moral: to this principle his great co-worker
Henry Barnard readily subscribed.

Certainly what is most impressive in the McGuffey Readers is the morality. From the First Reader on through the Sixth, that morality is pervasive and insistent: there is rarely a page but addresses itself to some moral problem, points some moral lesson. The character of the morality propounded has sometimes been associated with the character and needs of the West, as if the Readers were themselves, somehow, a product of the Ohio frontier, or of Jacksonian America. Actually the morality of the Readers was that of the Victorian age everywhere in the Western world. It can be read in almost all the children's books of that time—in the pious stories of Maria Edgeworth or Charlotte Yonge, of Mrs. Ewing and Mrs. Molesworth in England; in the scores of volumes written by our own Peter Parley (he was Samuel Goodrich) and by Jacob Abbott of *Rollo* fame, or in the Sunday-school papers that the young were expected to read, or in the pages of *The Youth's Companion*. Thus the prospectus of that famous magazine asserted (1827) that "this is the day of peculiar care for Youth. Let their minds be formed, their hearts prepared, and their characters moulded for the scenes and duties of a brighter day." And when Franklin Edmunds launched a little series of books for boys he assured anxious parents that "all stories of an exaggerated style and false sentiment will be avoided and nothing presented but what will be calculated to inculcate some moral lesson."

What was the nature of the morality that permeated the Readers?

It was deeply religious, and in those mid-century years, in America, religion meant Protestant Christianity. More, it was a Christianity closer to Puritanism than to that Unitarianism which was even then making its way out of New England and into the Ohio country. God was omnipresent. He had His eye on every child every moment of the day and night, watched its every action, knew its every thought. He was a just God, but a stern one, and would not hesitate to punish even the smallest children who broke His commandments. The world of the McGuffeys was a world where no one questioned the truths of the Bible, or their relevance to everyday conduct, and where the notion that the separation of church and state required the exclusion of religion from the schoolroom or from schoolbooks seemed preposterous. The Readers, therefore, are filled with stories from the Bible, and tributes to its truth and beauty.

Yet, for all its preoccupation with religion, the morality of the Readers was materialistic and worldly. It taught a simple system of rewards and punishments. Virtue was rarely its own reward: the kind old lady found out that the vagabond she had befriended was really a rich nephew returned from the goldfields; the honest farmer was given five hundred dollars by his rich neighbor as a reward for his honesty; the poor boy who helped the old man across the street was promptly provided with a job; the little chimney sweep who resisted the temptation to steal a gold watch was adopted by its enraptured owner. Wickedness, too, was invariably detected and punished, and once again the punishments were material and physical. The disobedient boy drowned; the greedy boy found himself in want; the rude boy, the meddlesome boy, the inquisitive boy failed to get the job, or forfeited the rewards that went to his more exemplary companions. Nothing was left to the imagination, nothing to chance, and nothing, one is tempted to say, to conscience. It is an intriguing—but unanswerable—question whether this kind of moral arithmetic eventually did more harm than good; those who are today infatuated with the morality of the Readers might reflect that the generation most elaborately and persistently exposed to it—the generation roughly from the forties to the eighties—was probably the most materialistic generation in our history.

It was a middle-class, conventional, and equalitarian morality, one that derived from Benjamin Franklin and his careful rules of good conduct, rather than from the Puritan austerity of a John Adams, or the Enlightenment of a Jefferson. Industry, sobriety, thrift, propriety, modesty, punctuality, conformity—these were the essential virtues, and those who practiced them were sure of success. Success, too, for all the patina of morality that was brushed over it, was clearly material. It was a job, a farm, money in hand or in the bank. Failure was, just as clearly, the consequence of laziness or self-indulgence, and deserved, therefore, little sympathy:

There is a class of people [asserted the Fourth Reader] who are the pest of every community, workmen who do not know their trade, businessmen ignorant of the first principles of business. They can never be relied upon to do well anything they undertake. They are always making blunders which other people have to suffer for, and which react upon themselves. They are always getting out of employment, and failing in business. To make up for what they lack in knowledge and thoroughness, they often resort to trick and fraud, and become not merely contemptible but criminal.

In all this the Readers performed for a rural America pretty much the function that the Alger books were to perform for an urban America.

The McGuffey morality had many similarities to that of Dr. Pangloss: no matter how distressing things might seem, all was for the best—the workings of Providence, the arrangements of society, the vicissitudes of the economy—all would come right in the end. Does the widow starve? It is not her fault, to be sure, but neither is it the fault of society, and if she bears up charity will take care of her. Are orphans bereft? Society has no responsibility for them, but there is always some greathearted man who will come to their rescue or some kind woman who will adopt them. Does the laborer lose an arm or a leg in the factory? His own fault, no doubt, but a generous employer will take care of him. Is the upright man out of work? That is one of the hardships of fate but, if he is willing to turn his hand to anything, someone will surely recognize his virtue and give him work. Life is full of hardships, but be of good cheer: God watches over His own, most men are kindly and generous, and in the end virtue will be rewarded.

All this was in the spirit of self-reliance and of individualism, and reflected, too, that distrust of the state which was implicit both in much of Puritanism and in Jeffersonianism. Yet the heirs of the Puritans in New England—even the author of "Self-Reliance" —did not carry that virtue so far, or release the state from responsibility for the operation of the economic order. McGuffey, and his collaborators and successors, lived in the midst of the greatest reform era in our history—an era when all the institutions of society were being called before the bar of Reason and asked for their credentials, and when the state was required to take on some responsibility for the welfare of the "dangerous and perishing

classes." But the Readers show no awareness of this ferment of
ideas, confess no temptation to challenge existing institutions, and
reveal no inclination to enlarge the concept of social or political
responsibility.

In nothing are the Readers more Victorian than in their pervasive sentimentality. As in so much of Victorian literature—on the
European continent as in England and America—sentimentality
washed over children, dogs, and horses, found expression in flowers and trees, adored the primitive, especially in Nature, and ro-
manticized the farmer; even its piety was romantic. Curiously
enough it was fascinated with death, and even children were expected to ponder the moral implications of death; one is sometimes
reminded of Poe's definition of the perfect subject of a poem as the
death of a beautiful woman. (Surprisingly enough, Poe himself is
represented in the Readers only by "The Raven.")

What of the contribution of the Readers to education?

Here they performed a signal service, but it was not the service
most commonly attributed to them by their admirers, and perhaps
not even the service designed by those who wrote and edited them.
For it was, in the event, intellectual rather than moral, and cosmopolitan rather than nationalistic.

We have only to turn to most of the textbooks and readers
current in mid-century America to see how great an improvement
the McGuffey inaugurated. That improvement was not merely
pedagogical—the rhetorical guide, for example, the elaborate exercises, the careful vocabularies, the rich body of illustrations, badly
drawn and printed, to be sure. More important was the marked
improvement in the content itself. The best examples of this are
the Fifth and Sixth Readers—the first to include a really substantial selection from literature.

What is striking about the Readers—it was probably not so
much a product of policy as of habit—was that they made so few
conscious concessions to immaturity. There was no nonsense about
limiting the vocabulary to familiar words, for example. There was
no effort always to be entertaining, and no policy of easy famil-
iarity between young and old. There was no drawing back from
many of the harsher experiences of the grownup world. If the

McGuffeys did not ransack literature quite as thoroughly as Hamlin Garland and Herbert Quick seemed to remember (the Readers are notable for the classics that they leave out as well as for what they put in), they did draw generously on modern English classics, and on such American books as might be supposed to be classics, and they took for granted that the young would understand them, or that teachers would explain them—something publishers never appear to think of today!

A second major educational contribution of the Readers was their cosmopolitanism.

It is customary to emphasize the ardent Americanism of the Readers, and Richard Mosier, in his *Making the American Mind,* has devoted a persuasive chapter to this theme. Certainly an emphasis on nationalism would not have been surprising, for this was the period of national self-consciousness everywhere, of Manifest Destiny, of the apotheosis of the Founding Fathers and the rediscovery of the Pilgrim Fathers, and of the struggle for Union. The temptation to use the Readers to inculcate patriotism and nationalism must have been well-nigh irresistible. Insofar as the Readers drew on the classics of American literature and politics they did doubtless contribute something to cultural nationalism. But what is astonishing is how little of this there really is. Though the original volumes of the Readers appeared when men could still remember the Revolutionary War and the War of 1812—McGuffey himself lived through that war, and on the Ohio frontier, too—there is no ardent hostility to Britain, no execration of George III, no atrocity stories about the Indians. And though new Readers, and revisions of old Readers, poured from the presses all through the era of the Mexican War, of Manifest Destiny, and of Young America, the Readers reflect none of this: even the Oregon Trail and the gold rush to California were not allowed to ruffle the serenity of their pages. Even more startling is the fact that those who later revised the Readers—this 1879 edition of the Fifth Reader is a good example—managed to avoid the Civil War! Aside from Francis Finch's "The Blue and the Gray"—a masterpiece of impartiality—the war might never have happened, as far as the Readers are concerned. The editors even brought themselves to omit the whole body of Civil War songs—"The Battle Hymn of the Republic," "Tenting Tonight," "Maryland, My Maryland," "The Conquered Banner"—though these were already the common property of the people, cherished then as now.

In the substantial attention the McGuffeys gave to American literature, in the celebration—or at least the affectionate recollection—of Washington and Franklin, Patrick Henry and Daniel Webster, they contributed no doubt to fostering a sense of patriotism in the young. But there was no deliberate attempt to do this. Perhaps the McGuffeys realized—what so many of our professional patriots do not realize—that in a sound and fortunate society patriotism can be trusted to take care of itself.

A more important contribution to nationalism was equally uncalculated, though by no means fortuitous. It lay in providing the schoolchildren of the mid-nineteenth century with a common body of allusion and a common frame of reference. Justice Holmes said of John Marshall that part of his greatness was in being *there;* so, too, we can say that part of the greatness of the McGuffey Readers was that they were *there* at the right time—they were *there* to be read by millions of children from all parts of the country, from all classes, of all faiths. They gave to the American child of the nineteenth century what he so conspicuously lacks today—a common body of allusions, a sense of common experience and of common possession. That, no doubt, was what made the Readers so cherished in retrospect: they were always there to be remembered and quoted, and you could be reasonably sure that your audience would share your recollection and recognize your quotation.

Here they are—to be taken seriously, to be taken humorously— but always to be taken and to be remembered: the boy who stood on the burning deck "whence all but he had fled"; the captain's daughter strapped to the mast in "The Wreck of the Hesperus"; "The Old Oaken Bucket"; the story of "Mr. Idle and Mr. Toil," which had the haunting simplicity of an Andersen fairy tale; Whittier's "The Fish I Didn't Catch," which was so useful as an aphorism; Abou Ben Adhem, whose name led all the rest; the easy rhymes of "The Death of the Flowers"; the declarations of a Patrick Henry; the wild courage of Arnold of Winkelried—" 'Make

way for Liberty!' he cried;/Made way for Liberty, and died!"; the
simple morality of the Psalm of Life; the touching story of Maud
Muller and the proud Judge: "For of all sad words of tongue or
pen,/The saddest are these: 'It might have been!' " and even a bit
of Shakespeare, just enough to whet the appetite.

It is here that the Readers made, perhaps, their greatest contributions, and it is here that they have something to teach us. For
one of the things that has gone out of much of current study of
literature and history on the elementary level is this common body
of allusion and of reference. That our children, today, are better
taught than were their luckless predecessors is generally conceded,
though we are sometimes puzzled that we have not produced a
generation of statesmen as distinguished as the Founding Fathers
—products of rural academies and embryo colleges—or a generation of men of letters as distinguished as those of the Golden
Day—products, again, of frontier schools, village academies, and
struggling colleges. But even people most confident of the virtues
of our current educational practices, and most proud of our textbooks, so handsomely printed, so lavishly illustrated, so elaborately
provided with pedagogical apparatus that they leave little to
either the child or the teacher, may wonder what has happened to
that body of common knowledge that was in fact common in an
earlier generation.

All of this was a benevolent, not a chauvinistic, expression of
nationalism—pride in the virtues or the beauties of the nation, not in its prowess or its superiority to other nations. Indeed,
the effect of the Readers was cosmopolitan rather than parochial—
something those infatuated extremists who seek to exploit them for
chauvinistic purposes might ponder. Children exposed to them—
particularly to the Fifth and the Sixth—could not but have a lively
sense of the past, and of the rich cultural tradition of other nations.
The Greeks were here, and the Romans, William Tell and Arnold
Winkelried, Hamlet and Shylock, and the Highland clansmen.
Irving described the Alhambra, and Southey celebrated the Battle
of Blenheim, and Thomas Campbell provided a sample of the
Scots dialect—not surprisingly, the Scots were favorites of the Mc-
Guffey brothers—and Charles Wolfe lamented the death of Gen-

eral John Moore fighting Napoleon in Spain—"We carved not a line, we raised not a stone,/But we left him alone with his glory!" Above all, the Readers provided an introduction, and more than an introduction, to the literature of England, and that literature, with its far-flung imperial interests, has always been more than national. Where McGuffey's great predecessor, Noah Webster, set himself to eradicate Anglicisms from the American language, and to foster a sense of American cultural independence ("America must be independent in literature, as she is in politics"), the McGuffeys refused to be distracted by cultural chauvinism. They saw no reason why political independence should cut young Americans off from their cultural heritage, and they deliberately gave to generations of boys and girls growing up on the prairies of the West a sense of membership in a larger community of history and literature.

The McGuffey Readers, then, are far more than a historical curiosity. They played an important role in American education, and in American culture, and helped shape that elusive thing we call the American character. If they did not themselves provide the stuff of culture and morality, they were one of the chief instruments for weaving this stuff into the fabric of American life. Their contribution was, on the whole, a beneficent one.

A PLEA FOR
DISCRIMINATION

9

I begin by recalling what might be called the Red Queen doctrine of reform. Alice, in *Through the Looking Glass*, ran very fast indeed, and when she stopped she discovered that she was just where she had started. "*Here*, you see," said the Red Queen, "it takes all the running you can do, to keep in the same place. If you want to get somewhere else, you must run at least twice as fast as that."

We have here almost an epitome of the history of reform in America. It was a little over a century ago that "the Great American Preacher" as he was then known, Theodore Parker, preached three famous sermons on "The Dangerous and Perishing Classes of Society" at the Music Hall in Boston. His preaching, his whole career, was part of that tidal wave of reform that surged across the Northern states in the forties and fifties of the last century, bringing with it more humane penal laws, sweeping improvements in public education, advances in the rights of women and of children, the amelioration of old injustices, and, eventually, the end of slavery. It was part of a crusade that took as its point of departure and as its philosophy the transcendental doctrine of the infinite benevo-

Address at Merrimack College, Massachusetts, 1965.

lence of God, the infinite beneficence of Nature, and the infinite perfectibility of Man.

Most of us still believe in the first of these articles of faith; of the second we are skeptical, and of the third, incredulous. For we have witnessed, in the century and more since Parker preached his sermons, and Dorothea Dix led her crusade for the feeble-minded, and Horace Mann lifted the level of education, and Garrison thundered against the iniquities of slavery, wave after wave of reform, all designed to put an end to poverty and ignorance and war and man's inhumanity to man. And we know that these evils are still with us, some of them in more acute form than when the crusade started. What can be the explanation of a situation which appears to fly in the face of reason? What can be done to speed up those ameliorative processes upon which we still rely to achieve those ends which our society still has at heart?

All of the problems that glare unceasingly upon us are, fundamentally, moral problems, but I do not suppose that they can be solved by moral admonitions or appeals: if they could they would no longer be with us. Nor shall I propose a plan of action: the American public has something of that kind in the program of the Great Society, and that has so far been no more successful than earlier crusades. I want to emphasize that aspect of the problem which particularly concerns all those who have enjoyed the privilege of a college education: the problem of discrimination. I want to make a plea for discrimination or—if you prefer—for counter-discrimination.

As we look back upon our long educational history, what is perhaps most sobering is the fact that notwithstanding great opportunities and substantial achievements, our educational accomplishments are still ragged and incomplete. They are ragged and incomplete because we have consistently practiced discrimination, and still do. We have tried to create a society that was both free and equal, but we have not tried hard enough; perhaps we have not tried sincerely enough. Now, after a century and three-quarters, we discover—with what should not be a shock of surprise—that our society has more built-in discriminations and inequalities than almost any other in the West.

With the most ostentatious of these discriminations, the deepest, the most persistent and intractable, we are all agonizingly familiar: discrimination against the Negro. And not against the Negro alone, but against other minority races and peoples: Mexicans, Japanese (let us not forget the concentration camps we set up for them during the last war), and Puerto Ricans. With the exception of slavery, and of the wartime restrictions on the Japanese, little of this discrimination has been deliberate, but the effect of it on children in Harlem or Watts is the same as if it were deliberate.

We have, in the past, discriminated against religious groups, notably Catholics and Mormons and Jews. To be sure, there has been substantially less of this in the United States than in almost any Old World country, and the United States was, we know, the earliest champion and practitioner of genuine religious toleration. But it took a long time to translate toleration into true equality, and some vestiges of discrimination linger on into our own day. This is not the place to discuss the vexed question whether our separation of church and state makes for discrimination against parochial schools, but it is not irrelevant to observe that the British and the Canadians do provide government aid to parochial schools, at all levels, and that our absolutism in this matter looks very much like discrimination to those who suffer from it.

More pervasive is discrimination in the economy. We started out, in America, with a rough equality—Franklin could boast with justice that in America there were neither rich nor poor, and that boast was not excessive even into the first half of the nineteenth century. But inequality has been growing steadily for the past century and more and is by now one of the inescapable facts of the American economy, and, to its victims, the most important fact. Our economic system, or chaos, condemns millions to poverty, and how astonishing that we seem only now to have "discovered" poverty in our affluent society, as if it had been hidden all the time! Is poverty an inescapable part of our kind of private enterprise? If it is, private enterprise stands condemned. More civilized, or perhaps more sophisticated, societies like those of Scandinavia, Holland, New Zealand do not tolerate the poverty we seem to take for granted.

Needless to say, part of this built-in discrimination is the consequence of poverty: discrimination in public health, medical care,
nursing, and psychiatric care, housing, employment, recreation,
and education.

It is the educational discrimination that cuts closest to the bone.
Here the Red Queen principle has operated with sobering regu-
larity. We have run very fast for a long time, and now, after well
over a century of dedication to the principle of universal education, find ourselves about as badly off as we were at the beginning
of the race. The disparities in our educational system not only
persist, they grow ever more violent. Of late we have concentrated
on something called "excellence" in education, never quite defined,
to be sure; it seems, in fact, to come down to a concentration on or
even an obsession with getting our young into the proper colleges
and universities, with the result that we have come to accept without a qualm discrimination against great masses of young people
who for one reason or another are not candidates for these institutions.

Some forty years ago Alfred North Whitehead admonished us
that

> When one considers in its length and in its breadth the importance
> of this question of the education of a nation's young, the broken lives,
> the defeated hopes, the national failures, which result from the frivo-
> lous inertia with which it is treated, it is difficult to restrain within
> one's self a savage rage. In the conditions of modern life the rule is
> absolute: the race which does not value trained intelligence is doomed.
> Not all your heroism, not all your social charm, not all your wit, not
> all your victories on land or at sea, can move back the finger of fate.
> [*The Aims of Education*, Macmillan, 1959, 26.]

Now, if we are to make up, even partially, for the injustices and
cruelties of the past, and somehow build a just society, we must
begin to practice counter-discrimination on a vast scale. We shall
have to compensate for the injuries, indignities, and injustices we
have done to the perishing and dangerous classes of our society—
the Negro, the Puerto Rican, the Mexican, the children of the
slums, the children of Appalachia and of much of the rural South,
the victims of poor schools, or of no schools, those who have been

denied proper medical care, those who have come from broken homes, or from no homes—the *disjecta membra* of our society and of our economy.

First is compensation in elementary and secondary education, first, and most compelling, for education is the beginning of social reform and regeneration. How do we go about such a program of compensatory discrimination? We start by abandoning many of our preconceptions about the relation of the home and education, and the sharing of responsibility between the two, and recognize that for many children in our society there are no homes, and no sharing of responsibilities. We must face the fact that children of the streets and the slums, the mining towns and the hard-scrabble farms of the South are already "deprived" when they first come to school and never really get over that deprivation. We must try to compensate for what they do not get in their homes or their communities.

Second, such compensation must extend from the secondary school to the college. We are even now in the process of creating junior colleges or community colleges which are designed to provide education and training for those whose talents are not primarily intellectual. It is perhaps the most encouraging experiment in the current educational scene. We shall have to abate some of our standards for admission to college, on behalf of the neglected and the disadvantaged. That experiment, too, is now under way, but in a faint and tentative fashion. The problem is difficult but not insoluble. It is true that most of the "disadvantaged" students of our schools are not able to come up to existing standards of admission to our colleges and universities. But these standards are not absolute, and they may be misleading in that they fail to allow for special talents, or for those whose inadequacy is the product of neglect rather than of incompetence. Standards can be modified for special circumstances and to special ends. Harvard and Duke, Amherst and Emory, California and North Carolina will not collapse because standards of admission are adjusted to compensate for the injustices and discriminations for whose amelioration and even eventual elimination these institutions were founded.

Third, we shall have to provide compensation or social security and social welfare programs. We should provide compensatory pay for the poor, and for the victims of industrial disorder and our reckless abuse of natural and human resources. How meager still is our compensation to the victims of our industrial system—the unemployed and the unemployable, the displaced, the old, the injured, and the broken. We need to use far more imagination here than we have shown in the past; perhaps we shall have to adopt the recommendations of Gunnar Myrdal or Kenneth Galbraith and pay the victims of industry as well as its beneficiaries.

Fourth, we must make compensation in the arena of public health. How astonishing it will seem, to future generations, that the medical profession, with some honorable exceptions, fought Medicare with sleepless hostility. Happily, this reform is now under way; but, until it operates in this country as universally beneficently and as graciously as it operates in the Scandinavian countries, we cannot rest satisfied. Public health is not just a matter of medical care; it extends to the causes of disease and of discomfort. How sobering are our statistics of preventable disease, of mental breakdowns, of industrial and automobile accidents and fatalities, of industrial and automobile pollution of air and of water, and how sobering, too, their implications for our morality.

Clearly, we shall have to make compensation in other fields as well—in housing, facilities for recreation, the treatment of delinquency, the administration of justice, which, as recent studies of the role of the ombudsman make clear, is shockingly discriminatory. Our nation was, doubtless, "dedicated to the proposition that all men are created equal" and, during most of the nineteenth century, it was (as far as whites were concerned) more nearly equalitarian than most others. But, whatever its political principles or its social standards, it is, in the twentieth century, less equalitarian than most Western societies.

These large-scale programs of compensatory discrimination will doubtless require an ever greater enlargement of the welfare state than we now know. It will require, too, an enlargement of the concept of welfare—we may even get back to Parker's ideal of welfare a century ago:

The welfare of a nation consists in these three things: first, possession of material comfort, things of use and beauty; second, enjoyment
of all the natural rights of body and spirit; and third, the development
of the natural faculties of body and spirit in their harmonious order,
securing the possession of freedom, intelligence, morality, philanthropy, and piety. It ought to be the aim of a nation to obtain these
three things in the highest possible degree, and to extend them to all
persons therein. That nation has the most welfare which is the farthest
advanced in the possession of these three things. [*The Present Crisis in
American Affairs,* 1856]

Many of us doubtless think that the welfare state has gone far
enough, and a reaction against it is clearly under way. But in fact it
has not gone nearly as far as it is bound to go, nor as far as it
should go, and there is little doubt that the next generation will see
an enlargement of the role of the state primarily in the realm of the
welfare of the underprivileged. It will see an enlargement, too, in
the concern for the beauty of city and of countryside, for the preservation of streams and lakes, for wild life and for Nature, and in
the concern for the arts. What this will call for is discrimination in
favor of those sectors of our life which have been neglected, as
well as in favor of those elements of our society which have been
neglected.

As we cannot afford the waste of natural resources, so we cannot
afford the waste of human resources, a waste that is irremediable.
We cannot tolerate it from a practical point of view, for our society
needs every resource it can summon to cope with the problems
that ceaselessly frown upon us. We cannot tolerate it from the
moral point of view, for a society that imposes or permits unjust
discrimination is an immoral society. The responsibility for creating a moral society lies with all of those whose lives have fallen on
pleasant places, all of those who have been, heretofore, not the
victims but the beneficiaries of our long-standing discriminations.

PART II

The University

THE AMERICAN
SCHOLAR REVISITED

1

Any discussion of the American scholar inevitably takes its departure from Ralph Waldo Emerson's historic Phi Beta Kappa address of 1837. "Thus far," said Emerson, "our holiday [an odd word, that, for the annual Phi Beta Kappa celebration] has been simply a friendly sign, a survival of the love of letters amongst a people too busy to give to letters any more. As such it is precious as the sign of an indestructible instinct. Perhaps the time is already come when it ought to be, and will be, something else." Thus far, well over a century later, our academic convocations, celebrated at more than a thousand colleges and universities, still give signs, friendly enough, of a love of letters or, to use Emerson's further phrase, of "exertions of mechanical skill." Something more is called for.

Emerson addressed himself, in his short essay, to two themes: the character of the scholar (mostly, as he observed it, dull), and the duties of the scholar. When we look to the historical record we discover how perspicacious Emerson was in definition and description. Where else do you get the definition of the scholar quite simply as "man thinking"—a definition democratic, equalitarian,

Address at the inauguration of the Boyd Lee Spehr Library of Dickinson College, 1967. Printed in the Wilson Library Bulletin, February, 1968.

and universal, suggesting neither special skills nor special interests, and granting credentials to every man, a definition, in short, both appropriate to and welcome to the America of the early Republic?

But, it might be said, if every man is a scholar, nobody is a scholar. In one sense this has always been true of the American scene. For the scholar, as such, has had practically no place in American society. If what Tocqueville said is no longer true—that there is no country in the world where, in proportion to the population, "there are so few uninstructed and at the same time so few learned individuals"—it was assuredly true for much of Emerson's age. But this general diffusion of knowledge and absence of erudition is but another illustration of the Tocquevillian principle that American society is a classless one. Just as we do not have, in the United States, a military, a bureaucratic, an ecclesiastical class, a peasantry, a proletariat, a bourgeoisie, or an aristocracy, so we do not have an "intelligentsia" or a body of what the French call *erudites*. Like the civil servant, the cleric, and—until recently at least—the soldier, the scholar is merged in the great ocean of American society; he has no stigmata, he scarcely has characteristics.

The fact that there is no discernible intellectual class in America, and that no special prestige attaches itself to the scholar and no special piety is expected of him, has troubled many European observers, and some American. Yet clearly there is much to be said for this condition. It means, as it has always meant, that the scholar, like the soldier and the cleric, has to earn his way. He cannot pull his brass, or flaunt his gown, for he has no brass and does not sport a gown. He cannot rely upon the prestige of a degree for, with two thousand institutions conferring degrees, the ordinary degree has no prestige. With rare exceptions he cannot rely even on the distinction of an academic chair; there are no regius professors in America, or their equivalent. He has to rely upon himself.

The circumstances of American life, in fact, create a new framework for the intellectual and the scholar, making demands upon him not made elsewhere, giving him advantages not enjoyed elsewhere, and, at the same time, denying him satisfactions commonly conceded elsewhere. As with so many things in America, the quantitative fact became a qualitative consideration. Because we have, in our own day, embarked upon a program of mass education, even at the highest levels—which is a contradiction, but no matter —we require something like mass production of those we call scholars. Most Europeans would deny that this is possible: scholars, they tell us, can no more be mass produced than artists; and when reminded that Florence mass produced artists and Vienna musicians, they point out, quite rightly too, that New York and Berkeley are not Florence or Vienna. Because we are committed to an equalitarian philosophy, we assume that every college is equal to every other college, though we know better; and because we cannot possibly distinguish among the tens of thousands who flourish the title "professor" we regard the title itself with indifference. When American professors complain that they do not enjoy the prestige of their colleagues in Britain, France, Germany, or Sweden, they are right. They do not and, what is more, they should not. Much of what passes for "anti-intellectualism" in the United States is merely a reaction to inflated claims. It is a reaction by no means confined to the realm of scholarship. We do not accept the claims of politicians to be statesmen, of clerics to be theologians or saints, or of Madison Avenue advertisers to be economists, and inflationary claims are no more effective in the scholarly than in the political, the religious, or the business world.

As the American scholar cannot expect to win salvation by grace, he must win it by works and, for the most part, by works that appeal to those who grant the rewards. This has long meant that American scholarship has been directed to the practical and the immediate, that it has addressed itself to the insistent demands of a growing society, and that it has pretty much accepted the standards of that society. The American scholar (and not the American alone) has long been prepared to do the bidding of his secular masters, not because he stands either in fear or in awe of them, but because his own interests and instincts are secular. This explains the otherwise inexplicable readiness of great universities and colleges, today, to accept the ignoble role of employment agencies for private corporations, or government bureaus like the CIA, which recruit on campuses and assume that the colleges will cheerfully lend their facilities to this wholly nonacademic business. Alas, they do. The American college and university has long been a service station for society, providing it not only with medical and law schools—something universities have been doing since the thirteenth century—but with schools of retailing, hotel management, and journalism, not entirely because legislators or benefactors will it so, but rather because American educators share with other segments of American society a passion for service. Just as the intellectual in America dresses, talks, and drinks like a businessman, so the average college or university blends happily into the social landscape. Even the academic vocabulary confesses this. In the United States and alone in the United States professorial studies are called offices, and scholars keep office hours, while teaching itself is called a "teaching load."

There is a strain of anti-intellectualism in much of American education, as in much of American philosophy. There was some of this even in Emerson, even in those transcendentalists who invoked Emerson for inspiration. For anti-intellectualism is inherent in an intuitive and *a priori* philosophy, one which starts out by repudiating Lockean sensationalism. It was Emerson himself who said that "man thinking" must not be subdued by his instruments. "Books," he said, "are for the scholars' idle times, when he can read God directly. The hour is too precious to be wasted in other men's transcripts of their readings." And, again, he said that "books are for nothing but to inspire."

There was some truth here, to be sure, as there is always some truth to be gleaned from Emerson. If you can indeed read God directly, then what a waste of time it is to read anything else. And, if it is inspiration that you want, what a waste of time to read things that are not inspiring—the statistical abstract of the United States, for example, or government propaganda.

Emerson's scholar was a poet rather than a philologist or an economist, and perhaps the most persistent charge against the scholar is that he is by nature a mystic and a visionary, removed from the everyday affairs of society. This criticism persists, and we put the matter more crudely now: the scholar has never met a payroll. But in fact the circumstances of American life and scholarship vindicate Emerson here, for mostly they have exposed the scholar to the criticism that he is not nearly visionary enough; that the world is too much with him; that he is altogether too ready to help figure out—for others—how to meet payrolls and not nearly ready enough to challenge the desirability of having payrolls in particular enterprises; that he is too ready to figure out for some government department how to mobilize resources for war, and not nearly ready enough to examine critically the war itself.

We can see something of the practical character of the American scholar in our attitude toward science. The emphasis has been, for the most part, not on what is called pure but on what is called applied science. Americans are supreme in the field of technology and they have even imposed the curious phrase "know-how" on their associates overseas, but until very recently (things are changing now) it was the British and the Germans who seemed to have the know-why. Every college president knows that it is easier to get money from legislators, or from private donors, for buildings than for men, and for applied science than for pure research. This is just another way of saying that in the United States the ideal scholar, or scientist, is the man who can get things done.

It is not perverse to assert that in some ways American universities are themselves anti-intellectual, or, at least, non-intellectual. Admiration for things rather than for ideas pervades much of the university community. Our greatest academic achievements appear to be material, and we take immense pride, some of us, in numbers. The emphasis has been on the student rather than the scholar, on teaching rather than learning, on practical subjects like business and engineering and schoolteaching rather than on more general or theoretical subjects.* In a good many institutions extracurricular activities overshadow and overbalance the curricular: and it is not the metropolitan press and television alone that celebrate the football game rather than the learned mono-

---

* In 1965, the last year for which we have statistics, American colleges and universities granted a total of 539,000 degrees. Of these, 120,000 were in "education," 63,000 in business, and 37,000 in engineering.

graph; the college papers and the alumni journals do so too, and in some areas of our country—the South and the West—presidents, trustees, administrators, students, and faculty unite in resisting any serious deflation of competitive athletics at many of our institutions of learning.

It might indeed be possible for some modern-day Veblen to argue that the American universities themselves do not fully or generally understand the nature and the function of the scholar. The failure of trustees and regents and, in some cases, of presidents and deans to defend academic freedom against the assaults of McCarthy, Congressional committees, state un-American activities committees, filiopietistic societies and, occasionally, misguided alumni, is a melancholy reminder of this. The readiness of some universities during the McCarthy era, and now again under the pressure of Vietnam-war psychology, to accept the shabby function of a kind of extralegal law-enforcement agency, to punish where the law itself is unable to punish, not for crimes but for dangerous ideas, is a confession of failure to understand the nature and purposes of scholarship. It is only fair to add that the most courageous and the most eloquent defense of freedom of speech and press, dissent and criticism, has come from the universities, and that in the last decade American universities have written a bright page in the history of academic freedom.

There are of course advantages as well as disadvantages to the scholar in these very American aptitudes and attitudes. If the refusal to accord the scholar a special status deprives him of some of the prestige he might enjoy abroad, the readiness to accept him as part of the social and business community brings him rewards that he does not elsewhere enjoy, and not material rewards alone. In most matters except the intellectual the American scholar is a favored, even a pampered figure. He is normally sure of a professorship, and this without waiting until he is ready to retire, as in so many of the universities of the Old World. He is paid if not better than the businessman at least not very much worse, as in all Continental countries except the Scandinavian and in Holland. Society provides him with ample facilities, not out of affection, but out of an impersonal passion for efficiency. He has larger and better libraries available to him than have scholars in any other countries on the globe; the libraries stay open every day and part of every night, their collections are admirably catalogued and classified, and their books actually circulate. We take this for granted, but the situation is unprecedented, and unique.* Nowhere else does the scholar command better laboratory facilities than in the United States, and it is this, rather than money, which accounts for the so-called brain drain from Europe. University presses stand ready, though not eager, to publish the scholar's most esoteric findings, and scores of learned journals compete for his most vagrant thoughts. Students, millions of them, hear him, if not gladly then of necessity; a thousand organizations clamor for his services, or even his lectures; and great foundations as well as the national government stand ready to support him in a style to which he is rapidly becoming accustomed.

The American scholar, like the American politician or businessman, is a product of and a function of American history and society. American society required him to fit the needs and fulfill the purposes of democracy; to provide a fairly high level of mass-education, train substantial numbers of young people to useful skills and vocations, and meet the miscellaneous and not too exacting demands of culture. It expected him to do a great many of the things that were done, abroad, by more specialized professions and institutions, and it was reluctant to indulge him in that leisure which was, in the Old World, one of his prerogatives. American conditions produced thereby a scholar different in many and important respects from the representative scholars of the Old World —a scholar very different, too, from that which Emerson described.

The conditions and imperatives which called into being this different kind of scholar have all but disappeared, but the habits and expectations of an earlier age persist. Here, as elsewhere on the academic scene, there is a cultural lag. Just as the high-school

* No one has ever taken a book out of the Bodleian and the splendid library of Cambridge University is available only to those who have an M.A. Cantab. following their names.

year is still geared to an anachronistic routine of farm chores and harvests, just as colleges are still supposed to act *in loco parentis* for students old enough to marry and raise families, so scholars go on functioning pretty much as they were expected to function in the nineteenth century, and go on, too, intoning the old litanies, as if they were as valid today as they may have been in 1837. But the demands which our own day makes upon the scholar, the temptations to which it exposes him, and the pressures to which it subjects him, as well as the opportunities which it offers him, are very different from those which operated in Emerson's day.

Perhaps the most striking difference between Emerson's ideal scholar and the scholar of our day is that Emerson's scholar was, or appeared to be, a solitary individual, whereas our scholar is a member of a community of science and learning. Emerson gave his address to the Phi Beta Kappa Society of Harvard College, but there is no mention in that address of Harvard, or of any other university. It was "the importance of the single person" that was the "signal sign of the times." "Everything," said Emerson, "that tends to insulate the individual, to surround him with barriers of natural respect so that each man shall feel the world is his and man shall treat man as a sovereign state—tends to true union as well as greatness." That kind of solitary enterprise was suitable for the poet in Concord, but not very effective for his neighbor, Judge Story of the Harvard Law School. Not only did Emerson ignore what has come to be the central and essential institution of scholarship, the university, but by implication he warned against it. Beware of books, he said, and he admonished the young to remember that when they read Cicero, Locke, and Bacon they should remember that "Cicero, Locke and Bacon were only young men in libraries when they wrote their books." As all three of these examples were totally erroneous we may suspect that the principle which they purport to support is equally misguided. Cicero, Locke, and Bacon were not young men sitting in libraries when they wrote their books: they were, on the contrary, mature men who had held high office, who had been bruised and buffeted by the waves of politics and whose writings were forged in the hot furnace of war and public affairs.

Emerson himself did not really mean that the scholar should withdraw into the life of the mind, and never emerge: indeed, whenever we read Emerson we must keep in mind that it was he who said that "a foolish consistency is the hob-goblin of little minds." Elsewhere, in this same essay, he asserts that the scholar must go out and embrace life, that "inaction is cowardice" and he has an obligation to be bold, that, indeed, "he is the world's eye, he is the world's heart." What Emerson really meant was that the scholar is to meet society on *his* terms, that he is to pursue the studies that *he* thinks important, that he is to preserve at all costs his moral integrity. Clearly Emerson is right. It is not the duty of the scholar—though it may be his pleasure—to serve the current needs of society or government. And the reason for this is obvious. Society almost inevitably thinks of the useful in narrow and immediate terms. It wants answers, preferably easy answers, to concrete problems, and wants them at once. It tends therefore to deflect the scholar from that work which he is peculiarly equipped to perform: the disinterested search for truth. Since the university—the corporate personification of the scholar today—is almost the only institution that exists to serve and safeguard the interests of mankind, and of future generations, if it is distracted from its true task, that task may go by default.

The scholar cannot divorce himself from his society but he should refuse to become a prisoner of it. It is his business to distinguish between the transient and the permanent, and to serve the permanent. Was this not what Emerson himself meant when he observed of the scholar, "Let him not quit his belief that a popgun is a popgun though the ancient and honorable of the earth affirm it to be the crack of doom"? So we may say of our present-day scholar, let him not quit his belief in the efficacy of freedom though the public and the government clamor for limitations on freedom as the price of safety. Let him not quit his belief in the dignity and integrity of the academy though every corporation and governmental bureau comes with an impudent claim to its services for recruiting purposes. Let him not quit his belief in the community of learning though every government insists on conscripting its scholars and scientists into national armies and marching them into battle under national flags. Let him not quit his confidence in a unity of mankind dictated eventually by science and technology, though he is assailed from all sides by those who argue and labor for disunity and fragmentation.

No, Emerson's scholar was not really a recluse who turned away from life; he was the world's eye and the world's heart. Emerson himself tried for a time to live to himself and protect himself from the world, but he found himself caught up in the swift current of events and the turbulent passions of controversy. He counseled civil disobedience—a dangerous phrase that, in our time; he wrote of John Brown that he made the gallows glorious like the cross, and the scholar he admired most among his contemporaries was Theodore Parker, "the Great American Preacher," as he was called. There can be no scholar, he said, without the heroic mind, and Parker had scholarship and the heroic mind. He was the most learned man in America, so it was said. His library was the largest and the richest in New England, and he had read it all and knew it all, and he wrote a dozen stout volumes himself and a hundred famous sermons. A crusader for freedom, he spoke from every pulpit and forum against the wickedness of slavery: championed every good cause; advised and counseled every statesman, Lincoln among them.

Only rarely in our history has the scholar been an isolated and lonely figure: even Emerson's scholars—the scholars of his actual world, not of his essay—were deeply engaged, intellectually, morally, and politically, in the great affairs of their time. Certainly in our day the scholar is not isolated. He is connected with the university, the foundation, the international commission, and dependent on these for much of his intellectual nurture. He is dependent on his colleagues and associates not at his own institution alone, or even in his own country, but throughout the globe. The scholar of today, no less than of Emerson's, is dedicated to the search for truth, but that search is a public affair and a cooperative affair.

We are confronted in, and outside, the academy, with the question of the role of the scholar in politics. It is not, as is sometimes supposed, a new problem, but very old, and it is sufficient to recall again that the three scholars whom Emerson cited were all involved in the politics of their own and of future generations. It would be presumptuous to make any pronouncement on the duty or obligation of the scholar either to participate in or to withdraw from public affairs; decisions of this kind are personal. Two observations are relevant. First, the scholar has the same right, and duty, to concern himself with public affairs as has any other citizen. He does not take a vow of continence when he assumes the academic gown. To the hackneyed objection that the scholar should not bring his political and social preconceptions into the classroom, it is sufficient to say, first, that no sensible scholar needs to be reminded of this, and, second, that if the scholar who feels strongly about public issues is encouraged to express his sentiments freely outside the classroom he will be that much less tempted to express them within the walls of the academy. To the familiar argument that the scholar who participates in public affairs thereby commits, or may be mistaken as committing, his institution to a particular position it is sufficient to say that there cannot be a double standard in these matters. No one supposes that a senator who expresses an opinion commits the United States Senate, or a lawyer the Bar Association, or a businessman his corporation. If the public has not yet learned that no professor can commit a college to a public position, if legislators have not yet learned that no scholar can commit a university to a public position, they may never learn.

The second observation is more fundamental. Ideally the scholar has attributes to contribute to public discussion that society needs, attributes that are his by virtue of a training so rigorous and a tradition so long that they can be described as instinctive. The first of these is the inductive habit of mind—the habit of distrusting general propositions and doctrinaire positions, and looking to evidence. The second, almost nonexistent in the political arena, is the habit of taking the long view, of thinking in terms of evolution, not of catastrophe; the ability to know that the particular crisis of the moment does not necessarily spell the doom of mankind; the habit of looking ahead, not a few years, but a few generations. A third quality we associate with scholarship is the instinct of disinterestedness, objectivity, judiciousness; the habit of weighing issues and arguments against each other, the readiness to concede good intentions and virtue to both sides of a dispute. A fourth quality is tolerance—tolerance for what appears, especially in others, to be error, tolerance for alien peoples, races, societies, economies, and civilizations, tolerance even for those ideas which, in the words of Justice Holmes, are "loathsome and fraught with death."

Needless to say, the scholar can function as "man thinking" or as "the heroic mind" only if he is free. Emerson took this for granted. "Free should the scholar be," he said: "free and brave. Free even to the definition of freedom, without any hindrance that does not arise out of his own constitution." And he added that "it is a shame [to the scholar] if his tranquility . . . arise from the presumption that his is a protected class" or if he diverts his thoughts from vexed questions by "hiding his head like an ostrich . . . peeping into microscopes, and turning rhymes, as a boy whistles to keep his courage up." Emerson himself was immune to pressure and to threat; he was independent and aloof and went his own way, but he had seen his associates threatened and intimidated: William Ellery Channing ostracized by his own parishioners; Theodore Parker read out of the Unitarian Church; Dr. Follen dismissed from Harvard for his abolitionist enthusiasm; Garrison dragged through the streets of Boston with a halter around his neck.

In our own day the problem of freedom for the scholar is more urgent than in Emerson's, in part because the threats are more frequent and more formidable, in part because the scholar has taken on, or has had imposed upon him, a larger responsibility for the shape and the conduct of public affairs. It might fairly be said of the New England scholars of Emerson's day that they had not made the Mexican War and bore no responsibility for it; it cannot, alas, be said of the scholars of our generation that they have not made the sentiments, the policies, the very tools and weapons that go into our current wars. It is indeed a tribute to the role and the power of the scholar today that men in high office ceaselessly attack them. They are denounced, almost every day now, by a president, a vice president, a secretary of state, and presidential candidates as "alienated intellectuals" or perhaps as "pseudo-intellectuals," and one putative candidate, Governor Wallace, has proposed the easy solution of shooting them when they dissent from official policy.

As the library is the center of gravity and the powerhouse for the scholar, attacks on scholars are inevitably attacks on libraries. This is no mere implication or by-product but the real thing. Every scholar knows that the attacks upon this citadel of enlightenment are relentless. Every librarian, public and private, is bombarded with demands that he remove books from the shelves, label or lock up all books that are dangerous, burn books, cancel subscriptions to subversive magazines. People who are afraid of ideas are, naturally enough, afraid of books which contain and spread ideas.

It is sometimes argued by those avid for censorship and eager to protect others—never themselves, to be sure—from dangerous thoughts that even the most inflammatory books are all right for the mature, but that they should not be put into the hands of the young, who might misuse them. A student who is not old enough to read any book that has ever been published is not old enough to be in a college or university. A student who is not old enough to be exposed to the most dangerous ideas is not old enough to be exposed to any ideas, for all ideas are dangerous.

The dedication of this new library is, in itself, a profession of faith in the freedom of learning and of science. It dramatizes the fact that the library is the heart of the academy. It proclaims confidence in the processes of the transmission of knowledge from generation to generation which is at the heart of education. It welcomes every student, and lays open to him all that has been thought in the past, and it conspires with him to persuade him to think new thoughts for future generations to build upon. It welcomes the future Ciceros and Bacons and Lockes and wishes them well in their inquiries, their discoveries, and their proclamations.

On a more familiar level, the library is the major link between teaching and research, which are, in turn, the business of the academy. Oddly enough, Emerson ignored the role of the scholar as teacher, perhaps because he thought it too obvious for comment. It is no longer obvious. We witness today a growing separation between teaching and research. It is no doubt possible to carry on

research without teaching—as in textual criticism, or field anthropology, though even in these areas it is surprising that there are
scholars who do not want disciples. But it is not really possible to
teach well without engaging in research, or, if that is too pompous
a word, in scholarly investigation. Professors who try to teach
without immersing themselves continually in some scholarly
project of their own soon grow stale, and so do their students.

Now this fusion of the scholar and the teacher implies a kind of
mutual-assistance pact between the university (which here represents society) and the scholar. The university is under obligation to
make it possible for the scholar to engage in research by providing
libraries and laboratories, and reducing what might be called the
housekeeping activities of its scholars. The scholar is required, in
turn, to recognize his obligation, and his opportunity, to teach.

"The American Scholar" has long been regarded as an intellectual declaration of independence—a kind of cultural counterpart to
Jefferson's great declaration. Doubtless there was some justification
for the emphasis on nationalism in the literature and the scholarship of Emerson's day. But how odd, now, the warning against
tradition and the past; how almost quaint the warning against "the
courtly muses of Europe." The scholar of today does not feel himself threatened by the weight of the past: it is the present, rather,
that weighs most heavily upon him. Nor is the task of the American scholar today that of proving the independence of American
science and learning, or resisting the infection of European muses,
courtly or otherwise. It is rather that of resisting the ravages of
cultural nationalism and of ideological antagonisms, and restoring
or recreating the community of science and learning that was one
of the glories of the age of the Enlightenment. In this arena the
scholar of today does not turn to Emerson for inspiration, but
rather to the great cosmopolitans of the eighteenth century: Franklin, Tom Paine, Priestley, and, above all, Thomas Jefferson, patron
saint of libraries, as he is of universities.

This may be the major obligation as it is doubtless the major
opportunity confronting the scholar today: to rebuild the community of learning fragmented and shattered by the World War, by
ideological and national animosities, and by revolution. The

scholar—and here it is the scientist who is most important—has played a decisive role in the creation of nationalism, and in the vast and turbulent revolution now sweeping the globe. He has a corresponding obligation to persuade his society to understand nationalism and revolution, and to help direct their torrential currents into peaceful channels.

There can be little doubt that our scholarship has been, and is, provincial. We have concentrated on *American* history, politics, and literature to an extent both unnecessary and misleading—unnecessary because there are so many agencies prepared to familiarize the young with things American, misleading because such concentration distorts the nature of the modern world. This concentration reflects, to be sure, prevalent attitudes of the whole society which is (like most societies) self-contained and even self-satisfied. The obvious comment here is that the scholar should not fit himself unquestionably into prevalent patterns, but consider them critically, and that scholarship, like education, is often most useful when it represents a countervailing force.

I am not readily persuaded that what is taught, or not taught, in the schools automatically translates itself into national character or public policy; often it is the other way around and it is national character and public policy that determine what is taught. Certainly I do not believe that by tinkering with the curriculum we can be confident of producing tolerance, virtue, and internationalism. Yet may we not conjecture that part of the responsibility for our seeming inability to understand and to control some of the vast forces that are sweeping the globe, to understand a global revolution, to understand why we are bogged down in an Asiatic war and why we seem to have forfeited the confidence of most of Asia, to understand why we seem unable to grasp either the dimensions of power or the limits on power—that some of the responsibility can be laid at the door of a scholarship too eager to dissociate itself from the muses not only of Europe but of the rest of the world; too ready to encourage, and even to pander to, those instincts of nationalism, of power, arrogance and conceit which now distinguish our character in so somber a fashion?

The American scholar today lives in desperate times. Yet as

Emerson wrote: "This time, like all times, is a very good one, if we but know what to do with it." And elsewhere he said, "If there is any one period one would wish to be born in, is it not the age of revolution?"

All of us have been born in an age of revolution, the old and the young alike, the revolution of half the human race seeking to emerge, in a single generation, from centuries of ignorance, poverty, and exploitation. Most of us in the United States are frightened by this revolution: we did not used to be frightened by revolution, but in this we have changed. Most of us are trying to deny, or even to repudiate and resist, the revolution. That indeed is our official policy; that is the meaning of the cold war we have been fighting for twenty years, and the hot war we have been fighting for almost five. More and more the American people fear revolution of all kinds—the revolution of the underprivileged peoples of South America and Africa; the revolution of old peoples of Asia, throwing off centuries of misrule; the revolution of expectations on all sides which threaten our own superiority, our wealth and our power; the revolution of new ideas about the equality of men, about the application of science and technology to human welfare, about war and international relations.

To listen to our elected leaders, to listen to our commentators and editorial writers, this is a very bad time for the young among you to be born in. But it is in fact a very good time—if we but know what to do with it.

What to do with it is *not* to repudiate it but to embrace it. It is *not* to adopt anti-policies instead of policies, anti-principles instead of principles, as we have been doing for twenty years. It is *not* to repudiate our own history of revolution and equality and justice, as we are in fact doing. It is *not* to substitute the ostrich for the eagle as the American symbol, as we are doing.

Certainly what to do with it is not to take refuge in those melancholy lines of William Butler Yeats, so familiar now:

> Things fall apart; the centre cannot hold;
> Mere anarchy is loosed upon the world,
> The blood-dimmed tide is loosed, and everywhere
> The ceremony of innocence is drowned;

> The best lack all conviction, while the worst
> Are full of passionate intensity.*

Better by far in this time of revolution for the scholar to recall the lines from Pericles' Funeral Oration:

> Draw strength from the busy spectacle of our great city's life as we have it before us day by day, falling in love with her as we see her, and remembering that all this greatness she owes to men with the fighter's daring, the wise man's understanding of his duty, and the good man's self-discipline in its performance. . . . For you now it remains to rival what they have done, and, knowing the secret of happiness to be freedom, and the secret of freedom a brave heart, not idly to stand aside from the onset of the enemy.

* Reprinted with permission of The Macmillan Company from *Collected Poems* by William Butler Yeats. Copyright 1924 by The Macmillan Company, renewed 1952 by Bertha Georgie Yeats.

THE EMANCIPATION
OF THE COLLEGE

2

Stark Young has said in *So Red the Rose* that it is essential to belong to something bigger than ourselves, and that applies to institutions as to individuals. This College, still in the vigor of its youth, is part of a larger institution that is venerable in its antiquity: the community of learning. There is something moving in contemplating the genealogy of our colleges and universities, a genealogy which carries us back from the bright modernity of California to the romantic obscurity of the Middle Ages. For we can tell that tale in almost biblical terms—that Bologna begat Paris, and Paris begat Oxford, and Oxford begat Cambridge, and Cambridge begat Harvard, and Harvard begat Yale, and Yale begat Pomona—with Amherst, another offspring of Harvard and Yale, standing as one of the godfathers. And of each of these begettings can we not say what Sir Walter Mildmay so bravely said to Queen Elizabeth of the founding of Emmanuel College: "I have set an acorn which, when it becomes an oak, God alone knows what will be the fruit thereof"?

As in all families, each generation has a family resemblance, but each generation, too, has strong individual characteristics. The

Address at Pomona College, 1962.

differences between Paris and Oxford are familiar enough, and so, too, between the American colleges and their European or English ancestors, and between the different generations of the American colleges. It is a test of an institution of learning that it achieve a character of its own. What we sometimes fail to realize—so accustomed are we to this feature of our academic landscape—is that the college itself is a distinctively American institution.

The American college came directly out of the English background, but almost at once, and of necessity, it took on its own character. It is relevant to note that what America created was a college, not a university, and what America had for another two hundred years was the college, not the university. The Continent did not, and to this day does not, know the college as an academic institution. The Oxford and Cambridge colleges were parts of universities, and derived much of their character and function from that relationship. Harvard College was modeled on Emmanuel of Cambridge, and on Edinburgh too, but could not be either. It took its color almost at once from its American environment; it had special functions to perform and a special character to attain. One of those functions, one which Oxford and Cambridge neglected disastrously until modern times, was that of colonization. Our colleges and universities have never been content merely to serve their own immediate community; they have consistently accepted responsibility for the extension of learning throughout the country. Is there in the whole of our cultural history a more touching spectacle than the spread of the New England college—and of Princeton as well—into successive wests, onto successive frontiers, the founding, by pious and hopeful men, of hundreds of little colleges from New York and Pennsylvania and Georgia to the Pacific coast? Each was bravely dedicated to undertaking for its own community what the founders of Harvard had set forth as their duty—to advance learning and perpetuate it to posterity. Each was dedicated to service to God and the commonwealth.

From the beginning, the American colleges departed from their English antecedents in important areas, taking on new forms and new functions in conformity with the American social, intellectual, and moral environment. As President Tyler of Amherst College said over a century ago: "Scarcely anything in America is more distinctively American than the relation between the colleges and the common people. The people have made the colleges what they are, and the colleges have in no small measure made the people what they are." This might have been said of the Scottish universities, and perhaps of Leipzig and Halle and Göttingen, but not of Oxford or Cambridge.

The American colleges broke at once with the English tradition of exclusiveness. They could not be exclusive, either theologically or socially—hardly even intellectually. They took their students where they could find them and pretty much as they found them, at almost any age from thirteen to twenty, with almost any preparation, and of almost any faith. Contrast this with the situation in England, where as late as the 1860's only those who belonged to the Church of England could be admitted to Oxford and Cambridge, and, with a few exceptions, only those from the great public schools. American colleges could not afford religious barriers; there were no social barriers (except, for a time, against women and Negroes); and it was easy to hurdle the economic barriers. Like the political party and the churches, the college was democratic and evangelical.

They were required, by the circumstances of their creation, to be small, rural, and regional. Because they were created by voluntary associations, and because they flourished in a society that was rural and impoverished, they could rarely rise above the level of their surroundings. They could not select their students; they could not insist on high scholastic standards (but they did insist on high moral standards); they could not build up great libraries; they could not concentrate very effectively on the intellectual task. They were, almost all of them, involved in a struggle for existence—the mortality of colleges before the Civil War was something like 80 percent—and in the course of that struggle made compromises and concessions on all sides.

What is more, the American colleges were called on from the beginning to do things not required of, nor permitted to, the colleges of Oxford and Cambridge or the universities of the Continent. And throughout our history, up until our own day, they have been required to do things not associated with universities in the Old World. From the beginning they were called upon to fill three roles:

They were expected to be preparatory academies. How many colleges, down almost to yesterday, maintained preparatory departments or academies in order to get students competent to do college work, or in order to finance the college operation? They were called upon to be colleges, in the Cambridge tradition, and to provide education and moral training at the same time. They were expected to be professional schools as well, and to turn out clergymen, teachers, lawyers, engineers, even businessmen.

Clearly, they could not perform all of these tasks well. It is almost a miracle that they performed any of them well. Yet that they did somehow provide both intellectual and moral training, and that of a high order, no student of our history can deny. As S. E. Morison wrote a generation ago:

> For an integrated education, one that cultivates manliness and makes gentlemen as well as scholars, one that disciplines the social affections and trains young men to faith in God, consideration for his fellow men, and respect for learning, America has never had the equal of her little hill-top colleges.

Then, in the decades of the seventies and the eighties, America at last created the university: Cornell under White, Harvard under Eliot, Hopkins under Gilman. Thereafter in rapid succession came Stanford, Clark, Chicago, Columbia, and others, private and public alike. Since that time it is undoubtedly the university that has been the dominant feature on the American educational scene, but a university cast in a distinctively American mold and ordinarily embracing a vast number of colleges within its catholic grasp.

In the twentieth century it is increasingly the university that sets the pace. This shift in the center of academic gravity to the university is not only natural but inevitable. For a new kind of society and economy implacably requires what the university alone can provide—specialized and professional training of the highest standards. It is a new order quantitatively and qualitatively that we face. Quantitatively the American university is now called on to service not only a vastly enlarged American society, but much of the non-European world too. Qualitatively the new world of science and technology makes almost limitless demands on knowledge and skills so advanced that they cannot possibly be supplied by the college alone.

Education is now called upon to prepare the young to function in a world that requires professional and graduate training in almost every field. The whole level of education has moved upward three or four years. Our better high schools occupy the place in the educational hierarchy that our colleges occupied forty years ago; our colleges are today what our universities then were. Students know this, even if their parents do not, and in all first-rate colleges—it is the simplest test of the quality of the college—they move on as a matter of course from college to graduate or professional school.

What this means is an increasing distinction between the work of the college and the work of the university. It means that the responsibilities of each will be heavier than in the past and more sharply defined.

Who can doubt that this is the best thing that has happened to the colleges since the rise of high schools three-quarters of a century ago? It is, in a very real sense, a kind of emancipation from all the improper things that they have been called upon to do in the past, a kind of declaration of independence from the burdens and impositions that have been fastened upon them. It leaves the private independent college free to do what it has always been expected to do, what it is so well equipped to do, and what no other institution in our society is prepared to do.

The college is now free to promote three things. First, imaginative communication between the old and the young in the transmission of the heritage of the past, and in exciting and encouraging intellectual curiosity on the part of all who are involved in the enterprise of learning.

Second, discipline of the mind, character, and body—and Alfred Whitehead has wisely reminded us not to ignore the claims of the body—training in habits of study, in the use of the tools of research in library and laboratory, and in the exercise of discrimination and judgment.

Third, acquaintance with and understanding of the seamless web of knowledge, embracing music, art, literature, and science. Sir Charles Snow has admonished us that we have permitted two cultures to grow up, and that the twain never meet. The university tends, almost inevitably, to accentuate the division among cultures; it is in the college that young people should learn the interdependence of all disciplines and the interrelations of the cultures.

It is equally important that we consider some of the things that colleges are no longer called upon to do and that they are not qualified to do. First, the college is no longer called upon to be a preparatory school. It should not teach subjects appropriate to the high school. I have in mind not only such absurdities as remedial reading, but the teaching of elementary tools of language, English or foreign. Colleges should not be expected to dissipate their resources in teaching elementary writing skills, or elementary French or German or Spanish; clearly there is a common-sense case to be made for the less familiar languages, whether Greek or Russian. Indeed, much is to be said for eliminating almost all merely introductory courses most of which rehash information which can and should be taught in the high school, or acquired by the student on his own.

Second, the college should not try to be a university or a technical school or a professional school. It should not undertake to train for business or for engineering, for library science or for nursing. These are not appropriate subjects for the college; they are the concern of the technical, the professional or the graduate school.

Third, the college should not feel under any obligation to entertain or to placate its community by athletic spectacles or other distractions. Athletics should be directed solely to the physical welfare and the pleasure of the young; they should not be exploited for the psychic satisfactions of the old, or for the pecuniary welfare of the community, or for the convenience of the press or of television. The sole criterion by which all extracurricular activities are to be judged is the criterion of relation to the mind and health of the student.

Fourth, the college should not be under obligation to fit the young to their society, to make them into interchangeable parts so that they can fit in anywhere. What society needs is more people who do not fit into the existing pattern, but who will challenge and even change the pattern. Almost all the geniuses of the world were eccentrics who did not fit in. One of the most gratifying functions of the college is to maintain the principle of the countervailing force; knowing that most of the forces in society make for conformity and adaptation, to encourage nonconformity and nonadaptation.

Fifth, the college is not called on to train for citizenship, or to indoctrinate with particular political or economic ideologies. It is not called on, for example, to dissipate its resources or distract its energies by participating in what may be popular crusades for or against some form of government or some political philosophy. If the young are to adopt what we may think the right principles, they must arrive at these on their own, not under pressure of indoctrination. That a sound education will help produce sound results is at least an allowable assumption, but the college should not intervene to dictate the results.

What scope then for the small college, what special role in our society and our culture? What can the college do better than the university—usually large and under public control?

First, it can remain small, with all the advantages that should ideally follow from smallness. They do not always do so. Oxford and Cambridge have insisted on retaining small colleges within the framework of larger institutions, and the Oxbridge principle of a federation of colleges, popular now in California and spreading throughout the country, is one solution to the problem of reconciling numbers with autonomy and distinction. Smallness can —again it does not always do so—provide a more tightly knit academic community; it can subject the whole educational process to continuous exposure and criticism; it can provide for communication between old and young; it can encourage faculty (and student) control of the educational process, so important in our society.

Second, the college can set and maintain high standards. There is little excuse for the existence of the private college if it does not do this. The colleges should set the pace that public institutions will be called upon to follow. I do not suggest that the standards of a Pomona or an Amherst be higher than those of a California or a Michigan, but I suggest that in most parts of the Union the small college has been, and is, in a better position to select students, insist on high performance, concentrate on intellectual activities, and resist pressures for irrelevant activities, than is the publicly supported teachers' college or university.

All the irrelevant activities, let me add, are not on the football field or in the fraternity houses; a good many of them take place in the classroom or in the dean's office. One of the contributions the private college can make is to take the lead in ridding higher education of some of the extraneous paraphernalia that now encrust educational institutions like barnacles. Partly because colleges in earlier days were often preparatory schools, partly because they were often competing for students, partly because parents were commonly more interested in the social and moral aspects of education than in the intellectual, colleges and universities permitted triviality and irrelevance to take over. I have in mind the detailed insistence upon such matters as attendance, credits, grades, and similar bookkeeping activities that belong more properly in the secondary schools. If students are still children these things are necessary; if they are adult, they are an irrelevance and an indignity.

Third, the college can, indeed it must, experiment. "Experimentation" conjures up novelties, but need not; indeed it is something of a novelty now to concentrate on essentials. It is probable that most of the significant experiments in higher education in America have originated in private colleges or universities; it is relevant that many of the great figures in the history of higher education in America were innovators and experimenters, and that many of these were connected with private colleges or universities—Jefferson, Wayland, Eliot, White, Gilman, Harper, Butler, Meiklejohn, Hutchings, Aydelotte, for example. Need I remind you of the connection of coeducation with Oberlin, the elective system with Harvard, the honors program with Swarthmore; summer sessions, the quarter system, and extension work with Chicago; study at foreign centers with Smith, Sweet Briar, Stanford, and others; active participation in programs of creative arts with Sarah Lawrence, Bennington, Brandeis, and Dartmouth; the separate honors college with Wesleyan; the work-study program with Antioch; the deliberate infusion of large numbers of foreign students with Brandeis; the so-called New College program with Amherst, Smith, and Mt. Holyoke; the federation of colleges with Pomona, and what might be called confederations with the colleges outside Philadelphia, those of the Connecticut Valley, and others?

Of all the areas of experimentation it is probably this last that is most urgent and most rewarding—cooperative arrangements which will preserve the integrity of the small college and achieve access to the resources of the university. Oxford and Cambridge are the original models here, but the problem in our country is more intricate and novel. For here we have to deal with space, with different standards of education from state to state, with mixtures of private and state control, and many equally vexatious matters. It is a tribute to the resourcefulness of our educational statesmen that so much progress has already been made; it is a challenge to them to advance that progress far more rapidly in the next generation.

These experiments, in turn, have made several things reasonably, and encouragingly, clear. First, that as colleges establish higher standards, high schools strive to meet them and professional schools adjust their programs to them. Thus, they help lift the level of the whole educational enterprise. Second, that students in general—and perhaps scholars, too—are capable of far greater efforts of mind than are customarily expected of them by our society, and that they will almost inevitably rise to whatever demands are made upon them. Third, that there is a vast untapped reservoir of intellectual interest, creative ability, and idealism in the student body today.

We recognize this, but only in part. As Santayana said, our minds are like geological strata—one part in the Pliocene, one part in the Silurian era. We expect our students to be mature and responsible, but treat them as if they were immature and irresponsible, and we are constantly surprised when they react by believing what we do, not what we say. Student responsibility is not merely a matter of student self-government, or of taking the games away from alumni and townspeople and giving them back to the students. It requires that students be called on to play a larger role in the academic and intellectual life of the college and university. Let us recall two relevant historical considerations; first, that the very concept of academic freedom originated as *Lernfreiheit*—freedom for the student to direct much of his own intellectual and professional career; and second that the English and American tradition of the college as *in loco parentis* emerged at a time when young men went to college at the age of fourteen or fifteen. If students are to be responsible, we must give them responsibility; if they are to be mature we must make every aspect of higher education far more a cooperative enterprise than it is today.

What presents itself to us, then, is a prospect both formidable and exhilarating—one, I hasten to add, by no means limited to the small or the private college. First, to do on a larger scale, for a far more numerous citizenry, what the small colleges of eighteenth- and nineteenth-century America did so well: that is, to encourage that service to the commonwealth which animated the generation of Jefferson, Madison, John Adams, Hamilton, Jay, and other products of the infant colleges of America. I do not think it possible to *train* for this kind of service in a formal fashion—not in the college anyway—but I do think it possible to provide for the young a pervasive climate of opinion which holds public enterprise more precious than private, and service to the commonwealth higher than the attainment of wealth.

Second, to discourage that narrow nationalism and that parochial culture which is urged upon us so stridently from almost all quarters, and to encourage the restoration of that larger community of learning that flourished in the eighteenth century—not least in America. This is peculiarly the task of the college and the university, which antedate modern nationalism and which will probably outlive the current form of nationalism; whose members are part of the cosmopolitan society that stretches from ancient times into the farthest allowable future; and whose acolytes and disciples are peculiarly the guardians of the heritage of the past, and of the free movement of ideas in the present.

And third, to encourage and participate in what is surely the most enthralling educational enterprise of modern times: that of spreading the college and university of the West to three-quarters of the globe that has not heretofore known such institutions, and that now desperately needs and wants them. Just as in the early years of the Republic the young men of New England colleges carried learning to the new West, so our generation will see a more sophisticated but no less idealistic group carrying to the far corners of the globe the institutions and practices of American higher education. What we will witness is the formation of an intellectual peace corps—a Minerva Corps—which will carry to other parts of the globe something of the American belief that education is for all who can profit from it; and something of American practice of academic freedom and intellectual independence.

It has long been fashionable to say that we in America are the Romans of the modern world. So we are, in a sense. But may it not turn out that we are the Greeks as well, and the Elizabethans, too, for good measure? May it not be that we are to perform, in the next century, those benign tasks which Athens and other Greek city-states performed in the ancient world of the Mediterranean? May we not, if we are seeking historical analogies, find ourselves playing the role which the city-states of Italy played in the Renaissance, which Elizabethan England played in the sixteenth and seventeenth centuries, which France played in the eighteenth? Perhaps it is our destiny to serve as the training school for skills and the powerhouse for ideas for the non-European parts of the globe; to help restore in the West, and to extend to the East, that great community which science and learning demand, but which politics and nationalism and war have hitherto so often frustrated.

THE PROBLEM IS
BRAINS, NOT BRICKS

3

College and university enrollments, stationary for some years, have already begun to respond to prosperity and to higher birth rates, and we may confidently anticipate an increase to four million students in the next ten years, and perhaps to six million in the next twenty. The problem of coping with numbers far exceeding anything in New or Old World experience has quite naturally excited lively attention and deep concern.

The first question—Should the colleges and universities accept and provide for these vast numbers, or should they cut down on the total number by raising entrance requirements and standards? —has been answered; or perhaps it has gone by default. There is no practical alternative to accepting however many students are qualified by current standards, and there is little likelihood that the qualifications will be changed. Nor is there, for that matter, anything in our experience to indicate that a limitation on enrollments would substantially improve educational standards; after all, the products of our universities today compare favorably with those of a generation ago when total enrollment was less than half that of the present time.

The New York Times Magazine, January 29, 1956.

Because the responsibility of the universities to take on whatever number of students are qualified seems generally recognized, almost all discussions of the future of higher education have focused on the material problems. Can the existing universities absorb another million or two million students, or will it be necessary to create still more universities? Can we, in the next decade, provide the dormitories, classrooms, libraries, gymnasiums and fieldhouses (to say nothing of parking lots) for a student population of four million—a population larger than the whole of Ireland or Norway? And where is the money coming from?

These are important and urgent questions, but they are not difficult questions. For excessive concern with the material aspects of the problem of higher education is merely distracting. In so far as the problems are material, they can be solved materially. This country is rich enough to acquire the campuses, build the dormitories, stock the libraries, equip the laboratories, lay out the playing fields—do all that is necessary for the physical well-being of a vastly enlarged student body—and it is rich enough, too, to pay the bills for maintaining this vast educational enterprise.

Far and away the most serious problem of expanding enrollments is one that has received curiously little attention. It is the intellectual problem, the problem not of bricks or books but of brains. It is already difficult enough to find teachers competent to serve in our high schools. Where are we going to find the brains and skills that will be required to serve the needs of four to five million mature students in colleges? First-rate colleges and universities try to maintain a proportion of one instructor for each ten students; if this is to continue we will need, in the next decade or so, between four and five hundred thousand scholars competent to teach at the university level. Add to this another hundred thousand librarians and administrators, and the dimensions of the problem become clear.

Where and how are we to find the half million scholars needed? That there are half a million first-class minds, capable of teaching at the university level, is doubtless true, but that the universities will be in a position to command their services is highly improbable. The universities and colleges are not turning out enough trained scholars to take care of even current needs. And they are facing the sharpest kind of competition from national and state governments, industrial research laboratories, the great foundations—from a score of institutions clamoring for brains and skills, and prepared to pay well for them.

What is the solution? One solution, of course, is to water down the intellectual content of higher education to the point where it becomes glorified secondary-school education. It will always be possible to find enough young men and women to teach elementary English or French, geography or chemistry, and if we ignore the question of whether these things ought to be taught at all in college, we can doubtless take care of great masses of students for at least two of the four years of college.

This lamentable process is already under way in many of the larger universities; it is becoming increasingly difficult to distinguish between the last year of high school and the first year or two of college. If the products of our high schools actually need such elementary instruction it is all to the good that they should have it, but it is absurdly expensive and illogical to provide for it in universities.

Another solution is larger and larger classes, with squadrons of student assistants taking on much of the burden of instruction. With the aid of microphones it is just as easy to lecture to five hundred as to fifty, and student assistants can deal with the more clamorous needs of the five hundred in small quiz sections. Or perhaps the new audiovisual techniques can be used for mass instruction, or as a substitute for professorial teaching. These devices are doubtless valuable in certain areas of instruction like mathematics and language, but appear to have little relevance to the encouragement of intellectual activity or to training for professions. What is needed in American education is more rather than less intellectual content, higher rather than lower standards.

One reason for our current difficulties is that we are, in a sense, the prisoners of our own traditions and habits, and, particularly, the prisoners of one tradition that has come down through centuries—the tradition of the lecture. We still tend to think of teaching as it was centuries ago, before the rise of the university library and the development of library science—a science more highly developed in the United States than anywhere in the world. We still refuse to learn what Oxford and Cambridge, for example, have taken to heart, that lectures often interfere with learning, that professors cannot be expected to do all the teaching, and that a major part of education is and should be performed by the students themselves.

The first thing required, then, is a reconsideration of the lecture system. That system has come down to us from the days before the printing press made books generally available and when clerics had a monopoly on learning. To this day university teachers in England who correspond roughly to our associate professors are called "readers," and students at Oxford and Cambridge do not "major" in, but "read," English or theology or law.

Now that students can read for themselves, the English universities have turned more and more from lectures to tutoring or to self-education; some years ago, when lectures appeared to be too popular, the history department of Cambridge simply "took off" its best lecturers! But in the United States, which has the best library facilities in the world and the best textbooks, the lecture system grows and flourishes, and professors go on "giving" courses as blithely as if no printed books were available.

One very simple way, then, to meet the shortage of teaching talent is to cut down on lectures and therewith reduce the number of professors that lectures call for. From the point of view of the student, the time spent going to lectures and preparing for course examinations can be more profitably spent in the study or the library. From the point of view of the scholar, the time spent preparing and delivering lectures, giving examinations, and attending committee meetings can be more profitably spent on conferences with students, or on research.

Not only do we rely far too much on lectures, we rely on lectures to do far more than it is possible or desirable for them to do. The ideal of the American university seems to be the encyclopedia; that is, it attempts to cover every branch and department of knowledge. Yet it is neither possible nor desirable to cover everything adequately. It is not essential that each major university have professors in Chaucerian, Elizabethan, Restoration, eighteenth-century, Victorian, and modern literature, to say nothing of American or Celtic or Old English. It is not necessary for a university to provide lectures in every area and period of history. No European university attempts to do this. The University of Uppsala is content with two medievalists and one economic historian, but Swedish historical students give a good account of themselves; the University of Copenhagen provides three professors, all in Danish history, but Danish students are not ignorant of the history of other times and countries. Almost all the historians at Göttingen specialize in German history, but the students there are held responsible for the whole range of history from ancient times to the present. Even Oxford and Cambridge do not attempt to cover literary or historical ground with the thoroughness of Columbia or Minnesota, but their students manage pretty well.

Not only should university administrators realize that printing and library science have made a great deal of lecturing superfluous and a great many elementary courses useless; they should realize, too, that the vast increase in the range of knowledge makes it quite impossible for any one university to be in fact universal and that learning is of necessity a cooperative affair.

Many of our major universities nevertheless persist in acting as if the burden of maintaining the whole corpus of learning rested upon them. Whether through vanity, zeal, or mere habit, they attempt to cover the whole range of learning and scholarship. There might have been some excuse for this ambition when universities were comparatively few in number and when travel was slow and difficult; there is no justification for it now.

Certainly it is far more satisfactory—and far cheaper—to send students to the centers of specialized study of such subjects as Sanskrit or Byzantine history or classical archaeology than for each major university to provide instruction in these subjects. It is not merely that universality is so expensive; it is rather that there are not enough first-rate classical archaeologists or Byzantine scholars to go around.

A third method of cutting down the costs and burdens of teaching is a drastic reduction in the paraphernalia of education—required courses, attendance, course examinations, grades, credits, and so forth. Universities elsewhere in the world get along largely without these time- and energy-consuming interferences with the business of learning, and there is no good reason why American universities cannot manage to get along without them. Substitute for most of them thorough examinations at the end of the third or fourth year and the result to colleges would be not only a saving in man and brain power, but an improvement in the end product.

Another way to counterbalance the cost of numbers is to cut down substantially on administrative overhead. All too commonly the most impressive buildings on a university campus are the gymnasium and the administration building, and this architectural preeminence is not too misleading. The tendency of administration to take over the primary function of any institution—educational, religious, economic, or political—is familiar enough. Yet English and European universities manage without an administrative bureaucracy; it is only in the United States that the administrative tail seems so often to wag the educational dog.

Cutting down on administration would have two happy consequences: substantial savings of money that might better be devoted to the main job of education, and savings of time that might better be devoted to thinking about education. Perhaps our colleges cannot really hope to attain the ideal which President Harold Taylor has set forth:

> The image of administrative virtue which I cherish is of Sir Richard Livingston as president of Corpus Christi College and vice chancellor of Oxford University seated at a twelve-foot desk, partly hidden from view by piles of books, manuscripts, flower pots and papers, answering his mail by hand and calling upon a member of his faculty with a head for figures to deal with the items of the annual budget.

Clearly they cannot achieve this, but they can try, though in all fairness we must confess that even Oxford and Cambridge colleges now have to have large staffs for administrative work, and that bureaucracy is overwhelming both universities.

All in all, our colleges and universites make too little intellectual demand on students and far too many nonintellectual demands— class attendance, for example, or a fixed number of terms and of years. And, conversely, they place too little responsibility on the students themselves. Given the right atmosphere, the appropriate facilities, and time, students will educate each other. We should see to it that they are given the time, the facilities, and the atmosphere.

In short, if faculty and administration are to do less, students must do more.

This is perhaps the hardest lesson of all to learn, for most Americans persist in thinking of college students as children who must be provided with intellectual, physical, and moral guidance to fit them for just the kind of world they have come out of and will go back into, and who must be protected against ideas and associations that might make them dissatisfied with that world or reluctant to conform to it.

But if students are to educate each other, and if they are to get their education outside the classroom, the universities must concede them far more autonomy than they do now. They must be treated as adults, not adolescents, and they must be encouraged to act like adults, not adolescents.

The young tend to do what is expected of them. If they are expected to yell themselves hoarse at football rallies, to act like oafs in fraternity initiations, to spend their spare time hovering over juke boxes and drinking Cokes, and to follow a pattern of dating thought up by Hollywood, they will do so.

If they are expected to read Donne and Proust, collect recordings of Pergolesi, stay away from gladiatorial contests, they will at least try to do so. If they are expected to get violently excited about fraternity politics and shun national politics, they will do so; if it is taken for granted that they will interest themselves in national and international affairs, they can be counted upon to do this, too.

It is essential, therefore, that we fix our standards and our expectations high. If students are to join the adult world rather than linger on in the world of adolescence, society itself must treat them as adults, not as adolescents. If students are to prize things of the mind and the spirit, society itself will have to show that it prizes and rewards things of the mind and the spirit.

Parents, faculty, and administrators, then, must be prepared to concede to students themselves a larger role in education than they now play. And to this end they must provide not only the intellectual stimulus but the material environment.

What does this involve? One thing is the residential college, preferably in small and manageable units, such as those at Harvard or Bryn Mawr or Grinnell today. For if students are to create their own community, they must live together, work together, play together, act together. They should, preferably, manage their own games and sports, their own papers and journals, their own musical and theatrical productions, their own political as well as social and religious activities.

They should even, as far as is practicable, manage their own academic program. "Academic freedom" originally meant freedom for the student rather than for the professor, and academic freedom today should mean respect for the intelligence, the individuality, and the maturity of the student.

The prospect in higher education, serious as it is, is far from desperate. It is one that calls for bold and original thinking, inventiveness, and vision. If we are prepared to reconsider the nature and function of our universities, to eliminate what is elementary, useless, or trivial, cut down on the administrative mechanics and nonintellectual clutter, concentrate on the creation of an atmosphere of learning and of respect for and excitement about learning, and encourage the young to play a vigorous and creative role in higher education, problems that now loom so portentously may take on a less forbidding character.

We are always going to have "problems" in education; let us at least see to it that it is the intellectual, not the material, problems that engage our interest and challenge our ingenuity.

THE URBAN UNIVERSITY,
OR IS IVY NECESSARY?

4

Historically and traditionally the university is urban. Bologna and Padua, Paris and Toulouse, Prague and Cracow, Heidelberg and Leipzig, Copenhagen and Leyden, Glasgow and Edinburgh—these set the pattern. By the eighteenth century almost every major city on the Continent, and every capital except Stockholm and London, boasted a university. The urban tradition persisted into the nineteenth century with the foundation of London, Manchester, Berlin, Bonn, Christiania and Toronto.

Oxford and Cambridge were the most notable exceptions to this association of the university with a major city, and they remained the only English universities until well into the nineteenth century. American colleges were modeled on these; the first was planted not in Boston or Salem, but in the village of Newtown, hopefully renamed Cambridge. Some of the later colonial foundations were located in towns—the College of Pennsylvania, for example, and King's College in New York—but for the most part circumstances reinforced the inclination to fix the American college in a rural frame. The circumstances were, and remained, decisive; after all, the nation was rural, and as colleges followed the westward-moving frontier, they blossomed in villages and in the country-side.

But the rural setting of our universities resulted from preference as well. Land was cheap in country villages, and space ample. Students were young, and it was thought easier to protect boys—and, by the nineteenth century, girls—from moral temptations and frivolous distractions in the countryside than in the city. Further-more, there were, or came to be, political considerations: farmers and villagers were jealous of cities, and demanded that universities —like asylums and penitentiaries—be located for the benefit of local interests. Thus, in the nineteenth century, state universities were commonly established in small towns: at Ann Arbor, not Detroit; at Urbana, not Chicago; at Columbia, not St. Louis; at Amherst, not Boston.

A combination of circumstances—the English rather than the Continental background, the Colonial and frontier experience, the American passion for prolonging youth, the early advent of co-education, the habit of exploiting education for local profit—all went to fix a pervasive pastoral stereotype for the American college and university. To this day the pastoral image persists; the less sophisticated among us still think of college in terms of spreading lawns and giant elms, of ivy-clad halls, of cozy rooms festooned with pennants, of happy students. The French, the German, the Italian student is not supposed to be carefree—when he is, we believe, it is at a café on some boulevard, or in a beer cellar, or perhaps engaged in a duel or a riot—but the American undergrad-uate is perpetually young and carefree, perpetually lounging on well-cropped lawns, strolling beneath giant oaks and elms, strad-dling a traditional fence, cheering on brightly clad warriors to crash right through the line. So powerful is this stereotype, so powerful the pastoral urge, that most of our urban universities yearn to be rural and try to provide themselves with the trappings of a country college. A few—such as Goucher, or Colby, or the Johns Hopkins—have moved physically to what they hoped would be the countryside; others try to create islands of peace within the grim urban surroundings.

Yet Harvard, Columbia, and Pennsylvania flourished in or near large cities, and new universities sprang up in cities all through the nineteenth century: Pittsburgh, the City College of New York, Boston, Buffalo, Rochester. The twentieth century has seen an enormous expansion of older urban universities, and an enormous increase in the foundation of new ones; today it is the urban university that most faithfully represents higher education in America. Of the fifty-two universities claiming more than ten thousand students, thirty-two are in large cities, fifteen in smaller cities, and only five in the countryside. The population of the great city universities is twice that of the others. The typical American college and university student is—in his physical surroundings—not unlike the typical German or Italian university student.

There is every reason to believe that this urban pattern, already typical, will become dominant in the next generation. Not only are urban universities growing most rapidly, but cities are growing out to embrace—or engulf—suburban and rural institutions.

It is time we gave up our pastoral image here—as elsewhere— and accepted the fact of urbanization and made the best of it. We cannot return to the pastoral world of the nineteenth century, nor can we spread a pastoral patina over our city institutions. Perhaps we can even be persuaded to give up Oxford Gothic: in the 1890's no one seemed to ask why the University of Chicago's *"battlemented* towers should rise, beneath the hopeful western skies," but perhaps we are today more conscious that Paris and London universities manage to command prestige even without battlemented towers.

How can the urban university best play the educational role which history and circumstances have assigned to it?

A university is a community of scholars, old and young, and its function is to provide scholars with the environment and the facilities conducive to the discovery and transmission of ideas and to their application to the larger community, present and future. This requires that the university be a physical as well as an intellectual organization; that it provide the physical facilities for the meeting of minds, research and study, social intercourse. Education is in part the imaginative relationship between old and young, and the university must provide for that—in classrooms, in more spacious studies (let us abandon the business term "office"), in libraries and laboratories, and—what is so commonly overlooked—in facilities for ceremonial occasions as well. Students educate each other— that may be the most important part of undergraduate education— and the university must make that possible: by residence halls, clubrooms, theatres, music rooms, dining facilities, and playing fields.

Clearly our city universities cannot hope to house all their students, or even a large portion of them, but they should house a nucleus of full-time students who would constitute the core of the community and provide continuity. Clearly, too, the urban university has to make a special effort to keep the rest of the student body on the campus—a term we may fairly use, as it was originally applied to fields in cities. It can do this by building student unions, and making them more than convenient places to install juke boxes; by providing for sports and recreation, music, drama, lectures, conferences, exhibits—all the things designed to catch the imagination of the young.

More than students are involved. The urban university must make a determined effort to keep faculty members on or near the campus in order to enable them to play their role in the maintenance of the intellectual community. Oxford and Cambridge think this so important that they have long required residence within four or five miles of the university. But the American scholar is like other members of the professional classes; he lives—by choice or by necessity—in the suburbs. And since few of our city universities provide adequate studies, clubhouses, dining halls or other amenities, he tends to spend as little time as possible on the campus. He is part neither of a university nor of an urban community, nor do circumstances encourage him to take on more than his formal duties in the educational enterprise.

Universities must make strenuous efforts to reconstruct the academic community. This may call for large-scale faculty housing; it may even call for university initiative and cooperation in the rehabilitation of extensive parts of cities: Chicago, Columbia, and Pennsylvania have already embarked on such programs. It may involve university schools for faculty children, and playing grounds and recreation facilities for young and old alike. Given the cultural aridity of most of our cities, it will probably involve responsibility for a wide range of cultural and social activities and amenities. One of these, important to student and scholar alike, is a good bookshop. What with first-rate libraries and floods of paperbacks, the bookshop is almost an anachronism in America. We have only to reflect on what Blackwell's and Parker's mean to Oxford, what Heffers and Bowes & Bowes mean to Cambridge, what Thin's and Grants mean to Edinburgh, what the scores of bookshops on the Left Bank, or in the university quarters of Copenhagen or Utrecht mean to these communities to realize what we are missing. The bookshop is as essential a part of the university community as the library or the laboratory, and a good deal more important than the stadium, and has the added advantage that it would be used somewhat more than thirty hours a year. American universities should maintain bookshops even at a loss, just as they maintain theatres, music, and athletics at a loss.

The distressing fact is that most of our urban universities are singularly lacking in any of the amenities of cultural life. How unlovely, how discouraging, are most of our great urban universities! The "bookstores" filled with textbooks and athletic equipment and toilet articles. The hideous cafeterias with their clutter and noise and dirt, the food antiseptic but tiresome, popular music piped in relentlessly to drown out all conversation. The residence halls with their Coca-Cola machines (the impoverished English provide every student with facilities for making tea in his room), and their television, and the students packed three to a room. The student unions designed to look and feel like hotel lobbies, with the local paper (never the *New York Times*) and *Confidential* for sale at the newsstand and a bowling alley in the basement. The student newspaper invariably featuring the most recent athletic contest or the forthcoming prom. One would as soon look at a Hearst paper for news of the world of scholarship as at a university paper. Even the playing fields are closed to all but members of the varsity teams; the best facilities of the gymnasium are set aside for teams; the hours of access to swimming pool or squash court rigidly fixed for the convenience of the coaches or of the teams.

What is the explanation of what has been called the mucker pose in so much of higher education in America—of its anti-academic and anti-intellectual character? It is twofold. First is the widespread illusion that education is something that goes on in the classroom, something that comes by way of a "course" that a professor "gives" and a student "takes." This leads to the natural conclusion that when the classroom is closed the process of education is over, and that the professor might as well go home and cultivate his particular garden, the student might as well go to the union and watch television. It is no exaggeration to say that if all lectures were abandoned Oxford and Cambridge would go on much as they have been going on for centuries; perhaps the time is coming when we, too, will have to abandon "courses," as a kind of desperate gesture to prove that education consists in more than taking notes and accumulating credits. An educational system centered on the lecture course will, inevitably, disparage and neglect those other and more significant aspects of the educational enterprise, and this is particularly true of urban universities, where all the material circumstances encourage such disparagement and neglect.

The second explanaton is one common to all higher education in America, but whose effectiveness—or burden—increases almost geometrically with the size of the institution. It is that while European universities are run by their faculties American universities are run by administrative bureaucracies, many of whose members have not the remotest notion what a university is about. The power elite of many of our large city and state universities consists of the deans (often only the dean or the vice president in charge of education is supposed to be interested in that enterprise), the personnel of the buildings and grounds department, the public-relations officers, the coaches and athletic staff, the scores of minor officials who keep the machinery going. We take for granted that bureaucracy takes over in politics, and perhaps we should not be too surprised that it so often takes over in education as well. It is clear that a substantial part of this administrative bureaucracy makes no perceptible contribution to education. Oxford and Cambridge, Paris and Heidelberg have managed without public-relations offices for a good many centuries, and seem to get along pretty well. No universities outside America maintain paid coaches for sports, or fritter away money and energy on stadia and field-houses. And, clearly, most of the bureaucrats who fix the dining hour (five to five forty-five!), who assign air-conditioned offices to administrators and cubbyholes to professors, and provide them-selves with staffs of secretaries, who make so many of the ground rules that control university life, are concerned primarily with their own convenience and not with education. Just as we shall never eliminate the gross evils of intercollegiate athletics until we reso-lutely give the games and the playing fields back to the students, so we shall never eliminate the crudeness, the anti-intellectual rules, the mucker pose in higher education until we give the universities back to faculty and students. One reason why Oxford and Cam-bridge colleges are admired by the whole world is that they are largely administered by their dons—in finances, gardens, student life, libraries, playing fields, food, and drink. The first act of any university president who wishes to restore academic amenities to an urban institution will be to put the bureaucracy in its place.

Yet, no matter how enterprising or imaginative our urban uni-versities are, they are nevertheless conditioned by the elementary fact of their location. American students who go by preference to semi-rural colleges, such as Smith or Leland Stanford, gladly spend a junior year (and sometimes more) in Paris or Madrid or Flor-ence. Distinguished scholars who can rarely be lured to teach in Syracuse or Dayton, Kansas City or Denver, Houston or San Diego, cheerfully accept a call to Bologna or Turin, Heidelberg or Edinburgh or Copenhagen. What is it that attracts the American student and scholar to urban universities in Europe?

It is not the universities alone, for these are often not as good as the American. It is in part the chance to be abroad, and to enjoy a different kind of life. But when Americans go abroad for study or for teaching they do not search out the universities in smaller towns—Exeter, let us say, or St. Andrews, or Aarhus, or Pau. They head for the big cities. And this is because they know that in almost every country of the Old World they can count on an exciting relationship between university and community. What lures the American student is the life of the boulevards, the cafés, the bistros; it is the Latin Quarter; it is the opera and the ballet, the theatre and the experimental film; it is the bookshops, the half-dozen newspapers in every city; it is the mature student body, educating itself, joining in the risks of life, taking an active part in literature, journalism, art, and politics. It is, too, the beauty of the cities that they know they can count on—not just the beauty stored away in museums, but the beauty of houses that have been allowed to grow old, of parks and squares instead of parking lots, of riverbanks not given over to industry but to pleasure, of gardens in the heart of town, of bridges that one can walk across without risk of life, of bicycle paths that parallel busy boulevards, of sidewalk restaurants, and of carnivals in the streets.

This is not the place to inquire into the causes of the blight that has fallen on American cities, but it is relevant to emphasize one or two considerations that concern the position of the university. One of them is (like the rural college) in part an inheritance from England; in part, too, it is a consequence of a classless society and over-rapid industrialization: the elementary fact that we have neither a patriciate, happy to identify itself with the cities, nor an aristocracy rich enough to maintain great town houses. It is the patriciate that gave character and culture to so many of the proud cities of the Continent—the burghers who beautified Florence and Venice, Frankfurt and Hamburg, Geneva and Copenhagen and Bordeaux and Prague and a hundred other places. For centuries now the patrician class has been content to identify itself with its city, to take responsibility for the government, the schools, and the cultural life in its community. There are few private houses with gardens in the very heart of New York or Chicago or Philadelphia (Boston and Washington are still exceptions), but think of the private houses, the mansions and palaces, that grace the heart of London and Paris, Vienna and Rome.

The European patriciate usually patronized the urban university, and rejoiced in its scholars and its opportunities. Not always, to be sure; Oxford and Cambridge got in the way of London and some of the other "provincial" universities, but the first families of Manchester, Edinburgh, and Glasgow identify themselves gladly with their universities. So, too, with the patriciates of cities like

Bologna or Dresden, the cities of the Low Countries or of Scandinavia. And everywhere—even in London and Paris—the relationship between the university scholars and the community is intimate and lively.

Not so in the United States. New York City is an exception, to be sure; and possibly—though not certainly—Boston and San Francisco. But elsewhere urban universities make very little impact on their communities. What effect do the local universities have on the newspapers of Chicago or Detroit? What role do the universities play in the musical or theatrical life of Los Angeles? To what extent are university scholars a significant part of the social and club life of Pittsburgh or Houston? It is impossible to imagine Edinburgh society without its contingent of university scholars, or the government of Sweden without the contributions from the universities, or the journals and publishing houses of Paris aside from the scholars of the Sorbonne, or even the financial and corporate life of Copenhagen without the university contributions. But where in America do universities play a comparable role?

It is not enough for academicians to wring their hands and look wistfully to Edinburgh and Zurich and Stockholm. Most of our urban universities, it is safe to say, command just about the position they merit in their communities. If they cut themselves off from their communities to try to ape rural and ivy-clad colleges, they should not be surprised if the community ignores them. If they adopt the policy of playing up athletics and social activities and playing down matters intellectual, they should not expect to command intellectual prestige. If they fail to maintain high academic standards or to attract a first-rate faculty, they should not be astonished if that segment of the community interested in education invests its loyalties in older or better colleges and universities. If they place their public relations in the hands of people who think a baseball victory more newsworthy than a translation of Virgil, they must not be surprised if the community takes them at their word. Many of the problems that now afflict the urban university will take care of themselves if the university first sets its intellectual house in order.

But there remains the question of the relationship between the university and the community. That relationship should be intimate, but not dependent. How far can the university assimilate to the city without becoming parochial in its character? How far can it identify itself with the city without becoming a service station for local interests? These are difficult problems—more difficult with new American than with older European universities, more difficult in a framework that regards the university as primarily vocational than in one that takes for granted its scientific and philosophical character. Yet the experience of such institutions as Harvard, Columbia, the Hopkins, Chicago, Minnesota, and California suggest that these problems are by no means insuperable.

The first responsibility of the university is not to serve its immediate community but to serve the much larger community of learning of which it is a part, not to serve its immediate generation, but future generations. It is reassuring to reflect that those urban universities that resolutely act on this principle are also those that command the most ardent and generous support from their communities—London and Paris, let us say, or Harvard and Columbia and the Hopkins. The first purpose of the university is not to serve the practical and vocational needs of the local community—to turn out hotel managers or pharmacists, or to investigate the supposed needs of local industry ("Both the University of South Carolina and Clemson College as well as the private institutions, have made known their willingness to make their facilities available for industrial research programs of *practically every kind,*" read an advertisement in the *New York Times* last year), but to serve the needs of society at large and in the realms of basic research. It is reassuring that the universities which act on this principle are those which, in the end, enjoy both affection and prestige.

Yet the obligation to be part of the community remains. Perhaps the simplest formula here is that while the university itself must not merge its identity with the city that houses it, the individual members of the university should be far more active in and take far more responsibility for community affairs. They should live, if possible, in the city and participate actively in the cultural life in the city—its music, art, and theatre, its newspapers and journals. They should be encouraged to take an active part in politics and public affairs. In all of these activities the university itself should cooperate, by making it convenient for its members to live in the city; by making its facilities available for civic purposes; by encouraging political or journalistic or cultural involvement by members of its faculty. All of this requires a bit more boldness than most of our urban universities now display. It means that (as in Italy, for example) members of the faculty might be encouraged to edit newspapers. It means that the university administrations should not be frightened if their economists play an active role in labor unions, or help run the local Civil Liberties Union, or the local branch of the Foreign Policy Association. It means that the university should work closely with the local libraries, museums, and other cultural institutions.

If our universities are to enjoy the advantages of their urban position, if they are to be to American society what the great urban universities of Europe have been to their societies, they must assume responsibility for the development of urban and regional civilization. They have, most of them, a large domain and immense potential wealth: think how the urban universities of Italy and Germany jostled each other; think what they contributed to the civilization of those people and countries! They have, most of them, great cultural resources in the cities themselves. What they need is an awareness of their opportunities and potentialities; what they need is a philosophy. They should foster the spirit that animated Pericles and his fellow Athenians:

Ours is no work-a-day city. No other provides so many recreations for the spirit. . . . We are lovers of beauty without extravagance and lovers of wisdom without unmanliness. Wealth to us is not mere material for vainglory, but an opportunity for achievement. . . . Our citizens attend both to public and private duties, and do not allow absorption in their own various affairs to interfere with their knowledge of the city's. . . . Let us draw strength not merely from twice-told arguments —how fair and noble a thing it is to show courage in battle—but from the busy spectacle of our great city's life as we have it before us day by day, falling in love with her as we see her and remembering that all this greatness she owes to men with the fighter's daring, the wise man's understanding of his duty, and the good man's self-discipline in its performance. [Alfred Zimmern translation of Pericles' Funeral Oration, in *The Greek Commonwealth*, Oxford, 1931.]

IS TUITION
EVER JUSTIFIED?

5

Back in 1960 the Heald Committee recommended a modest tuition charge for the New York City colleges, traditionally free to students from the city high schools, and at the same time the trustees of the University of the State of New York recommended tuition charges for all students at state institutions of higher learning. In 1967 Ronald Reagan, elected to the governorship of California on an economy platform, announced tuition charges for students in all the universities and colleges of the vast California higher-education system. And almost everywhere states, confronted by rapidly rising costs of higher education, are in process of imposing higher tuition or higher "fees"—a kind of euphemism for tuition—on students. Is this a sound development, or a departure from sound principles? Is higher education a private luxury, a privilege, an investment, which those who enjoy should pay for, or is it an essential function of and service to society which the society should support?

So far the answer has been, characteristically enough, that it is both, and that it should be paid for by the beneficiaries and supported by the state. We have, that is, not a single but a dual or mixed system of higher education: tax-supported state and municipal institutions which charge no, or only nominal, tuition, and

The New York Times Magazine, February 26, 1961.

private institutions which are supported by endowments, gifts, and tuition. Actually, as so often the case in this country, the two have been growing closer together every year. Many of our tax-supported institutions charge "fees" which are almost the same as tuition, and boast large endowments; private institutions on the other hand provide scholarship aid to take care not only of tuition but of all other costs, and draw increasingly on public funds for support. The American reluctance to work out a solution on logical principles is nowhere better illustrated than in this realm of the support to higher education.

With five million students now crowding into the colleges and universities, and additional millions on the way, no one will challenge the statement that higher education is not a thing apart but an integral part of the entire educational system of the nation, and should be harmonized with that system.

The system itself has never been harmonious—it has never even been a "system." But what is impressive, as we contemplate some three centuries of history, is that from the very beginning education was regarded as a public responsibility. The Puritans who came to the Bay Colony were an extraordinarily well-educated group (they boasted perhaps the highest proportion of university graduates of any community in the world), and as early as 1635 they established a Latin school and the following year a college. It is interesting that provision for secondary and higher education antedated provision for elementary education by some years. The public-school laws of 1642 and 1647—the earliest in the Western world—were directed to public purposes. The Act of 1642 was designed to preserve "that learning which may be profitable to the commonwealth," and the "Olde Deluder Satan" Act of 1647 required schools in every town, "that learning may not be buried in the graves of our fathers in the church and the commonwealth." The Founding Fathers displayed a similar concern—we might almost say passion—for education. The philosophy of men like Jefferson and Noah Webster and Benjamin Rush was clear enough: that only an enlightened citizenry could make self-government work and that it was therefore the responsibility of the state to provide the enlightenment.

Until well into the nineteenth century public support was con-

fined to elementary—and some "higher"—education; it was not until the second quarter of the century that the philosophy of public
responsibility broadened out to embrace secondary education.
Until that time education, after the elementary grades, was provided for by academies and church schools: in 1850 there were
alleged to be some six thousand of these, most of them publicly
supported though usually with some tuition charge. The first public high school was opened in Boston in 1821, and Massachusetts
enacted the first high-school law six years later; notwithstanding
lively interest by Governor DeWitt Clinton, New York State did
not get around to requiring towns to maintain high schools until
after the Civil War. As late as 1890 there were only some twenty-
five hundred high schools in the entire nation. And the argument
that the community had no right to spend tax money on high
schools persisted until finally silenced by a famous decision by
Chief Justice Cooley of Michigan in the Kalamazoo case of 1872.

From the beginning Americans appeared to consider higher
education both a public and a private responsibility. Both Harvard
College and William and Mary were quasi-public in character, and
it is interesting to recall that as late as 1818 state and federal courts
had a hard time deciding whether Dartmouth College was a public
or a private institution. The dual, or mixed, pattern of higher education persisted after independence. By the time of the Civil War
denominational zeal and private philanthropy had founded some
two hundred private colleges, but it was in this period, too, that
Americans invented the state university, and launched municipal
colleges on English or European models. Thus, early in our history,
municipal, state, and federal governments, churches and philanthropy all combined to provide for the American people a varie-
gated pattern of public and private higher education, which has
persisted to this day.

The distinction between the two is more apparent than real, just
as the distinction between denominations or between classes in
America is more apparent than real. All higher education is private, whatever its legal or fiscal character. Regardless of whether a
board of regents or a board of trustees appoints a professor, he
pursues his research in his own way and teaches in his own way;
regardless of whether a young man goes to a private or a public

college, he learns in his own way. Both teaching and learning are individual: neither the teacher expounding Macbeth nor the student reading it is aware of the legal auspices which preside over his work. All higher education is public, too, no matter how financed. No private institution—no matter how lavishly endowed— is free from the influence of the state. It depends on the state for its charter, for tax exemptions, and for an interpretation of tax laws that makes possible gifts and inheritances. It draws its students chiefly from high schools supported by the state, and sends them out to graduate and professional institutions that are state-supported, or into society where as voters and office holders they will control future relations between government and education. What is most interesting is the way in which our colleges and universities have accommodated themselves to these pressures for uniformity in American life: in the United States the general has triumphed over the particular. Thus Harvard and California are far more like each other than they are different, and so, too, New York University and the College of the City of New York, or Duke University and the University of North Carolina; compare—or contrast—Oxford and Liverpool. Perhaps the chief distinction that obtains in America is quantitative: few public institutions can resist pressures to grow big, and the "small" college is almost invariably private. Yet even here—in New York State, Michigan, California—there are attempts to duplicate, or to imitate, the small college in public institutions: thus Riverside in California and Oakland in Michigan were originally designed along collegiate lines, and the new university at Santa Cruz is designed to be a "cluster" of colleges, as at Oxford or Cambridge.

As education developed in America it became increasingly a public responsibility. Elementary education was everywhere free; academies—already quasi-public—gave way to public high schools; and by mid-twentieth century more students attended public than private colleges and universities. In the next two decades the disparity of numbers grew: the figures for all institutions of higher education from junior college to universities for 1965 are 3,500,000 in public and 1,900,000 in private schools. "Private" institutions, meanwhile, became increasingly involved in public services. Thus MIT and the University of Chicago are, indubitably, private institutions, but both are in a sense instruments of public policy, both are deeply involved in research sponsored by and financed by the national government; and both spend more government than private money.

The rising cost of higher education in the last quarter century has laid a heavy burden upon taxpayer, private philanthropy, students, and parents; expenditure per pupil in the public schools has doubled even in the past ten years, and so has tuition in many colleges and universities. As costs soar and students crowd into academic halls, even public institutions are forced to look about for new sources of revenue. The University of Vermont has long charged tuition; many universities collect substantial fees; the recommendations of the Heald Committee is a portent of what may come. The proposed tuition charge is modest, but experience suggests that modest charges have a way of becoming importunate.

What is the argument for tuition in public colleges and universities?

First, that those who can afford to pay for education should do so, just as they pay for other services that are advantageous to them: medical, musical, theatrical, and so forth. After all, so the proponents of tuition assert, a college education is not only a good in itself, but a good investment; those who can flourish college degrees are sure to command higher earnings than those who cannot. To call on the taxpayer to finance the whole of this expensive education is to favor an educational elite at the expense of the masses of young people in the country. Second, public funds are not, after all, limitless. Indeed, we have already reached the limit —or we are close to it. Such money as is available should go to elementary and secondary education, where it is so desperately needed, rather than to higher. To withhold money from new school buildings, teachers' salaries, libraries and equipment in order to finance a minority of fortunate young men and women in college is undemocratic. As for the needy student, the new plans for tuition will not affect him. No one will be denied an education because he is poor; it is only those whose families are well able to pay tuition who will be called on for their fair share.

This is all persuasive enough. Yet it has aroused heated and determined opposition. What are the arguments against tuition in college and university—arguments that apply logically not only to state but to private education?

First, the principle that controls the relation of the state to education is both clear and simple. Education is not a luxury in which we indulge the privileged few; it is a necessity for the commonwealth. Society requires higher education because it has a paramount interest in an educated citizenry. That is the principle that justifies state support to elementary and secondary education, and compulsory school attendance; that is the principle behind state-support to higher education in most American states and in every nation of Europe. If it is a valid principle, on what ground should private or public college education alone be exempt from it? Surely the logic that applies to the high school applies to the college.

That, in any event, is the American tradition. States began to establish tax-supported universities even in the eighteenth century, and as early as 1802 the federal government recognized a responsibility to higher education by granting each Western state two townships for the support of "seminaries of learning." The Morrill Land Act of 1862 reaffirmed this principle and vastly enlarged its scope, by providing public lands as a subsidy for agricultural and engineering education in every state. Meantime, too, a number of cities—Charleston, Cincinnati, New York among them—had established tax-supported colleges. With World War II came that remarkable educational enterprise known as the G.I. Bill of Rights, whose costs ran at one time to three billion dollars a year. The G.I. Bill has run out, but federal subsidies to fellowships and to research are now roughly one billion dollars annually. It is a bit late in the day to challenge the interest of society in higher education, or the propriety of local, state, and federal grants to cover costs of tuition.

A further consideration is relevant here—not only relevant but decisive. The college is today what the high school was in the nineteenth and early twentieth centuries. In 1900 when our population was 76 million, our total high-school population was 519,000; roughly one student for every 150 persons. But as of 1965, with a population of 200 million, there are between 4.5 and 5 million students in colleges and universities (the exact figure depends on whether you count teachers' and junior colleges); roughly one student for every 40 or 45 persons. Again, as late as 1920 only 20 percent of youngsters between the ages of 14 and 18 went to high school; today the percentage of those between the ages of 18 and 21 who attend college is almost twice that high. In New York State it runs to 55 percent and the educational authorities of New York and of California predict that it will rise to 70 percent in the near future.

Not only is the college now what the high school was a generation ago from the point of view of students; it is pretty much what the high school was from the point of view of society and of social functions as well. We are entering an era when automation and the nature of the economy make few demands on little skills but urgent demands on great skills. We are entering an era when we are going to need incomparably more experts than ever before to perform the complicated duties of a highly complex society and a sophisticated economy. We are confronted with staggering shortages: a shortage of doctors, engineers, psychiatrists, social workers, librarians, administrators—you can extend the list almost indefinitely. These shortages promise to become more acute with every passing year. If we are to meet the demands of the new society, if we are to train technicians and administrators for ourselves and for the backward areas of the globe, we must see to it that far more students go to college and to graduate and professional schools than now do, and we must keep them there until they become expert.

All very well, it will be said, but why should the taxpayer subsidize those who are able to pay for their education and who will in the end profit greatly from that education? If education is indeed a good investment why should not its beneficiaries pay the bill?

It is a plausible argument, this, and one that gains strength from a contemplation of the affluence which so many students seem to enjoy—the shining cars parked in front of the handsome fraternity houses, the weekends at ski resorts and the summers abroad. We should not allow ourselves to be distracted by these irrelevancies, but keep in mind the controlling principle. The important thing about higher education, as about fire or police protection, good roads, slum clearance, national parks, old-age pensions and unemployment compensation, is not the private but the public benefit. We do not tax parents with children more heavily than those without because they benefit more from public schools, or remit taxes to those who may not qualify for unemployment insurance.

But more, it is a fallacy to suppose that those who enjoy the advantages of a university education will not eventually pay for them. If their education does in fact bring them enhanced income —and statistics tell us that only 15 percent of elementary-school graduates earn over $6,000, but that 66 percent of college graduates do—then they will inevitably pay substantially higher taxes on those incomes. If they do not return to society the full cost of their education, income taxes can be adjusted to the point where they will do so. But in fact doctors, lawyers, engineers, architects, and others whose education enables them to command a substantially higher-than-average income will pay back, over the years, far more than the state ever spent on their education. Indeed, if the figures of the monetary value of education which are so smilingly submitted to us are sound, it follows with unanswerable logic that society can make no better financial investment than in higher education.

Burdened as we are with taxes that grow heavier every year, can we meet these additional demands?

Actually the sums involved are not as high as might be supposed. The 1957-58 figures reveal that in that year state and local governments contributed $1.206 billion to higher education, the federal government $710 million, gifts and endowments $826 million, and tuition $939 million. Figures for 1965 show increases in all of these categories, but a particularly large increase in federal contributions: Mr. Howard Babbidge of the Office of Education estimates it at between $1.5 and $2 billion. In short, tuition constitutes roughly one-fourth of the income of our colleges and universities; if the total cost of tuition were to be absorbed by state and federal governments, the additional charge would be far less than what has been added since 1957.

In this connection it is not irrelevant to note the experience and practice of other countries. Poorer nations like France, Germany, Denmark, and Norway (with smaller student bodies to be sure) provide not only free education all the way through the university but, ordinarily, room and board as well. So does Britain, with larger numbers of students; even at those ancient citadels of privilege, Oxford and Cambridge, 90 percent of all students are on government scholarships which provide not only all academic fees but contributions to room and board. Russia, with some three and one half million students in her universities and technical and scientific schools, provides free tuition and room and board for all students maintaining certain minimum scholastic standards, and pays the students pocket money besides! The United States, the richest country on the globe, is the only one that is seemingly not rich enough to subsidize the education of its university students.

There is one final objection to free education that scarcely rises to the dignity of an argument: that young people will not value what comes to them so easily and so cheaply.

Is it necessary to observe that it is not, for the most part, the young people who pay for their education, but their parents? That the young will respond if their parents foot the bills, but regard with contempt what comes from the community, is not an argument that will stand examination. But we are not left to speculation here. There is not the slightest evidence that students at Oxford or Manchester, Paris or Copenhagen, cherish their education less than do those privileged to pay in the United States. It is suggestive that no European university thinks it necessary to put on vast athletic displays in order to win community support for education, and that the average European student has a higher sense of responsibility to his university than does the average American student. Nor—if we look to the American scene—is there any reason to suppose that students at the University of Michigan or the Iowa State University value their education less than those who pay tuition at Princeton or Stanford. The notion that we value only what we pay for directly is false to experience and false to morality.

Needless to say no one proposes to put Harvard or Chicago, Oberlin or Amherst out of business, or to deprive them of any income. The thousand and some private institutions that depend on tuition will, of course, continue to draw a large part of their income from that source. This is not the place to deal with the mechanics which should operate to transfer the burden of payments from the individual to society. In all likelihood the best solution is the one with which we are most familiar from experience with the G.I. Bill of Rights—payment directly by government to students who win admission to college. In all likelihood, too, the federal government will come to be the chief source of such payments, for only that government can command adequate tax resources and can assure some degree of equality between states and regions. But there is no reason why state and even local authorities should not continue to bear a substantial part of the costs of higher education. They will of course maintain their own institutions; they can, as well, subsidize study at private institutions. Illinois and California already do so, and educational authorities in New York, Pennsylvania, and Missouri have recommended such programs for their states. This makes sense economically as well as intellectually, for it is a good deal cheaper for a state to pay full tuition for its students at private institutions than to duplicate buildings, grounds, facilities, and faculties in public ones. And who can doubt that academically, too, it is wise to preserve and strengthen the private colleges which have so much to contribute of devotion, tradition, and love of learning, rather than to concentrate all education in mammoth state institutions?

There is every reason to agree with Professor Seymour Harris that the tuition which private institutions charge should correspond more closely than it now does to the real costs of education, so that underpaid teachers, librarians, and maintenance men and women are not called on to make special sacrifices to education that other members of the community do not make. The logical and sensible solution is for governments—national, state, and local—to extend to all students who qualify for admission to accredited colleges and universities (itself a difficult problem) the kind of tuition support that was provided for by the G.I. Bill of Rights, or—better yet—the kind of grants that are provided by the Woodrow Wilson Fellowships for graduate study.

Far from harming the private institutions, such a program would greatly help most of them by placing them on a basis of financial equality with public institutions. It would have the effect of raising the educational level all along the line, for colleges would be called on to compete for students on other than financial grounds. It would eliminate irrelevant financial considerations from advanced and professional education.

Taxes to support higher education are like taxes to support elementary education, strengthen national defense, build roads, maintain hospitals, provide medical care, operate libraries and museums, and maintain public order. The principle that underlies all of these enterprises is that they are essential to the well-being of society. Once we concede that the whole community—the community of the future as well as of the present—has an overriding interest in education at every level, that the whole community requires the scientists to maintain national defense, the engineers to build the roads, the doctors to serve the hospitals, the social workers to cure juvenile delinquency, the librarians to safeguard the treasures of the past, the judges to maintain public order—once we concede this familiar principle, the whole problem of the cost of higher education falls into its logical place in that heroic enterprise, the American Commonwealth.

GIVE THE GAMES
BACK TO THE STUDENTS

6

Almost every year the public is startled by revelations of some new scandal in college athletics—the bribery of basketball players, the open purchase of football players, the flagrant violation of rules by the college authorities themselves.

It is regrettable that these scandals should excite so much attention, for, by dramatizing the ostentatious immoralities of college athletics, they tend to distract attention from the more permanent and pervasive immoralities. Indignation at the more overt manifestations of corruption thus becomes a kind of moral catharsis; having expressed it, we can contemplate with apathy the conditions which almost inevitably produce the corruption.

Thirty years ago a report of the Carnegie Foundation on college athletics concluded that:

> The paid coach, the special training tables, the costly sweaters and extensive journeys in special Pullman cars, the recruiting from the high schools, the demoralizing publicity showered on players, the devotion of an undue proportion of time to training, the devices for putting a desirable athlete, but a weak scholar, across the hurdles of the examinations, these ought to stop and the intramural sports be brought back

The New York Times Magazine, April 16, 1961.

to a stage in which they can be enjoyed by a large number of students and where they do not involve an expenditure of time and money wholly at variance with any ideal of honest study.

"These ought to stop." Instead, they have become all but universally accepted and legalized—nay, the malpractices themselves have become respectable, and we can look back upon our old view of them with a certain nostalgia. For today's malpractices are more extreme and more widespread. Worse yet, they have percolated down to the high school and they have corrupted large segments of our society.

For almost half a century now, educators have talked hopefully about de-emphasizing college athletics. And every year the emphasis has grown greater, not weaker. The problem is not one of overemphasis. It is not even one of emphasis. The problem is the enterprise itself—intercollegiate athletics. If we are going to solve that problem, we must begin by restating principles so elementary and so obvious that they should not have to be stated at all:

The function of colleges and universities is to advance education. Whatever contributes to education is legitimate. Whatever does not contribute to education is illegitimate.

The only justification, therefore, for games, sports, athletics, is that these do in some way contribute to education.

By education we mean nothing narrow. Clearly, it involves physical and moral as well as intellectual well-being. But these are by-products of education. There are a number of institutions that have responsibility for the physical and moral well-being of the young, but the schools and colleges are the only institutions that have primary responsibility for their intellectual well-being.

Does our current system of intercollegiate or interschool athletics contribute either to the central function of education, or to its by-products? Clearly, it does not. As now organized and directed in most colleges and in a good many, if not most, high schools, athletics contribute nothing whatsoever to education. They simply distract the time, energy, and attention of the whole community from the main business of education—and from its legitimate by-products.

Our system of athletics does not contribute to the physical fitness of the young. On the contrary, it concentrates on physical training for a mere handful of students—whom it often harms by overtraining—and reduces the great majority of students to the role of passive spectators, or television viewers. Even the facilities provided for physical training are often monopolized by the "teams," to the detriment of most of the student body. Thus, in many colleges, the swimming pool is "reserved" during the prime hours from three to six every afternoon for the swimming team. Imagine excluding all but Phi Beta Kappa students from the library for three hours every afternoon—or any afternoon!

It does not contribute to sportsmanship—which was one of its original purposes. On the contrary, the tremendous emphasis on winning the game has largely destroyed sportsmanship and has corrupted both players and spectators.

It does not contribute to initiative, independence, alertness, and other desirable qualities. Instead, by centering authority in paid coaches whose primary interest is winning games, it has gone far to destroy initiative and independence on the part of players.

No impartial student of college and high-school football and basketball—these are the chief occasions for corruption—can doubt that, on balance, these sports, far from making any contribution, actually do immense and irreparable harm. It is not only physical training and sports that are corrupted by the current malpractices; it is the whole educational enterprise. And, since the whole community is involved in the educational enterprise, it is the whole community.

Educational institutions themselves are corrupted. They publicly confess that their athletic functions are more important than their academic, and acquiesce in malpractices that they would not tolerate in any other branch of their activities.

Colleges that spend more money on athletics than on the library, that excite more interest in basketball than in music, that cater to the demand for "winning teams" rather than for sportsmanship are faithless to their moral and intellectual obligations. Moreover, the community itself is corrupted by being bribed with athletic spectacles to support educational programs which should be supported on their merits. Perhaps worst of all, the boys and girls of the country are corrupted: here is the real corruption of the innocent. Almost every newspaper, every weekly magazine, every television network makes clear to them that what is most important in education is athletics, and what is most important in athletics is winning.

No newspaper ever celebrates the scholarly achievements of local students in its biggest headlines. Why, then, should we expect the young to believe us when we tell them, on ceremonial occasions, that it is the scholarly achievements that are important? Alumni demand a winning team, and so does the community. Not long ago, a North Carolina coach was quoted as asking, "How can I be proud of a losing team?" Would he also say, "How can I be proud of R. E. Lee?" Can we expect young people to take us seriously when we tell them that it is the game that counts—not the victory?

What is the explanation of this deep and pervasive corruption of games and sports? What has happened to us?

What has happened is that we have taken games away from the students, to whom they belong, and given them to adults, to whom they do not belong.

We now require of high-school and college boys—and, sometimes, girls—that they provide entertainment for the community and bring money to local shopkeepers and restaurants and other businessmen. (Recently a New York City official said of an Army-Syracuse game that "the restaurants reported business to be fabulous . . . the Transit Authority reported 28,000 extra riders that day . . . immensely increased hotel business.") They are expected to provide copy for the local newspapers, for magazines, and for TV and radio.

We do not permit children to work in shops or factories for our profit. Why should they be expected to make money for business interests in the community?

We do not permit our daughters to put on performances in burlesque shows or night clubs for our entertainment. Why should we require our sons to put on gladiatorial spectacles in stadia for our entertainment? We do not expect the young to pay school taxes, or to support the chemistry department of a university. Why should we expect them to earn money for the athletic programs of the local high school, or to support the athletic departments of our colleges and universities?

The problem is deep and pervasive, but fortunately not complex. The solution is drastic, but fortunately not difficult: all that is needed is the will to apply it. The solution is threefold:

First, give games back to the students. Second, eliminate all outside pressures to win games. Third, take the dollar sign entirely out of school and college athletics. Let us elaborate on these.

First: Let students manage their own games, as they do at English universities. Let them play their games for the fun of it, not to entertain adults, or make money for the community or win glory for old Pugwash.

An end to games as spectacles. An end to bands in uniforms and drum majorettes and well-trained cheering sections, all of them artificial and all giving a fantastically exaggerated importance to the games. An end to vulgar ceremonies like singing "The Star-Spangled Banner" before the kick-off; no one sings the national anthem before a swimming match—or an examination; why should patriotism be invoked for football? An end to the recruiting of players by coaches or alumni, to coaches who play the games from the sidelines and, for that matter, to formal coaching. If there must be coaches, let them depart on the day of the game and permit the players to play their own games. After all, professors do not help the students pass examinations.

Second: Eliminate all outside pressures. Alumni letters about the football team should go into the wastebasket, where they belong. An end to pressure from coaches; their jobs should not depend on victories. An end to pressure from newspapers; let them report professional games, and leave students alone to play as well or as badly as they please. An end to pressure from public-relations offices of colleges; let them report academic activities or go out of business. An end to pressure from townspeople; they can get their entertainment, find emotional safety valves, and get rid of their vicarious aggressiveness elsewhere.

Third: Eliminate money—all the way. No more paid coaches. Let students do their own coaching, or let school teams draw on "old boys," or get such aid as they need from members of the teaching staff who are primarily and legitimately teachers. After all, paid coaches are both new and singular in history; they did not exist until this century, and they do not now exist in English or European universities.

An end to all athletic subsidies, direct and indirect; to athletic "scholarships," a contradiction in terms. No student should be encouraged, in high school, to subordinate studies to athletic prowess. No student should be admitted to college on any grounds but those of academic competence; no student should be allowed to stay in college unless he is intellectually competent.

An end to separate athletic budgets: to admission charges for games; to the expectation that football or basketball will somehow "pay for" other parts of physical training. Games should be as much a normal part of school or college as music or drama or the college newspaper, and should no more expect to be self-sustaining.

An end to the building or maintenance of costly stadia used only a few hours each year. Let us make drastic reductions in expenditures for athletic equipment, for uniforms, for other superfluities. No more travel expenditures for spring training camps, for fall training camps, for airplane junkets to the other end of the country. Let schools play their neighbors in the same town or—at an extreme—in the same state.

Adopt these policies and nine-tenths of the evils that plague intercollegiate athletics would evaporate overnight.

Of course, if they *were* adopted, the games would deteriorate— as spectacles. Those who want to see brilliant performances in football or basketball can then go to professional games, as even now they go to professional rather than to college baseball games. Let the fans—the subway alumni of Notre Dame or the vicarious old grads of Michigan—organize city or state football and basketball teams, just as the English have city or county soccer teams.

Naturally, student interest in organized athletics will decline; it should. Sensible students already know that if they are going to get on with their education—if they are going to get into a law school or a medical school—they have little time for organized athletics.

European universities have managed to survive for centuries

without the benefit of "teams," and doubtless American colleges and universities can learn to do so.

Of course, there will be a falling-off in enthusiasm for old Siwash among certain kinds of alumni. Perhaps, in time, colleges can produce alumni whose interest is in intellectual rather than in athletic programs. In any event, there seems to be a pretty close correlation between high-powered athletics and low-powered finances. It is a sardonic commentary on the current scene that public pressure for winning teams rarely finds expression in lavish gifts or in generous appropriations. Institutions such as the Massachusetts Institute of Technology and Amherst College, at any rate, seem to manage pretty well without the exploitation of athletics, and institutions such as Ohio State, which has yielded to pressure for winning teams, are treated with niggardliness by an ungrateful legislature. Nor does an inability to mount athletic spectacles seem seriously to handicap the educational functions of Wellesley, Radcliffe, and Vassar.

These are negative consequences which we may anticipate from the elimination of money and of pressures from college athletics and the return of games to the students. The positive consequences which we may confidently anticipate are exhilarating:

This simple program will restore integrity to athletics, making clear once more the now blurred distinction between the amateur and the professional. And it will enormously improve programs for physical education for the young people in schools and colleges, an improvement desperately needed. It will release the energies of educators and students for the primary job of education. The colleges will be freed from improper pressures and influences and permitted to do what they are best equipped to do and what they have a moral responsibility to do: educate the young.

Is all this a counsel of perfection? Can this program of cleansing and restoration be achieved? Well, it has been achieved at the Johns Hopkins, the University of Chicago, and MIT. It has been achieved at Swarthmore and Oberlin and Pomona and Reed. Somehow, all continue to flourish.

No halfway measures will do. As long as nonacademic organizations have an interest in athletics, as long as games belong to coaches or alumni or townspeople or the business community instead of to the young people who play them, all the evils which have afflicted school and college athletics in the past will continue.

Radical surgery is needed. But it is radical surgery from which the patient is sure to recover and which guarantees good health and good spirits.

THE TWO CULTURES:
THE INDUCTIVE
AND THE DEDUCTIVE

7

It is a commonplace recognized by, and indeed enjoined upon us, that ours is the age of science. It is the scientists who—as C. P. Snow put it—have the future in their bones. I hasten to add the kind of observation expected from historians: there is nothing new about this. The seventeenth and eighteenth centuries were an age of science; the sovereignty of science was even greater then than it is today, more generally acclaimed, more widely shared. In that familiar quarrel between the ancients and the moderns which agitated western Europe for almost a century, it was the moderns who were triumphant, and the claims of the moderns were largely the claims of science. It was the age of Newton; indeed, he gave his name to it, and to the way of thinking which came to be all but universally accepted. Who would write now, of any scientist, what Pope wrote, "God said, Let Newton be! and all was light"?

It was the age of Linnaeus, the sovereign of the North, who organized and ordered the world of nature. It was the age of Buffon, who reigned like a king in his royal gardens, gazing at his own statue and musing on his own immortality. It was the age of the encyclopaedia, with its pervasive concern for science and tech-

Address at University of Wyoming, 1967.

nology and its indifference to history or religion. The great men of
the Enlightenment were, most of them, scientists, or pretended
they were: D'Alembert and La Grange and La Place and Lavoisier
and along with them Diderot and Voltaire; the great Leibnitz, who
invented integral calculus, and Immanuel Kant, who thought of
himself as a scientist, and Goethe, who wrote on almost everything
and even dared challenge Newton himself. In America, too, it was
the age of science or of nature; most of the statesmen were natural-
ists or scientists—Franklin, of course, and Jefferson with his experiments in chemistry and in scientific farming, and Benjamin
Rush, who combined medicine with education and statesmanship,
and Rittenhouse, of whom Jefferson wrote that the world has but
one Rittenhouse and never had one before, and that astonishing
Benjamin Thompson, who later became Count Rumford of the Holy
Roman Empire and who put science to the use of politics.

It is relevant too that what we call the social sciences—particularly economics and sociology—emerged out of science and tried to
conform to its rules and habits. History, politics, and law, to be
sure, had their roots deep in the past and belonged quite clearly to
the world of the ancients, but from the eighteenth century on their
practitioners tried increasingly to assimilate them to the world of
nature, to bring them under the operation of those same laws
which controlled the operations of the physical world.

And how arresting that so many of the great seminal ideas of the
social sciences should have been drawn from science: the idea of a
universe ruled by law to which society as well as nature con-
formed, which we associate with Newton; the idea of evolution,
which embraced society and all of its interests as well as nature;
the idea of the role of the unconscious, the subconscious and the
irrational which we associate with Sigmund Freud and his successors.

The shift from the world of Newton to the world of Darwin and
then to the world of Freud—and perhaps too the idea of relativity
and uncertainty which derives so much from Einstein and Heisen-
berg—involved convulsive readjustments. But there was continuity, and that, too, was drawn from the world of science. For all of
these epochs of modern science had in common the application of

the inductive method. It is precisely the method of science, and all of the modern social—what it is fashionable now to call the behavioral—sciences, use and depend on it.

We are, all of us, bemused by Sir Charles Snow's notion of two cultures, the culture of science and the culture of the humanities, with the so-called social sciences hovering uneasily in a twilight world between the two. No one can deny that the analysis is accurate, or the problem of communication between the two cultures acute. But I venture to suggest that the real distinction between scholars is not so much professional as philosophical, and that the line of demarcation here is not to be drawn by faculties, as it were, but by principles. Historians and physicists do indeed have trouble communicating with each other—witness the difficulty Henry Adams had in communicating with himself, or his readers, when he took up physics—and so do biologists and literary critics. But mathematicians also have the greatest difficulty communicating with each other, and so do literary critics and poets and painters. The fundamental difficulty is, I suggest, that of communication between those who cling to the deductive and those who profess and practice the inductive method of thought and investigation. A little learning, or a little patience, or a bit of mutual trust and confidence, can bridge the gap between the scientist and the social scientist; but what can bridge the gap between those who start with a body of preconceived ideas about man, nature, and God and their interrelations, and those who prefer to cut loose from such preconceptions and start with what they consider to be facts?

I need not enlarge upon the nature of these distinctions nor on the significance of these divisions. The deductive world starts with the absolute—with laws or principles that are part of the cosmic system, as it were, with truths that are at once intuitive and transcendental. You will recall that the very essence of American transcendentalism was belief in a number of intuitive truths such as the infinite benevolence of God, the infinite beneficence of nature, the infinite perfectibility of human nature. But the inductive world starts with William James's admonition: "Damn the absolute." It rejects the intuitive, the transcendental, the *a priori*, the theoretical, the deductive, and embraces with unlimited fervor the experimental, the organic, the verifiable, the functional, the progressive, the scientific. The world of the deductive was, to quote William James once more, "Buttoned up and white-chockered and clean-shaven," while the world of the inductive was—and is—formless and uncertain and unfinished, but everlastingly alive with possibilities of change.

It was the use of this inductive method which enabled the social sciences to be effective for perhaps the first time. In law the inductive method forced the abandonment of natural-law doctrines in favor of sociological jurisprudence, the abandonment of the conviction that law was a kind of brooding omniscience in the sky and the acceptance of the notion that law was an instrument of society. In politics the new principle forced the abandonment of the assumption that the constitution was somehow part of the cosmic system and of those subjective notions which had for so long befogged political thought and conduct—fixed concepts of sovereignty, for example, or of the character of political parties—and the acceptance of constitutions and laws as instruments to be used for secular purposes. In economics it meant a shift from such classical concepts as that of economic man, or the law of supply and demand, or the sanctity of property, to the recognition of economic practices, functions, and even vagaries and to a new and livelier concern for the welfare of those who had heretofore been regarded as inert pieces of the economic machinery—workers, farmers, or slum dwellers. In sociology it brought the repudiation of Spencerian concepts of *laissez-faire* as identical with the cosmic system, and the acceptance of social dynamics, a revolutionary shift from passive acquiescence in the notion of cosmic determinism to active control over nature and the processes of evolution through the instruments of government and society. In education the new principle brought a shift from teaching to learning, from the concept of education as a preparation for life to that of education as an integral part of life, from education as the handing on of a body of knowledge to education as a continuous and dynamic explanation.

We have, in this first substantial chapter of the history of the impact of scientific thought on social thought, a spectacle of the liveliest interest for our own generation.

It was the use and abuse of science and technology which brought about the industrial revolution and was responsible for the eruption of those many social, economic, and moral problems which clamored so insistently for solution in the nineteenth century. It was the imagination, sympathy, compassion, faith, born of and nourished by the humanities—that is, religion, philosophy, art, literature—and the practical efficiency of the social sciences, which combined to provide partial solutions of these problems, and which staved off catastrophe and gave a stay to desperation.

We are confronted now with a revolution that is deeper, broader, more comprehensive, and more insistent than that of the nineteenth century, a revolution once again brought about by the findings and the application of science, and by technology. No one can doubt that science and technology are ultimately responsible for the revolutionary crises of our time: the vast and disorderly increase in world population which threatens to crowd us all off the globe; the convulsive effort of three-fourths of the peoples of the world to catch up in one generation with the European fourth —catch up materially and politically; the capacity of militarists to destroy civilization, indeed to wipe out life on this globe. These are the problems that glare at us continually: overpopulation; chauvinistic nationalism and race war; atomic warfare. It is not science and technology which are responsible for these problems, for science and technology are neutral. But it is science and technology which made it possible for these problems to emerge, and it is man's abuse as much as his use of science which has given to these problems their inescapable urgency.

But science provides too the possibility of solving these problems. Science *can* solve the problem of overpopulation: *can* provide enough food and material goods to raise the standard of living for the majority of mankind who now live on the verge of starvation: *can* wipe out many ancient diseases, save the lives of babies, prolong the lives of the old, restore to usefulness millions now incapacitated. Science can desalinate the oceans and provide water for irrigation and for industry; can extract food from the seas; can furnish vast new resources of power for industry. It can even help fill the emptiness of leisure time for our own affluent society.

Atomic energy can be applied to peaceful purposes as easily as to destructive.

Needless to say, "science" is an abstraction; it is almost a semantic delusion. Science does not function by itself; by itself it neither creates problems nor solves them. It is an instrument, and in our kind of society it is an instrument chiefly of politics.

But politics and its multifarious activities—international organizations, the conduct of foreign policy, provision for the general welfare, health, education, justice, the conservation of natural and of human resources—all of these are the domain of the social sciences, inspired, counseled, and tempered by the humanities.

The role of the social scientist in our time is not only clear, it is almost mandatory. It is to educate society to the nature of the problems which confront it—to educate a parochial society to global problems, to educate Western society to non-Western problems, to educate an affluent society to the problems of poverty, to educate a predominantly white society to the realities of race, to educate a powerful society to the limitations on power. And it is to provide the mechanisms of politics, administration, and education which will enable science to fulfill its beneficent capacities.

In short, the social sciences are called upon to perform once again, on a world scale, and for ultimate stakes, the tasks which they performed so well in the generation of Lester Ward and John R. Commons, John Dewey and Charles W. Eliot, Robert La Follette and Woodrow Wilson. They are called upon to address themselves to problems which in one sense are as elementary as those raised by the industrial revolution. For it may well be that we overly sophisticate the nature of the task which confronts the social sciences. As C. P. Snow reminds us:

> We cannot know as much as we should about the social condition all over the world. But we can know, we do know, two most important things. First we can meet the harsh facts of the flesh, on the level where all of us are, or should be, one. We know that the vast majority, perhaps two-thirds, of our fellow men are living in the immediate presence of illness and premature death; their expectation of life is half of ours, most are under-nourished, many are near to starving, many starve. Each of these lives is afflicted by suffering, different from that which is intrinsic in the individual condition. But this suffering is un-

necessary and can be lifted. This is the second important thing which we know—or, if we don't know it, there is no excuse or absolution for us. [*The Two Cultures: and a Second Look,* Cambridge University Press, 1963, p. 77.]

The problem of confining atomic energies to the tasks of peace presents, to be sure, grave difficulties. Lincoln said of slavery, a century ago, that ". . . we, even we here, hold the power and bear the responsibility." Today, we not only bear but share power and responsibility, and we have yet to learn how to do this.

Yet, in dealing with these prodigious problems, with the life or death of our civilization in the balance, we are still bemused, we are still plagued, we are still paralyzed, by the importunities of those who cling to the deductive approach. Thus, to the demand that the state provide for the general welfare, as the constitution admonishes it to do, they invoke the well-worn shibboleths of Manchester liberalism and social Darwinism. To the efforts to ameliorate the intolerable tensions of the cold war, they intone the arguments of isolationism and of chauvinistic nationalism, or some apocalyptic visions of history and of a historical Armageddon in which we alone battle for the Lord. To proposals for reknitting those ties which for so long bound us to the largest and potentially most powerful nation on the globe, they respond by insisting either that China is not really there at all or that she is damned and therefore to be banished forever from the company of the saved as Lucifer was banished from heaven. And to the appeal for a general nuclear disarmament before we are confronted with the nightmare prospect of twenty nuclear powers, they respond—some of them— with what is perhaps the most irrelevant *cri de coeur* in the history of politics, "Better dead than red."

It is a relevant, but paradoxical, consideration that those who cling to *a priori* assumptions about man and society tend to draw support not from historical experience with the inductive approach but rather from the history of the failure of the deductive. Those who take their stand on "human nature," who have no faith in the capacity of intelligence to solve problems, who put their faith in cosmic principles and eternal verities—always as interpreted by themselves, of course—rather than in expedients, accommodations and compromises, like to remind us how frequently we have been disillusioned in our hopes for progress. True enough, but the concept of progress was fabricated not by philosophers or historians rooted in science, but by theoreticians. It is, assuredly in its more general and ambitious form, an *a priori* concept, one based on faith rather than on trial and error. It was a noble faith and that society which cherishes it is better and more secure than that which rejects it. But the failure of man to come up to the hopes and predictions of a Condorcet, or a Comte, is a monument not to the failure of science and social science, but to that of doctrinaire principles and expectations.

Let us turn then to the humanities. It is true of course that the social sciences are in a very real sense humanities, in that they are concerned with man, not with things, with human nature rather than with nature. But where the social sciences are interested in man in general, the humanities are interested in man in particular. Where the function of the social sciences is to illuminate and perhaps to solve problems of politics and the economy, of education, crime, delinquency, poverty, administration, municipal and international law, and so forth, the function of the humanities is to understand and enrich individual life. The social sciences, like science itself, depend on mathematics and on statistics; it is not chance that the study of economics, sociology and politics is becoming increasingly mathematical. But with statistics the humanities have no serious concern. It may be relevant to the student of cultural anthropology that ten million Americans prefer the Beatles to Mozart, but it is not relevant to the humanist.

In this sense the role of the humanities—of art, literature, philosophy and music—remains much what it was before the rise of modern science. The social sciences are of necessity evolutionary and progressive, but not the humanities.

Perhaps the most elementary observation to be made about the humanities is that they are not required to be "useful" in any ostentatious sense. The traditional role of the humanities has not been to instruct but to inspire, to enrich life rather than to improve it.

Yet as a by-product of such enrichment may we not believe that lives enriched, minds excited, sympathies broadened, may help create a more humane society? As economic affluence imposes upon its beneficiaries an obligation to take care of those who are less fortunate, not only at home but in continents once but no longer distant—an obligation which Americans of this generation recognize and strive to fulfill—might it not be that intellectual and artistic affluence will in turn inspire a society, unconsciously perhaps, to livelier sympathies, broader tolerance, more humane conduct, in international relations? "In defeat, defiance," but "in victory, magnanimity"—may we not believe that Churchill learned this in large measure from the study of history and the reading of poetry?

Granted (as Dean Barzun reminds us somewhat sardonically) that affluent societies have not in the past consciously used their talents in this manner—not fifth-century Athens, not Renaissance Florence, not Elizabethan England—the test is not necessarily what is done deliberately or immediately, but what comes to pass, not necessarily in the present, but in the future. For surely it is clear that what is lacking in our relations to the poor and the desperate peoples of the globe, is not good will but understanding and the mechanisms with which to translate understanding into policy. None are deliberately hostile to the poor and the weak: none want war and few even want the panoply of war; none are prepared to champion disease and ignorance. What is lacking is imagination—the ability to enter the minds and souls of others, to see and to feel life as it is lived by those hundreds of millions for whom hunger and cold and misery and disease are familiar companions.

It is in part for this reason that we have the extraordinary spectacle of a double standard in our foreign policy. We have a double standard in what we assume is right and necessary for ourselves, and what we take for granted is enough for others, and we do not stop sufficiently and ask ourselves whether the exceeding bounty of nature which we enjoy is so clearly our due that we are not called upon to share more of it with others. Even in the formal conduct of foreign relations we act upon, if we do not subscribe to, a double standard. It is right for us to violate the neutrality of Cuba or of

China, because our intentions are peaceable and noble, but wrong
for Cuba or China to violate international law. It is right for us to
intervene in the Civil War in Vietnam or in the Congo, but pernicious for others to do so. It is, if not right, at least necessary, for
us to have atomic superiority, but it is dangerous and wicked for
others to enter the atomic race. We are, so far, the only nation ever
to use thermonuclear power and even now, twenty years after
Hiroshima, we establish nuclear mine fields along the German
frontier; but it is Russia and now China who are dangerous, not
we. When we undertake to spread the American way of life, we
are engaged in a holy mission; when Communists attempt to spread
Communism they are guilty of subversion. All this comes in large
part from an inability to see ourselves as others see us, to imagine
the point of view of others; that is, from a poverty of the imagination. All this comes too from the lack of a sense of history, and of a
cosmopolitan point of view.

Who can doubt that this lack of imagination is associated with
the deductive and the doctrinaire attitude of mind? Those who
embrace absolutes rarely find it possible to sympathize with those
who do not share their confidence in these absolutes. Those who
are sure that their convictions are somehow part of the cosmic
system—their convictions about communism, the position of China
in the society of nations, loyalty and subversion, the sanctity of
private property, and so forth—are inclined to believe that any
who differ from them are challenging cosmic truths, and that nothing, therefore, is too bad for them. For as Justice Holmes said
almost half a century ago, "If you have no doubt of your premises
or your power, and want a certain result with all your heart, you
naturally . . . sweep away all opposition." This is the history of all
fanaticism in the past, religious, political, racial; it is the rationale
of much current fanaticism.

It is the humanities which should teach us patience, understanding, sympathy, tolerance for different philosophies and different
ways of life. Yet it cannot be said that the humanities now perform
this affluent function. Indeed they are, in large measure, in revolt
against these traditional functions. Separated from their historic
roots in religion, and, from the familiar roles assigned them both

by the Enlightenment and by Romanticism, they appear rather to be engaged in a convulsive dissociation from all those things which gave them character and purpose in the past, and we are confronted with the extraordinary spectacle of the humanities divorced not only from religion, philosophy, and morality, but from the experiences and values which have for centuries been their chief preoccupation.

What we have, today, is a full-throated revolt of the humanities against what is human, a kind of nihilism which implicitly and explicitly repudiates what men have valued in the past. What we have is the non-novel and the non-drama, the expulsion not only of the hero but of the villain as well; the repudiation of form, narrative, plot, and meaning. In the world of literature we seem always to be waiting for Godot, or wandering in the nightmare imagined by Kafka, or involved in the masochistic humiliations of a Jean Genêt, or entranced by the illusions and evasions of a Robbe-Grillet. In painting, in the plastic arts, in music, the record is much the same. As Dean Barzun has written:

> The modern artist finds himself doing the work of dehumanizing he abhors. By mirroring, as plastic artist, he shows man attenuated and anonymous. . . . Man broken up and disfigured . . . By building, as modern architect, he overwhelms and belittles man in gigantic upended coffins of steel. By composing, as modern musician, he destroys the inner rhythm and concord of feelings through the insistent beat of harsh combinations of sound. . . . By writing, as modern poet or novelist, he gives no quarter to either intellect or sensibility, pitting them against each other in words wilfully flat and opaque and sordid and clinical—in short reiterating to the point of nausea the proposition . . . that the life man has made for himself is not worth living. [*Science, the Glorious Entertainment*, Harper, 1964, pp. 235-236.]

In a curious way, most of this, too, for all its experimentalism, represents a revolt against the inductive and the pragmatic approach. The nonrepresentational painter, the abstract sculptor, the practitioners of anarchy and nihilism in the novel and the theatre are not observing life, but rejecting it, and therewith rejecting, too, the findings of science and the heritage of civilization. Nihilism is by no means confined to literature and the arts, but permeates the social sciences as well. Here too, in much of academic economics, politics, sociology, and law, we find that fascination with the technical, the mathematical and the professional, and that indulgence in a private vocabulary, which are deliberately designed to discourage interpretation, and to frustrate those educated on Montesquieu and Burke and the *Federalist Papers*, on Tocqueville, John Stuart Mill, or Lester Ward. History, which has never really known whether it belonged to the humanities or the social sciences, is in danger of being rejected by both. More and more it seems to flourish for itself alone, to be preoccupied with and fascinated by its own technical problems.

The role, even the responsibility, of the university in the present crisis is clear enough. Not all universities are in a position to play the role which circumstances have so insistently imposed upon them or to fulfill the responsibilities. But most of the American universities are, for, far more than universities in the Old World, the American reflect their society and perform the miscellaneous functions which society demands. This readiness to function as a social service station should have been fatal to scholarship, but was not.

We are entering now into a new era in the long history of the university, one that will draw more upon American than upon Old World experience. Already the Western university, and particularly the American university, is spreading with astonishing rapidity to all continents; and the American university is transforming education not only in South America, Africa, and Asia, but even in the countries of the Old World.

From the very beginning American colleges were dedicated to the service of God and the Commonwealth. Over the generations and the centuries they took this dedication seriously, and if the concept of God was secularized, the concept of the Commonwealth was, if anything, consecrated. The universities are now confronted with the obligation to expand that concept to embrace the commonwealth of learning, science, art and philosophy everywhere on earth.

It is the special obligation of the social sciences and the humanities to make us aware of the condition of man throughout the globe, and to provide us with the political, administrative, and scientific mechanisms which will enable us to improve that condition. Who can doubt that it is the university that is the most effective instrument for performing this task—the American university, above all, which has had long experience in the creation and administration of that wonderful network of intellectual and scientific resources formed by government, the academy, foundations, learned societies, the professions, and private enterprise. The university is the most effective of all organizations—more effective than government itself—for bringing to bear the varied resources of science, and the social sciences, on the problems of the backward areas of the globe. It is, too, the most hospitable of all institutions for providing a sanctuary for scholars and a haven for the arts. It is the most effective of institutions for fulfilling that task to which the late President Kennedy recalled it—that of combining power and poetry. This is perhaps but a different phrasing of science and the humanities. Where both are understood, where each penetrates and suffuses the other, there is no incompatibility, but a beneficent partnership.

THE UNIVERSITY AND THE
COMMUNITY OF LEARNING

8

When we consider the nature and the role of the university at the beginning of the twenty-first century, the history of predictions admonishes us to be both cautious and modest, for few of them have been vindicated by history. "And the things men looked for cometh not / And a path there was, where no man thought" seems to be the rule in history. How sobering to contemplate the utopias of the past, from Plato's *Republic* to Bacon's *New Atlantis* and Butler's *Erewhon;* how different the New World from the New Atlantis, how different Australia from Erewhon, how different even the real Israel from Theodor Herzl's *Altneuland* and from the plans of the Zionists. How misguided, for that matter, the prophecies of our own Founding Fathers of the development of the American society. And the difficulty, on the whole, has not been that the predictions were too visionary, but that they were too prosaic, not that they have been too ambitious, but that they have been too unimaginative. It is well, when looking to the future, to recall Daniel Burnham's admonition: "Make no little plans."

Address at University of Kentucky, 1965. Reprinted in *The University in the American Future*, edited by Thomas B. Stroup, Copyright © 1966 by the University of Kentucky Press.

It is a mere thirty-five years now to the year 2000, a single
generation, as generations go. Who, in 1930 looking ahead to 1965,
imagined, or could have imagined the development of the university and its associated institutions over this thirty-five-year period?
Who, then, would have imagined that this generation from the
thirties to the sixties would prove the most progressive and creative
in the history of higher education? Abraham Flexner had just published his mordant *Universities—American, English, German*, con-
trasting American universities unfavorably with the German, and
educators who imagined that the American university might be
something new under the academic sun were being put in their
place by Robert Hutchins. Almost everywhere the college was the
tail that wagged the academic dog, and in many colleges football
was the most important activity. Most colleges and universities
were worried about filling their classrooms and dormitories, and
paying their professors: the state of Kentucky, for example, reduced its biennial appropriation from something over three to less
than two million dollars in a period of four years. Notwithstanding
the threat of impoverishment, few educators called for federal aid,
and those who did were looked upon as the enemies to both learning and freedom, for it was an article of faith that federal aid
spelled federal control. And certainly it never occurred to anyone
in that innocent day that either the universities or the government
had any responsibility for education among the backward peoples
of the world.

What has happened in the past generation suggests the direction
which higher education in America (and perhaps in Europe) will
in all likelihood take in the next generation. The quantitative
changes are obvious. There was an immense increase in the number of colleges and universities, and if the new institutions are not
all Harvards or Chicagos, neither are they all built in the image of
Old Siwash or Canarsie, as some of our European friends seem to
think. There was a fivefold increase in the total number of students
and a proportionately higher increase in the number of students in
professional and graduate work. Appropriations increased some
tenfold and so did endowments. More important are the qualitative changes of the past generation: a decisive shift from the pri-

vate to the public university; the massive entry of the federal government into the academic domain; the steady raising of standards except where, as in the South, state policy made that difficult; a shift in the center of gravity to the graduate and professional schools; and an immense growth of the research functions of the university, sometimes at the expense of teaching.

More astonishing, perhaps, than the prosperity of the academic community has been the poverty of academic leadership. The generation after the Civil War had seen the emergence of a galaxy of great educational statesmen: Charles W. Eliot, Daniel C. Gilman, Andrew D. White, and after them Harper of Chicago, Butler of Columbia, Van Hise of Wisconsin, and Lowell of Harvard. There are more affluent universities now, but no academic statesmen to compare with these. Most of us will, I suspect, agree that in the last generation it is Robert Hutchins and James B. Conant who have been the most distinguished contributors to educational thought. But Hutchins' thought has been for the most part critical and even negative, and Mr. Conant has concerned himself almost wholly with the problems of secondary education. Pressure for change, expansion, experimentation, improvement has come rather from without than from within the academy; it has come in substantial part from that government traditionally feared: the federal. It has come in large part, too, from circumstances which educators have been most reluctant to recognize, the importunate demands of war.

The university is, by now, firmly established as the focal point not only of American culture and education, but of American life. It is, next to government itself, the chief servant of our society, the chief instrument of social change. It occupies something of the symbolic place of both the church and the state in the Old World, but it fills a role which neither church nor state can effectively fill; it is the source, the inspiration, the powerhouse, and the clearing house of new ideas.

All this is very much in the American grain. For as the Americans were the first people to use their schools primarily for nonacademic purposes, so they were the first to turn to their colleges and universities for general social services, often of a nonacademic nature. And as so many of those social purposes were new—the creation of a classless society, for example, or the separation of church and state—the universities early fell into the habit of taking new functions and new ideas in their stride.

We take this for granted, but Europeans cannot. "Universities," wrote Johann Grimm at the beginning of the last century, "are like gardens where wild growths are only reluctantly tolerated." Even that was putting the matter somewhat amiably. From the sixteenth to the eighteenth centuries most Old World universities were not only unsympathetic to new ideas, they were under pressure from both church and state to resist and suppress such ideas. The great Thomasius was forced out of the University of Leipzig at the end of the seventeenth century because he lectured in German, and a generation later his successor Christian Wolff was forced to depart Halle on pain of death for suggesting that Chinese philosophy was as benign as Christian. At the University of Paris the medical faculty was forbidden to teach the circulation of the blood until the eighteenth century. In Jesuit universities the rule of Acquaviva (head of the order, 1581-1615) that "the teacher is not to permit any novel opinions or discussions to be mooted . . . or to teach nor suffer to be taught anything contrary to prevalent opinions of acknowledged doctors current in the school" held good all through the seventeenth century and into the eighteenth. No wonder the universities were moribund in most of Europe in the seventeenth and even the eighteenth centuries, those in Holland, Scotland, and two or three of the German states being the only important exceptions. They had contributed little to the Renaissance and they contributed even less to the Enlightenment; how interesting that the University of Florence languished all through the brilliant fifteenth century, and that the University of Paris was the center of obscurantism all through the enlightened eighteenth.

Circumstances imposed a very different situation on the new United States, for here were none of those powerful institutions which in the Old World could be relied upon to encourage and patronize science and learning. No monarchy, no aristocracy, no church, no bench nor bar as yet, no great merchant companies and no guilds—whatever was to be done had to be done by the schools and the colleges. This circumstance, which might appear a serious handicap to the new nation, had its advantages: there was no crown, no government, no church, no class powerful enough either to control or to censor science and learning in the New World. To do the miscellaneous tasks which so desperately needed to be done, and which no traditional institutions were prepared to do, Americans invented a new kind of university.

I need not remind you that the university is a Western invention, one of the two or three most important inventions of Western man. The original university, that which grew up in Italy in the twelfth and thirteenth centuries and spread from Italy to France and Spain and from there to Germany and the North, was an institution designed to train theologians, doctors, lawyers, and—increasingly —students of philosophy who might conceivably serve society outside these three set professions. The original university was urban, nonresidential, professional, patronized either by the church or by the prince and controlled pretty much by these. The English created a second kind of university—the colleges of Oxford and Cambridge, located in the country rather than in the city; residential; with masters *in loco parentis* to students; designed at first to train churchmen but increasingly to train the upper class to rule. The Germans added to this, in the eighteenth century, the function of expanding the bounds of knowledge through research, and that came to be the distinctive mark which characterized the modern university.

Americans took over features from all three models, modified them, and added new functions, interests, aims, and activities to make something which—by the end of the nineteenth century— was really a fourth type of university. It was rural and urban, residential and nonresidential, collegiate and professional and just miscellaneous; it was religious and secular, private and public, and a combination of the two. Its most striking feature, however, was that it was not bound to the traditional roles, but took on whatever tasks society assigned to it: agricultural education, veterinary science, teacher training, commerce and business, architecture, librarianship, and scores of other miscellaneous activities. Nor did it become wholly professional. It undertook the old familiar tasks of teaching the young, and carried the doctrine of *in loco parentis* to lengths that others thought absurd, and that we now think absurd; it catered to the public interest with games and sports on a scale that conjured up images of the Roman arenas. It sponsored research of the most advanced character and built up research libraries and laboratories that were the envy of the rest of the world.

Now we are witnessing what might be called a new proliferation: the creation, in affiliation with existing schools, of semi-autonomous institutes to investigate the things society wants investigated. There are antecedents here in the Old World, but institutes such as the famous Max Planck Institute in Göttingen, for example, or the Niels Bohr Institute of Copenhagen, belong clearly in the framework of the traditional university. The American institutes are, in a sense, more secular and less academic. Here is an institute for the study of violence; there one that concentrates on urban development; here—it happens to be at Columbia—an institute for citizenship, and elsewhere—this is at Chicago—an institute for the study of race relations. How interesting, too, the recent and widespread trends making the universities the centers of the creative arts. Almost every college, now, has to have a poet in residence, or a painter, or a musician. Where in the eighteenth century a Haydn, a Handel, a Mozart was under the patronage of some prince like Esterhazy, or of the church, in twentieth-century America, a Hindemith, a Roger Sessions, an Aaron Copland, an Eliot Carter finds patronage—the very term is misleading—in some college or university.

In short the pattern of the American university—a pattern now spreading back to the Old World—is that of an institution large enough and prosperous enough to serve all the traditional functions of the university—teaching and character training and professional training; serve the needs of society and of government; engage in far-reaching academic ventures across national boundaries; and initiate, sponsor, and carry out research in every field that calls for investigation.

Every age thinks its crises the most urgent; perhaps there is some vanity here, for the sense of urgency is subjective. But complexity is another matter: that seems to increase by geometrical rather than by arithmetical progression. The problems confronting the next generation are surely as urgent as those which confronted the past; they promise to be even more complex if for no other reason than that they are so unavoidably world-wide. The basic and pervasive task is to grasp and control these forces of revolutionary change that threaten to overwhelm us, and to direct them into peaceful channels. The tasks are familiar, and they are tasks with which—for the most part—the universities are peculiarly equipped to deal: to save and replenish our natural resources and to discover new resources to meet the demands of a vastly increased population; to wipe out many of the diseases which afflict mankind, and to improve the physical standards of peoples throughout the globe; to abate race prejudices; to develop a public economy as affluent as our private; to lift standards of education at home and abroad at every level; to encourage and patronize arts and music; to work out mechanisms designed to avoid war; to cooperate in that prodigious revolution—the greatest since the Renaissance—whereby the backward and impoverished peoples of the globe are attempting, in a convulsive leap, to close the desperate gap which divides them from the prosperous and the fortunate. These and related tasks will make importunate demands upon our resources of organized intelligence, and the responsibility will fall, in larger measure than ever before, upon the scientist, the scholar, the expert, the trained administrator, and the enlightened statesman. That is another way of saying that the responsibility will fall upon the university, for in our country, and increasingly elsewhere, the university is called upon to provide these persons.

One of the elementary tasks of the university has customarily been neglected. That is, to seek out, train, and manufacture intelligence. Over the centuries in the Old World and in the New, the university, unlike the Church, has been a passive instrument rather than a zealous crusader. The Church has gone out to save souls, but the university has not gone out, in any corresponding manner, to save minds.

Now the American theory—I know of few Europeans outside

Russia who subscribe to it—is that talent is to be found every-where. It is the theory set forth most elaborately, and with most im-pressive scientific support, by that great educator-sociologist Lester Ward: that there is potentially the same talent in any hundred thousand people—black, white, or yellow, male or female, rich or poor—the same intellectual, the same social, the same artistic talent, and that it is the duty of the state—for he was our first great exponent of the welfare state—to seek it out and to create condi-tions in which it can flower. The accepted American principle does not go quite this far: it is rather that everyone has a right to as much education as he can profit from. But it is notorious that even in America there has been little organized effort to discover who could profit from what education; it has all been left to chance. Perhaps the greatest single waste of natural resources here and abroad has been in the resources of human talent. Only now are some of our colleges and universities—the impetus has come from the lower schools—moving to compensate for those discriminations and injustices which society has so long imposed upon large seg-ments of the population: Negroes, for example, or the impoverished and neglected children of the slums and of the rural South.

The next generation is going to need proportionately far more doctors, engineers, librarians, architects, biologists, psychiatrists, poets, musicians, and statesmen than the past, for the elementary reason that the tasks that have to be done require more and more expertise. Therefore, perhaps the most urgent task facing the edu-cational establishment in this or any country is the manufacture of intelligence.

Will this enterprise—this seeking out of talent, this trial and error—mean a leveling down rather than a leveling up? It was a question which troubled that most perspicacious of observers, Alexis de Tocqueville, and his answer still excites our sympathy.

Let us look briefly at some of the problems which will, unques-tionably, confront the university in the next generation.

The most elementary observation to make about the university in the year 2000 is that there is going to be a prodigious growth in the population and in the professional activities of the university. A population increase to three hundred million will in itself increase the number of students by over one third; the proportion of those going on past the high school to some form of higher education, already rapidly rising, will increase that total by at least another third. These two considerations alone will contribute to a university population of something like ten million. But that is merely the ostentatious expansion. The knowledge explosion, to use a cant phrase, is even more spectacular than the population explosion. We may get the population explosion under control, but it is neither desirable nor possible to get the knowledge explosion under control. Thus, as the university is called upon to cope with a doubling in the number of students, it will be called upon to cope with something more than a doubling in the body of scientific and scholarly knowledge, and in scientific and scholarly interests as well. In considering the task of the university, the new interests are probably more significant than the new knowledge. The physicist or the biologist, for example, can discard old data as he acquires new, but the historian cannot; and, even as he acquires new information about old subjects, he is called upon to familiarize himself with a host of new subjects. Who would have thought, thirty years ago, that every university worth its diploma would have a department of African, Latin American, Near Eastern or Far Eastern studies?

Scholars and administrators will have to find means to cope with this avalanche—one quite unprecedented in history. Universities cannot be expected to have all books in their libraries—most of them are unobtainable for the newer institutions. Technology will need to devise means of making the books accumulated at the Widener and the Bibliothèque Nationale speedily available to all. Professors cannot all be airborne, all attending conferences in Paris or Serbelloni, or advising governments in India or Mexico; some way will have to be found for making their talents available and making them physically available too. All universities cannot teach all subjects; some method must be worked out to allocate financial resources, which are never adequate, and intellectual resources, which are always inadequate.

Qualitative changes are no less inevitable than quantitative. The college is quantitatively today what the high school was in 1930; perhaps the never-ending proliferation of knowledge and the insatiable demand for expertise will make the Ph.D. of 2000 as much in demand as the A.B. is today. If the society of the future does not demand additional degrees, it will, beyond doubt, require some evidence of continuous exposure to new findings of science and scholarship in one way or another.

We are witnessing now two strongly marked tendencies in higher education. One is the spectacular growth of junior and community colleges; the other, the equally impressive development of graduate and professional studies. Will the traditional undergraduate college be squeezed out by these forces, as Dean Barzun has predicted? Is it desirable that we reorganize our "higher education" to recognize this situation? To do so would be an almost revolutionary departure from American experience, but harmonious with traditional European experience, where what we now teach in most of our colleges has long been relegated to the *lycée* or the *Gymnasium* or the technical school, and what we now teach in our professional schools has been accepted as the proper business of the university.

Much is to be said for an accommodation to what we might call the European system: it would free the university from many of the improper pressures which now play upon it—pressures to have winning football and basketball teams, for example, pressures to serve as a marriage mart for the young (who no longer need one), pressures for lowering standards in order to take in all comers, pressures from special-interest groups, or from filiopietistic societies to teach what should not be taught, or to teach in the wrong way what should be taught. But much is to be said, too, for the more traditional American compromise.

For to separate undergraduate and graduate faculties, for example, might drive away teachers and scholars, dry up library and laboratory resources, substitute for the love of learning among the young mere professional zeal, and by separating teaching from research, dry up the imagination of scholars, so essential to the highest flights of science or learning.

There is never any "solution" to "problems" of this nature, but it seems entirely probable that the problem will take care of itself. As the secondary schools do their proper job of preparation, the demands of scholarship make themselves felt ever more insistently in the college itself. "General," as distinct from "professional," education will come increasingly from the students themselves, from the library, from extracurricular and even extracollegiate activities.

The mounting requirements—and expense—of advanced and professional education will call for a more effective collaboration among universities and between universities and other institutions and agencies than now obtains. There will have to be a clearer division of labor—in library collections, for example, in specialties such as classical archaeology or Sanskrit or African studies or astrophysics—than now obtains. One of the more urgent tasks of academic statesmanship will be to arrange such cooperation, not only among universities, but among universities and all other research institutions.

In the next generation the university will, in all likelihood, be more and more a center and a sponsor for the creative arts. This enterprise, already well established, is something new in academic history. Universities in the Old World did not concern themselves with the arts, and do not; they supported no "poets in residence," no painters to induct the young into the mysteries of abstract art, no choreographers to teach ballet, no composers. Traditionally all of that was left to the court, the church, the aristocracy. But there were no comparable institutions in the New World to patronize the arts, and the arts were neglected until, quite recently, an aristocracy of wealth took over the patronage. But the patronage of a Morgan or a Frick was to historical, not to living art. Increasingly in the last quarter century the universities have taken over this delightful responsibility, and now most colleges and universities have a center for creative arts, a poet in residence, a theatre, a museum, and a school of painting and of sculpture. I have no doubt that this happy association between the arts and the academy will flourish, with immense advantage to the academic community and to the public and, let us hope, to the arts as well. Creative artists are fearful of the limitations of the academy, but surely of all patrons the academy is the least exacting, the most liberal, and, for those who have faith in youth, the most inspiring.

The responsibility of the university to such miscellaneous things as science, scholarship, public service, and the arts dramatizes the role which the university has achieved in America and which it will increasingly occupy here and elsewhere in the world—that of a clearing house for all scholarly and scientific and artistic interests. We need not accept Lord Snow's conclusion that there are two cultures and never the twain shall meet at any high table, to realize that the task of communication is becoming increasingly difficult, not only between cultures, but within: mathematicians are no longer able to communicate, and Hellenists have little time to speak to Latinists. But in the American academy they do speak to each other, if nowhere else than on faculty committees, and university and foundation administrators have somehow to keep ever in mind the units of learning. Nothing can prevent the fragmentation of knowledge, but the university can and will do more to restore harmony than any other institution.

All in all the most striking development in higher education in America in the past twenty years has been the role which the federal government has assumed. There are, to be sure, antecedents: the federal government began to sponsor state universities with the Morrill Land Act of 1862. Yet fifteen years ago the then president of Columbia University, Dwight D. Eisenhower, could exclaim in the most solemn tones against federal aid to higher education. Now the federal government helps finance practically everything but faculty salaries—student fellowships, construction, research, international exchange. We take for granted, here in the United States, that if the federal government is to sponsor research it should turn, as a matter of course, to the universities. Yet there were alternatives: the government might, quite logically, have turned to the Departments of Agriculture, of the Interior, of Justice, or it might have created new agencies to carry out scientific programs, as it once created the Library of Congress, the Smithsonian, the Geological Survey, the Surgeon General's Office, or, more recently, the Space Agency. But, wherever security is not a primary consideration, government has chosen to turn to the universities. Within another generation it is probable that a substantial part of governmental activities will be carried on by universities and that a substantial part of university activities will, in turn, be articulated to, if not responsive to, governmental needs, national and international.

All this conjures up an alarming picture of universities as mere agencies of society or of government, so deeply involved in current affairs that they are unable to serve the larger commonwealth of learning, so dependent upon government that they forfeit their independence. Doubtless there are dangers here, and the history of universities in other parts of the globe—even in Germany with its long tradition of academic freedom—admonishes us to caution and to vigilance. But happily there are countervailing forces operating in the American arena which permit us to take a more optimistic view. There is, first, the long tradition of academic freedom in the United States, a tradition stronger here than in any countries outside northern Europe, and stronger today than at any time in the past. Second, there is at least a margin of safety in numbers. We need not take too seriously our statistical total of some nineteen hundred institutions of "higher learning," nor even the figure of fourteen hundred listed in that otherwise infallible index *The World Almanac*, but surely there are between one and two hundred institutions which are regarded as proper universities even by the most exacting standards. The demands of government and society, importunate as they are, will be spread widely over these scores of institutions, and most of them will continue to devote most of their energies and resources to the traditional functions of the university. Furthermore, as government and society grow increasingly dependent on the university, it will be, in a sense, in command of the situation, able to impose its own standards on government and society.

The experience of universities in the past quarter century seems to confirm this reassuring view. It is in this era that universities have been most elaborately engaged in public service, most intimately involved with government, and most deeply indebted to government appropriations. Yet who, knowing the history of academic freedom, can doubt that it is in this era, too, that American universities have achieved their greatest degree of freedom and independence? As recently as ten years ago it was freely predicted that if the government financed university research it would insist on supervising and even controlling that research, that it would endanger the independence of the university laboratories, that it would gradually come to monopolize university resources. So far we can say that none of these fears has materialized in any serious fashion.

This experience, in the crucial quarter century since World War II, affords us ground for hope that an American university may escape in the future, as it has in the past, those national and ideological pressures which elsewhere so gravely imperil the independence of the academy. These pressures, familiar in totalitarian countries of the right or the left, are now particularly ostentatious in the many new nations whose universities—themselves often newly created—have no tradition of independence, no natural allies in sister institutions, and no arsenals of public support on which they can draw when threatened. By great good fortune the American universities have never been seriously menaced by church or state, by the demands of an arrogant ideology or by the specter of starvation. Their long experience with independence, their affluent intellectual and material resources impose upon them special responsibilities to sustain and guide the universities of the newly emerging nations throughout the globe, and help them achieve membership in the great community of learning. The re-creation, the strengthening, the expansion, of this community will inevitably be the major enterprise of the American university in the century ahead.

PART III

Aspects of Academic Freedom

IS FREEDOM AN
ACADEMIC QUESTION?

1

It was charged against Socrates that he was corrupting the youth of Athens, and it was on this charge that he was condemned to drink hemlock. The charge that teachers are corrupting the youth is a familiar plaint of every generation that identifies its own shibboleths with the eternal verities. As more young people are exposed to the teachings of philosophers (or doctors of philosophy) now than ever before, and more in America than in any other country, it is perhaps inevitable that the charge should be familiar in our own time and that it should sound and resound over the land. In New York City it was made against no other than Bertrand Russell and, what is more, sustained by the courts; in New Hampshire it was made against Professor Paul Sweezy and not sustained by the courts. We have heard it, just recently, from Texas, from Colorado, from Montana. We hear it now, most stridently, from across the plains of Minnesota. The youth of the University of Minnesota are being corrupted, and the man who is corrupting them, Professor Mulford Sibley, is, like Socrates, a political philosopher. His method, too, is that of Socrates: he stirs up the young to challenge the existing order; he admonishes them—

Saturday Review, June 20, 1964.

encourages is a better word—to take nothing for granted, to test all things, to find their own truths. It all started casually and almost facetiously. Last fall a spokesman for the American Legion, one Kenneth McDonald, challenged the credentials of Professor Sibley to serve as faculty adviser to the Student Peace Union—or to any student organization at the university. That organization, the Legionnaire asserted, was infiltrated with Communists and subversives. And whose fault was that? Was not Professor Sibley suspect —Professor Sibley, who was an avowed Socialist, and who had joined so many dubious organizations in his day? Was he fit to be an adviser to students; was he not a corrupter of the young?

It was in connection with these charges that Professor Sibley wrote a letter to the student newspaper, the *Minnesota Daily*, decrying conformity and celebrating the virtues of diversity.

We need students who challenge the orthodoxies [he wrote]. American culture is far too monolithic for its own good. Personally, I should like to see on the campus one or two Communist professors, a Student Communist Club, a chapter of the American Association for the Advancement of Atheism, a Society for the Promotion of Free Love, a League for Overthrow of Government by Jeffersonian Violence, an Anti-Automation League, and perhaps a Nudist Club. No university should be without individuals and groups like these.

If the professor's purpose had been *épater le bourgeois,* he certainly succeeded. Within no time at all the state was agog. What, Communists on the campus? What, the open advocacy of atheism? What, free love . . . and nudism? Is this what "our children" (the phrase was used by the critics) are exposed to when we entrust them to the university? (No one, it seems, was alarmed at the proposal of an Anti-Automation club.)

Soon militant groups like Christian Research and the American Legion, and editors of small-town newspapers, were in full cry. Fire Sibley—that was the simple solution. Fire Sibley, said Mr. Milton Rosen, public-works commissioner of St. Paul, who made himself spokesman for the patrioteers. "My God," he asked, "how long are you going to let these radicals run our colleges?" The American Legion, too, wanted Sibley fired, and Commander Kenneth McDonald urged an investigation of the University by former

FBI agents and the creation of a state un-American Activities to carry on the good work.

A number of provincial editors struck the same note. "Must we expose our young people to all the diseases in our political world just to prove how strong they are?" asked the Fairmont *Sentinel*, concluding, somewhat wildly, that "Professors have to be either for the American system or for the Communist system." A columnist, one Orlin Folwick, provided a fresh and perhaps historic definition of the function of the scholar in the American university. It was "to help students obtain an appreciation of their country and its objectives, so they can become normal tax paying citizens."

A St. Paul businessman objected to Professor Sibley's economic views. "He teaches and advocates that competition is disappearing from American business," said Mr. Henry Teipel. Clearly Mr. Teipel believed in competition—except in the realm of ideas. How society was to achieve free enterprise in the economy without free enterprise in ideas, he did not explain. It was left to Christian Research to carry its protests to their logical conclusion. It called for cleaning out the entire university, starting with President Meredith Wilson—who belonged to that subversive organization, the Council on Foreign Relations, which had received support from that other subversive organization, the Carnegie Corporation.

It is tempting to dismiss these reactions as puerile and insignificant. They are puerile, but they are not insignificant. After all, the state legislature was sufficiently impressed by them to vote an investigation of the university. Technically, to be sure, the investigation was limited to the personnel practices of the university. But, as the chairman of the Senate Education Committee, Senator Dunlap, made clear, "We're going to get very definitely into determining basically what this position is which is referred to as academic freedom."

That is all to the good—though it may be doubted that a legislative inquiry into personnel practices, especially one launched with such a rhetorical spray, is the ideal way to achieve this end. But the public *is* confused about "this position referred to as academic freedom." The public *is* confused even about the nature and the function of the university. The observations of Professor Sibley's critics—and even of some of his friends—confess that confusion.

Thus Senator Wright, who proposed the original investigation, asserted roundly that Professor Sibley was "an academic deviate." It is a fascinating phrase. It suggests, of course, that there is, or should be, an academic type from which the hapless professor has deviated. It suggests that those who do not conform to this type or standard have deviated. As we know, the term itself has curious overtones from the realm of morals. Surely nothing more sharply dramatizes Professor Sibley's plea for variety and pluralism than this tacit assumption of orthodoxy as proper in the academy.

To insist on orthodoxy and penalize ideas or arguments that deviate from that orthodoxy—even ideas and arguments that in Justice Holmes's great phrase are "loathsome and fraught with death"—is of course to set up prior standards by which to judge all ideas and arguments. How are we to know what ideas are dangerous unless we know what is "safe"? And who is to establish the criteria of danger and of safety? How are we to recognize "extreme" statements, unless we have some standard of "moderate" statements? How are we to recognize those who "deviate" unless we know what is the norm? Is it possible to obtain agreement on any such standards? Clearly it is not. What the Senate of Minnesota would consider a moderate and normal statement on human rights the Senate of Mississippi would consider extreme and dangerous. What Unitarians would regard as a common-sense statement on evolution members of Jehovah's Witnesses would consider heretical. What a Quaker—say Professor Sibley—would regard as a moderate statement about nuclear disarmament the American Legion would regard as un-American. It is unnecessary to belabor so elementary a consideration. As Justice Jackson said in the second flag-salute case:

> If there is any fixed star in our constitutional constellation, it is that no official, high or petty, can prescribe what shall be orthodox in politics, nationalism, religion, or other matters of opinion, or force citizens to confess by word or act their faith therein.

Mr. Rosen and many others object to Professor Sibley because he is a Socialist, or because he does not appear to believe in "free enterprise" in the economic system. Are these critics, then, prepared to require that all professors be either Republicans or Democrats? If not, what is the point of the criticism? And, for that matter, if it is misguided for Professor Sibley to criticize the free-enterprise system in the economy, why is it not equally misguided for Mr. Rosen to criticize the free-enterprise system in the realm of ideas? Certainly, of the two, free enterprise in the intellectual realm is incomparably more important to society than free enterprise in the economic, for the simple reason that it comes first, and without it there can be no enterprise in anything.

What Professor Sibley recommended was enterprise and pluralism. Granted his examples were "extreme"—deliberately so, no doubt. It is the principle we must judge, not the examples. What is the alternative to intellectual enterprise and pluralism in a university faculty? It is of course conformity and uniformity. Do the critics of academic "deviates" want conformity and uniformity? They may think that they do, but they delude themselves. They may rejoice in uniformity in the teaching of history or economics or politics, but do they really want conformity and uniformity in physics, chemistry, and biology? If they insist on history and government professors who all think alike, how can they expect to get physics and biology professors who think differently? Even if this paradox could be resolved, is it what the critics want? Do they want one and only one version of politics, economics, and history? Whose version is it to be?

Three assumptions are implicit in the arguments used by the critics of Professor Sibley and of the university itself for permitting wide latitude to professors and students. The first is that there exists somewhere a body of Truth—Truth about politics, about law, about economics, about morals. Second, that it is the function of the university to teach, indeed to inculcate, this body of Truth. And third, that students are passive receptacles into which teachers pour Truth as a mother pours milk into a baby.

These assumptions have a familiar ring. They underlie the principles on which all authoritative systems rely—all systems or governments that are certain that they know truth, that the truth they know is clear and final, and that their truths can be imposed, by persuasion if possible, by force if necessary.

It is scarcely necessary to add that all of these assumptions are mistaken. There is no fixed body of Truth about politics, history, economics, or law, any more than about physics, biology, or medicine. It is not the business of the university to hand down a body of agreed-on Truths, or to indoctrinate the young. If, in a moment of folly, the university or its professors attempted to do this they would fail, for young men and women intelligent enough to get into a university are too intelligent to submit tamely to indoctrination.

There is another aspect of this problem of censoring what professors may say or what students may write—one that the champions of orthodoxy do not sufficiently consider. It is this. Once you take responsibility for censoring what may not be said, you by necessary implication sponsor and approve whatever you *allow* to be said. If you assume responsibility for Professor Sibley you cannot stop there; you must assume responsibility for all the professors at the university—and at all institutions of higher learning. Anything else would be arbitrary and capricious. If you exclude some stories from student magazines—as Senator Wright wants to do— you give the stamp of approval to all those stories you have not excluded. Are legislators, are filiopietistic societies really prepared to take on this responsibility? It is well to remember that once you embark on the business of censorship you are in for a long and arduous journey.

Even this does not exhaust the errors or fallacies of Professor Sibley's critics, or of those who would "investigate" the university. There is, for example, the fallacy that it is the business of the legislature to supervise what is taught at the university. There are two errors here. The first is that the legislature is competent to decide what should be taught at a university, how it should be taught, and who should teach it. The legislature can no more do this than it can decide what medical practices should be adopted by a hospital and what doctors and surgeons should be admitted to the hospital. It is no more competent to do this than it is competent to decide who should be admitted to the ministry, and what doctrines should be preached from the pulpit. The second error is even deeper. It is that the university is somehow a subordinate bureau or department in the government, and that university professors are civil servants whose scholarly duties and activities are subject to legislative supervision. The regents of the University of Minnesota have resolutely rejected such notions, but not all regents are that enlightened. These widely held assumptions confess a deep misunderstanding of the nature and function of the university and of the nature and function of academic freedom.

What is the nature and function of the university?

What is academic freedom, and why is it essential to the well-being of the university?

Perhaps the best short definition of a university is that of Robert Maynard Hutchins. A university, he said, is a center of independent thought. It is, to be sure, more than that, but unless it is that, it is not a university. For only if it is a center for independent thought can it perform its three historic functions. Those are, first, to preserve and transmit knowledge and discipline from one generation to the next; second, to train scholars, scientists, doctors, lawyers, and other professional men and women for the service of society; and third, to extend the boundaries of knowledge, to discover new truths and new ways of thinking about old truths.

If the university is to fulfill these functions it must be free. That is the essential condition of its vitality. It must be free from outside pressures that would distract it from its true work—free from intimidation, free from harassment, free from arbitrary interference or controls. The university depends, to be sure, on gifts and appropriations, and many people carelessly conclude that those who pay the piper may call the tune. But appropriations to a university no more justify public control of its intellectual activities than appropriations to the judiciary justify control of the decisions handed down by the judges.

Freedom is not merely negative; it is not merely the absence of harassment. It is positive encouragement to independence. It is the provision of conditions ideal to the functioning of the independent mind. It is the creation and the preservation of a climate of freedom. It is in the fostering of the creed that the great Learned Hand imbibed at Harvard College in his youth:

You were not taught it in words; you gathered it unwittingly from uncorrupted and incorruptible masters. It was in the air; you did not proclaim it; you would have felt ashamed to demonstrate the obvious. You came to know that you could hold no certain title to beliefs that you had not won. . . . And chiefly, and best of all, you were in a company of those who thought that the noblest of man's works was the pursuit of truth; who valued the goal so highly that they were never quite content that the goal they had reached was the goal they were after. . . .

A university is not an abstraction. It consists of scholars and students. When we say that a university must be free, we mean not only that the great historic institution, the great intellectual enterprise, must be free, but that the scholars and students—and the administrators, too—who constitute it, must be free.

But what is academic freedom?

Academic freedom is not a special dispensation conceded by an indulgent society to a group of amiable Mr. Chipses. It is not a special privilege granted to professors. It is a device for getting on with the job of teaching, training, and research. Freedom is guaranteed to the scholar so that he will be able to inspire in the young a passion for truth, and so that he can present to them, in his own life and conduct, an example of the search for truth. It is guaranteed to the scholar so that he can train new generations of technicians and public servants who will freely exercise their intelligence on behalf of their society. It is guaranteed to the scholar so that he can engage, fearlessly and vigorously, in pushing outward the boundaries of knowledge in every field.

Academic freedom is, like other freedoms, a device for avoiding error and arriving at truth. We take this for granted in the realms of science. We should take it equally for granted in the realm of social thought.

Our society is not perfect, nor our government; it has not solved all of the problems that beset it, and it will be beset by new problems. It needs, therefore, critics and explorers in the social and political areas as well as in the physical ones. It needs a Gunnar Myrdal to make it aware of an American Dilemma before that dilemma becomes insoluble. It needs a Hutchins to challenge the organization of higher education, or a Conant to make it aware of the glaring contrast between the education available in slums and suburbs before that contrast poisons American society. It needs a Kinsey to expose the hypocrisy of legislation dealing with sexual conduct and misconduct. It needs a Neibuhr to remind us of our own heritage of injustice and of guilt, so that we do not adopt an attitude of moral superiority to other peoples while we indulge ourselves in immoral conduct. It needs a Kennan to challenge our policies toward Russia and a Lattimore to challenge our policies toward Communist China, for these policies may be mistaken. It needs a Pauling and a Szilard to warn us against the suicidal implications of our atomic program before that program gets out of hand. Without these critics and dissenters, and hundreds like them, our society may fall into irreparable error.

THE NATURE OF
ACADEMIC FREEDOM

2

Let us begin with the academy itself, and then consider the nature of the freedom which it enjoys. What is a university, and what are its functions?

A university is a place where young and old are joined together in the acquisition of knowledge and the search for truth.

Its functions are threefold. First, to transmit knowledge imaginatively from one generation to the next. Second, to provide society with a body of trained professionals—originally priests, doctors, lawyers, and scholars—which is why Old World universities still have only four faculties. In modern times, and particularly in the United States, the university is expected to train for many other professions as well—architecture, journalism, teaching, forestry, engineering, and so forth, but the purpose is the same. The third function of the university is rapidly becoming the most important: to expand the boundaries of knowledge through research and to discover new truths.

Now, these functions imposed on the university by history and by circumstances mean that the university is to be a special kind of institution. It is the only institution in Western society whose bus-

Saturday Review, August 27, 1966.

iness it is to search for and transmit truth regardless of all competing or conflicting pressures and demands: pressures for immediate usefulness, for social approval, pressures to serve the special interests of a government, a class, a professional group, a race, a faith, even a nation. If the university performs its duty it will, of course, serve all of these interests, for we must believe that the search for truth is useful to all groups, but this is a by-product of the larger achievement of the training of the young to wisdom and the search for truth.

The university is the chief instrument whereby society provides itself with independent criticism and advice, and with a continuous flow of ideas. It maintains the university as it maintains scientists, doctors, judges, and priests, not to minister to its passions but to serve its deeper and more permanent needs. Society does not impose its will on scientists, because it wants to discover the secrets of the universe; it refrains from bringing pressure on judges, because it wants to see justice done; it leaves doctors alone because it wants to discover the causes of and the cure for diseases; it permits religious freedom because it wants spiritual solace. Society provides freedom for scholars and for the university as an institution for the same elementary reason, because it wants to discover truth about as many things as possible.

It is out of this situation that the concept and the practice of academic freedom emerges, and on these principles that it rests. If society is to assure itself of a new generation trained to understand the world in which it will live, it must leave teachers free to transmit truth as they see it; if society is to have the benefit of disinterested advice, it must protect scholars who give that advice even when it is unpalatable; if society is to have the advantage of a flow of new ideas and discoveries, it must leave scholars to carry on research in their own way. At its peril does any society interfere in any way, at any time, through pressure, intimidation, distraction, or seduction, with these sovereign functions of the academy.

Once the nature of the university is clear, particular problems of "academic freedom" present few real difficulties. Consider, for example, two questions which have greatly agitated our society of late: the problem of student rebellion and student discipline, and the larger problem of alleged subversives on university faculties who justify their advocacy of unpopular causes—Negro rights in the South, opposition to the war in Vietnam, the recognition of Communist China—by the plea of academic freedom. The principles which must control our attitude toward these problems are rooted in the nature and function of the university.

We can dispose briefly of what now troubles a good many well-meaning people—manifestations of student freedom that seem (or are) excessive, bad-mannered, or unpatriotic. It should be remembered that academic freedom was born, some seven centuries ago, as student freedom, with the insistence by students in Italian and French universities on the right to have a decisive voice in choosing professors, arranging for courses of lectures, controlling all their housekeeping affairs, and securing certain political rights in their communities. The notion that the university should act *in loco parentis* to its students is a relatively new and limited one; to this day it is confined pretty much to English-speaking countries, and unknown elsewhere. The principle of *in loco parentis* was doubtless suitable enough in an earlier era, when boys went to college at the age of thirteen or fourteen; it is a bit ridiculous in a society where most students are mature enough to marry and raise families.

No one will deny that manifestations of student independence occasionally get out of hand, just as manifestations of adult independence get out of hand; we should remember, however, that if there is to be excess, it is far better to have an excess of interest and activity than an excess of apathy. But the solution for student intemperance is not for the university authorities to act in the place of parents. It is not the business of the university to go bustling around like some Aunt Polly, censoring a student paper here, cutting out indelicacies in a student play there, approving this club or that, accepting or rejecting speakers invited by student organizations, snooping into the private lives of students. These matters are the responsibility of the students themselves.

If they perform their duties badly, so much the worse for them, but perhaps they will learn by experience. If they go to excess and violate the law, let them be subjected to the penalties of the law.

Where they violate reasonable academic rules—rules designed to protect the integrity of the academic enterprise—they should be subjected to whatever penalties are provided for such violations. But they should not be treated as if they were children, nor should the university be expected to turn aside from its proper job, which is education and research, to the petty pursuit of discipline.

Granted that the expression of student independence sometimes causes pain or chagrin. But to those who deplore or denounce students who ostentatiously depart from commencement exercises when a member of the Johnson Administration is given a degree, we can put a very simple question: Would you rather have the kind of society where students were so indifferent that they lacked interest in politics, or the independence to differ with the administration? Would you rather have the kind of society where no student would dare assert his independence for fear of reprisal? If not, you must take your chance on independent thinking running to what you consider bad manners, just as adult independence often runs to bad manners: when members of UN delegations walk out of debates, for example, or when distinguished poets refuse Presidential invitations.

Turn, then, to the more important question of "subversives" on university faculties, or subversion in teaching. It is the fear of these which induced infatuated legislatures to require special loyalty oaths for teachers in the McCarthy era, and which accounts for the harassment of universities in backward states such as Massachusetts and California.

We may observe that there is no evidence of subversives on college faculties, or that the term "subversion" is so vague as to be drained of meaning, or that neither loyalty oaths nor inquisitions can prevent the contagion of ideas. But these observations, though just enough, are not really relevant to our central problem. What is of crucial relevance to that problem is quite simply that the academic community, if it is to be free to perform its beneficent functions, must be free to fix its own standards and determine its own credentials. No other bodies, certainly not an inflamed public nor an election-minded legislature, are competent to fix these standards or to determine whether or not scholars meet them. This responsibility is primarily one for specialists—fellow physicists, fellow historians—and ultimately one for the whole academic community, for sometimes specialists have a narrow or jaundiced view. But questions of fitness to teach and to carry on research are always academic questions.

Professional qualifications do sometimes involve questions of character, to be sure, but how, when, and where they do are matters for professional determination. And the reason for this is very simple. It is not merely that it is logical and just, but that it is the only method which can provide us with the kind of physicists and historians that we need. If other criteria than those of professional competence and the confidence of academic colleagues in the integrity of the scholar are invoked, the system itself will break down, just as medicine or justice will break down if surgeons or judges are selected by other than professional criteria. Needless to say, scholars will make mistakes in judgment, just as doctors and lawyers make mistakes in judgment. But the consequences of substituting irrelevant and pernicious criteria for professional ones in choosing academic colleagues are far more serious than any possible consequences of occasional incompetence in professional selection.

What shall we say of university teachers and scholars who outrage public opinion by advocacy of doctrines that seem to the great majority to be erroneous? What shall we say of teachers who persistently flout the public will as expressed by resounding majorities? Once again the underlying principle is simple enough. If scholars, or students, violate the law, the law should deal with them as it deals with any other members of society who violate the law. No scholar may claim that academic freedom gives him some special immunity from the law. But if what a scholar does or says does not violate any law, but merely outrages public opinion, then it is not the business of the university to do what civil authorities are unable to do.

The spectacle, common enough in the McCarthy era, of regents and trustees rushing in to punish teachers for conduct for which the civil authorities were unable or unwilling to prosecute—"taking the Fifth Amendment" for example—was a shameful one. In so far

as trustees join with public opinion to intimidate or silence scholars, however much they may be misguided, they violate and betray
their trust.

So it is with the punishment, by whatever means, of those who
exercise their right to express ideas that are unpopular and seem
dangerous—advocacy of the cause of the Vietcong, for example, or
of the propriety of Communism, or of the harmlessness of por-
nography. It may be thought deplorable that otherwise intelligent
men should entertain, let alone champion, notions of this sort, but
how much more deplorable if we had the kind of society where
they could not. A university is an institution where scholars are not
only permitted but encouraged to think unthinkable thoughts, to
explore intolerable ideas, and to proclaim their findings. There are
risks here, to be sure. The church saw that when it forced Galileo
to recant, or forbade the teaching of the circulation of the blood, or
the Linnaean system of botanical classification. But these are risks
that society must learn to take in its stride if it expects progress in
the realms of knowledge and of science.

If we are to have the kind of society where thought and expression are free, we must take our chances on some thoughts being, at
least potentially, dangerous ones. The danger, however, is not
really so desperate. After all, those who disagree with the loathsome thoughts are equally free to express thoughts that are beautiful.

Let us not suppose that all this is but a matter of theory. We
have ample evidence, in our own history, and in the history of
other nations, of what happens when government or society si-
lences, by whatever means, dangerous or loathsome ideas. And we
know, too, that ideas which one generation thinks dangerous are
regarded by the next as salutary; ideas which one society thinks
loathsome are accepted by another as noble.

The Old South persuaded itself that slavery was not only good
but a positive blessing, and that those who criticized slavery or
sought to undermine it were enemies to the Southern way of life.
As the slave interest had things all its own way, it proceeded to
dispose of its enemies. To protect the "peculiar institution," teachers who questioned the historical or ethnological credentials of

slavery were dismissed, preachers who denied the Biblical justification of slavery were expelled from their pulpits, editors who criticized the social structure of slavery lost their posts, books and magazines which contained antislavery propaganda were burned. To counter the abolitionist argument of the North—an argument which seemed to Southerners as pernicious as Communism seems to members of the John Birch Society—they formulated a proslavery argument and invested it with moral authority. Thus the South silenced serious discussion of its major problem; thus it foreclosed every solution to that problem but the ultimate solution of violence; thus it laid the foundations for a century of hatred and violence.

More familiar to most of us is the dark and tragic history of Hitler's Germany. The Nazis not only convinced themselves of Aryan superiority and of Jewish inferiority; they were so sure they were right that they looked upon anyone who spoke up for the Jews or who opposed Nazi policies as an enemy of the Fatherland. More systematically and more savagely than Southerners of the 1850's, they purged the universities, silenced the clergy, closed down the press, burned offending books, and wrote new books to replace them, and killed, exiled, or silenced all who dared question the justice of what they did. They destroyed not only dissent but free inquiry and discussion, and—like the Southerners—left no remedy for their errors but that of violence. Nor can we reassure ourselves that these manifestations of hostility to the university and to intellectual independence are a thing of the past. Even now, in South Africa, in Rhodesia, in the Argentine, those who fear freedom and democratic processes, move with sure instinct to control the universities and to destroy academic freedom.

Those who today assure us that academic freedom is all right in ordinary times, but that in time of crisis it must give way to the importunate demands of national unity, those who argue that academic freedom is all very well in time of peace but a pernicious indulgence in time of war, are like the Southern slave owners and the Nazis and the white supremacists of South Africa, if not in conduct, then in principle. They are saying in effect that discussion and debate are all very well when there is nothing to discuss, but that they must be abated or suspended when there are serious matters before us. They are saying that we can tolerate freedom when there are no issues that threaten it, but that we cannot tolerate it when it is in danger.

Do those who would suspend academic freedom in time of crisis because it imperils national unity really understand the implications of their argument? Are they prepared to decry those Englishmen who in the 1770's stood up for the American cause—men like Tom Paine and Dr. Price and Joseph Priestley and Lord Jeffrey Amherst, whom we have so long honored as friends of liberty? Are they prepared to assert that those Southerners who, in the crisis of 1861 rejected the claims of Southern unity and preferred instead to go against the stream of public opinion and stand by the Union, deserve only obloquy? Are they prepared to say that Germans who revolted against the iniquities of the Nazi government and sought to overthrow Hitler were traitors and deserve the detestation of mankind? Do they really think that the only test of true patriotism is support of a government, no matter what it does?

These considerations go far beyond the confines of the academy, but they bear with special force on the academy. For the university has a special obligation to act as the critic and the conscience of society. Society has indeed created it to play this role. It has said to the scholars who constitute the academy:

"It is your business to think and investigate and fearlessly to announce your findings. It is your business to be independent and scientific and impersonal, to stand aside from the awful pressures of public opinion and of interest, the persuasive pressures of nationalism and the compelling pressures of patriotism, and consider scientifically the validity of what your society does. It is your business to study politics and economy and history as scientists study physics and astronomy and geology. It is your business to look and to think far ahead, to look not to the immediate effects but the ultimate consequences of conduct.

"We require you, therefore, if you would not betray your historic function, to avoid all that is merely parochial, all that is interested, all that is prejudiced. We require you to avoid the temptation to serve those who may suppose themselves your masters, and devote your affluent talents to your true masters—the whole of society, the whole of humanity, the great community of learning, the sacred cause of truth. In order that you may do this we give you the precious boon of independence which is academic freedom. We know that some of you will abuse this independence, that some of you will fail to use it in the larger service of mankind, and that many of you will be mistaken in your findings. These are chances we are willing to take because we know that if we do not protect those whose task it is to search out truth, we may fall into irreparable error and thus lose everything that we hold dear."

HALFWAY TO
NINETEEN EIGHTY-FOUR

3

I

George Orwell's Oceania had a vast and efficient information agency; its name was the Ministry of Truth, and its purpose was to make every citizen of Oceania think the right thoughts. "The past is whatever the records agree upon," was its motto, and it wrote, or rewrote, the records. Now the information agencies of our own State and Defense departments, the USIA and the CIA, seem bent on creating an American Ministry of Truth and imposing upon the American people a record of the past which they themselves write.

It is the CIA whose activities have been most insidious and are most notorious, but the CIA has no monopoly on brainwashing. Consider, for example, the film *Why Vietnam*. It is "one of our most popular films"; it is distributed free to high schools and colleges throughout the country, and to other groups who ask for it—as hundreds doubtless do. Its credentials are beyond reproach; it was produced by the Defense and sponsored by the State Department, and President Johnson, Secretary Rusk, and Secretary McNamara all pitch in to give it authenticity.

The Saturday Review, April 15, 1967.

Now, the USIA is not permitted to carry on propaganda within the United States, and the reason it is not is that the American people do not choose to give the government authority to indoctrinate them. Government, they believe—and rightly—already has every method of communication with the people which it can properly use. The President, members of the Cabinet, the armed services—these can command attention for whatever they have to say, at any time. There is, therefore, no necessity, and no excuse, for government propaganda, no need for government to resort to subterfuge in its dealings with the people.

What we have always held objectionable is not overt publicity by government, but covert indoctrination. *Why Vietnam* is, in fact, both. It is overt enough, but while it is clear to the sophisticated that it is a government production and therefore an official argument, the film is presented not as an argument, but as history. Needless to say, it is not history. It is not even journalism. It is propaganda, naked and unashamed. As the "Fact Sheet" which accompanies it states, it makes "four basic points," and makes them with the immense authority of the President: that the United States is in Vietnam "to fulfill a solemn pledge"; that "appeasement is an invitation to aggression"; that "the United States will not surrender or retreat"; and that we—but, alas, not the other side—are always "ready to negotiate a settlement."

Government, which represents all the people and presumably all points of view, should have higher standards than private enterprise in the presentation of news or of history. But *Why Vietnam* is well below the standards of objectivity, accuracy, and impartiality which we are accustomed to in newspapers and on television; as scholarship, it is of course absurd. In simple, uncritical, and one-dimensional terms it presents the official view of the war in Vietnam, with never a suggestion that there is or could be any other view. When Communists sponsor such propaganda, we call it "brainwashing."

Let us look briefly at this film, for it is doubtless a kind of dry run of what we will get increasingly in the future. It begins—we might have anticipated this—with a view of Hitler and Chamberlain at Munich, thus establishing at the very outset that "appeasement" is "a short cut to disaster." Because the free nations of the world failed to stop aggression in the thirties, they almost lost their freedom and had to fight a gigantic war to survive; if we fail to stop "aggression" now, we too may lose our freedom. For "we have learned at terrible cost that retreat does not bring safety and that weakness does not bring peace, and it is this lesson that has brought us to Vietnam."

Here then is the first distortion of history, and it is a preview of what is to come throughout the film. The aggression of the great totalitarian powers in the thirties in fact bears little resemblance to the civil war in Vietnam, nor is the Geneva Agreement of 1954 to be equated with appeasement. The facts are almost precisely the opposite of what is implied by *Why Vietnam*. One of Roosevelt's objectives in the war was to get the French out of Indochina; the Eisenhower objective of the fifties was to keep them there. The French are out now and we are in, playing the role that the French played before Dien Bien Phu—and still fighting Ho Chi Minh.

But now the scene shifts to Vietnam. In 1954, says our narrator, "the long war is over, and the victorious Communists are moving in." It is a statement which has only the most fortuitous relation to reality. The long war was indeed over—the war between the Vietnamese and the French. But to label the Vietnamese who fought against the French "Communists," and to assume that somehow they "moved in" (they were already there) is a distortion of history. Yet there is worse to come. For next the camera is turned onto the Geneva Conference. It was, so we learn, "a victory for the Communist world," and there is no hint that we ourselves accepted the results of the conference. Vietnam, we are told, was "divided at the 17th parallel" and there is no suggestion that the division was to be a purely temporary one. Nor is there any reminder that the Geneva Agreements called for an election, that President Eisenhower himself said that in such an election 80 percent of the vote would have gone to Ho Chi Minh, and that we were chiefly responsible for putting off the election. No, what schoolchildren and students are given here is a one-sided story of a Communist conspiracy to destroy the peace of 1954. Worse yet, they are presented with the spectacle of a "reign of terror," in which "children are killed in their sleep." Clearly only Communists kill children; we do not.

Now we are presented with a scene of peace and plenty, liberty and reform, in South Vietnam: it is Eden before the fall. Staggered by the success of the South, the Communists launch "a furtive and remorseless war against the people," and Secretary Rusk appears to denounce this "cruel and sustained attack." Attack by whom? Presumably by Ho Chi Minh, though this is left, safely enough, to the imagination. Nowhere is there any mention of the Vietcong; nowhere any suggestion of a civil war, and nowhere any hint that until we began a substantial military buildup in Vietnam —in violation of the Geneva Agreements—there was no invasion from the north. And, as part of that corruption of the vocabulary familiar to students of Orwell's Newspeak, words like North Vietnamese and Vietcong give way to the generic word "Communist."

But worse is to come. What is it the "Communists" want? Shadowy hints conjure up terrors that even the narrator is reluctant to name. "The prize the Communists are after . . . South Vietnam . . . standing at the gateway to Burma, Thailand, Cambodia, East Pakistan." The imagination reels, as it is, of course, meant to. For here, looming up before us, is the menace of China. Says our narrator, "Spurred by Communist China, North Vietnam's goal is to extend the Asiatic dominion of Communists."

No wonder that in this phantasmagoric scene American "advisers" somehow become "fighting men," helping the outnumbered South Vietnamese resist Communist aggression. And if there are still any lingering doubts about the justice and the necessity of American participation, here are both President Johnson and Secretary McNamara to set the record straight.

Now we have a new theme: peace. "Fifteen times," no less (it is doubtless thirty by now), we have tried to open negotiations, and each time we have been rebuffed. All we want—there is a note of plaintiveness here—is free elections; curiously enough, just what the Geneva Agreements called for back in 1954. All we want is to limit the war. And how do the recalcitrant Communists meet our appeals? They attack us with "high explosives aimed at American air bases." They kill little girls (picture of little girl cruelly destroyed). They even attack the United States Embassy, clearly the crowning infamy. There is a kind of inarticulate assumption that we don't do anything as unsporting as using "high explosives."

Now we are invited to take a more philosophical view of the war. Why are Americans risking life and limb in this distant jungle? That is easy. To keep American promises—indeed, "to fulfill one of the most solemn pledges" in our history, a pledge made by three Presidents. Needless to say, this is nonsense. President Eisenhower refused to make such a pledge; President Kennedy insisted that the Vietnamese should fight their own war. It is President Johnson who made the pledge (though not, it might be remembered, in the campaign of 1964), and who is now busy conferring retroactive solemnity upon it by rewriting the historical record.

But there is still another reason why we are in Vietnam—self-defense. For if freedom is to endure in Chicago, Birmingham, and Dallas, it must be vindicated in South Vietnam. What is more it must be vindicated by us, for the non-Communist countries of Asia cannot, by themselves, resist the grasping ambitions of the Communists. What we have here is pretty clearly a rationalization of intervention against Communism everywhere, for Communism is, by definition, "grasping and ambitious." And the reason we must take on this heavy responsibility is that "there is no one else." How does it happen that there is no one else? How does it happen that, except for Thailand, the other members of SEATO are not taking on any responsibilities? Deponent saith not.

There is one final reason for fighting in Vietnam, and it is given us, again, by President Johnson. "We intend to convince the Communists that we cannot be defeated." This has, at least, the merit of frankness: we are fighting a war to prove that we can't be defeated. It is all a bit like William James's Italian woman who stood on a street corner passing out cards saying that she had come over to America to raise money to pay her passage back to Italy; but it is not so amusing.

We are almost through with *Why Vietnam.* Once again the audience is assured that we long for peace; once again that "as long as there are men who hate and destroy" we must keep on fighting.

Perhaps even high-school children are mature enough to wonder who it is who is doing the destroying. But are they mature enough to resist hate?

II

The dissemination of *Why Vietnam* in high schools and colleges is no isolated episode in the manipulation of public opinion by government, but part of a larger pattern. We must view it in connection with the publication program of the United States Information Agency, the clandestine activities of the CIA, the vendetta of the Passport Office against travel to unpopular countries, or by unpopular people, as part of an almost instinctive attempt (we cannot call it anything so formal as a program) to control American thinking about foreign relations. We had supposed, in our innocence, that this sort of thing was the special prerogative of totalitarian governments, but it is clear that we were mistaken.

Forbidden by law from carrying on propaganda in the United States, the USIA has managed to circumvent this prohibition. It does not confine itself to sponsoring books that give a benign view of American policies. It cooks up the books, finds the authors, provides the materials, and subsidizes the publication. "We control the things from the very idea down to the final edited manuscript," said Mr. Reed Harris of the USIA, his contempt showing through by the use of the term "things." The CIA—it, too, is forbidden by law from operating as an intelligence agency at home—engages in much the same kind of thing; thus the article in the distinguished journal *Foreign Affairs* defending the American role in Vietnam, by George Carver—an employee of the CIA who did not bother to make that connection known to the editors of the journal or to the public. How many other articles of this nature have been planted or insinuated in American magazines we do not know; one of the worst features of this clandestine activity is that it exposes the entire publishing and scholarly enterprise to suspicion.

It is, of course, not the sponsorship but the secrecy that is the vice. If books and articles sponsored by government agencies were openly acknowledged for what they are, they could be judged on their merits, which are often substantial. In the absence of such acknowledgment they are a fraud upon the public. What is needed is a Truth in Packaging Act for the United States government.

The massive involvement of the CIA in the opinion-manipulation business is too notorious to require elaboration. Noiselessly and insidiously the CIA moved into student organizations, churches, labor unions, newspapers and magazines, and Heaven and Mr. Helms alone know what else, not only corrupting these activities at the source but training hundreds of Americans to take intellectual corruption for granted, and to associate their own government with the dirty business.

What is perhaps most surprising is that many of those involved in these subterranean activities seem unable to understand what is wrong about them. They defend them on the ground that, after all, the Communists use deception, too, and we must fight fire with fire; they assert that the government got its money's worth in these investments; they argue that secrecy is essential to success in the Cold War; they even submit, with an air of injured innocence, that we should be grateful to the CIA for doing what Congress refused to do. They seem, many of them, wholly unable to grasp the essential point: the corruption of the democratic process.

All of these attempts to control the minds of the American people in order to win the Cold War violate the two great Kantian moral imperatives: to conduct yourself so that your every act can be generalized into a universal principle, and to regard every human being as an end in himself, never as merely a means to an end.

Consider the first. We can generalize the particular policies which CIA, USIA, and Defense have adopted into three principles. First, and most elementary, if government can indoctrinate schoolchildren, and their parents, about foreign policy it may, with equal logic, indoctrinate them about domestic policy. If the USIA and the CIA can sponsor books and finance organizations to fight Communism, they may, with equal justification, sponsor books and finance organizations to fight "socialism" or the "welfare state" or anything else that they think odious. Congress has quite deliberately withheld such powers from these and other organizations; if they circumvent these prohibitions, will we not have an end to genuine freedom of choice in American politics?

Second, if government can carry war propaganda into the classroom—even without a formal war—may it not with equal logic carry any other propaganda into the classroom? And if it has this power, what will happen to the American principle that the national government has no control over the substance of what is taught in the schools? If the principle of indoctrination of schoolchildren is once firmly established, may we not end up with the Napoleonic philosophy of public education—that the overarching purpose of schools is to produce loyal patriots?

Third, if government can control the thinking of its citizens, it can control everything else. Americans pride themselves on their tradition of "free enterprise," and some of them go so far as to equate free enterprise with "the American system." But the only free enterprise that counts, in the long run, is intellectual enterprise, for if that dries up all individual enterprise dries up. A government that can control the thinking of its citizens can silence criticism and destroy initiative, and a government that is exempt from the pressures of criticism and of political initiative is one that is in training for tyranny.

Governmental malpractices of thought control violate, just as clearly, the second categorical imperative—to treat all men as ends, never as means. For to exploit the integrity of school and university, science and scholarship, to the dubious ends of ideological conflict, is to subvert the very foundations of our civilization and our moral order.

The reason we are trying to win the contest with Communism, and indeed with all forms of injustice and oppression, is that we believe in the virtue of freedom, of the open mind, of the unimpeded search for truth. These are not only our ultimate ends; they are, equally, the indispensable means whereby we hope to achieve these ends. If we corrupt all of this at the very source, we may indeed win the immediate contest with "Communism" and lose the cause for which we are fighting. If we triumph over the enemy with the weapons of deceit and subversion, we employ his weapons, embrace his standards, and absorb his principles.

Without intellectual freedom, uncontaminated, unimpeachable, and categorical, we cannot achieve the ends to which our society is dedicated. This is ultimately why we cannot tolerate activities of governmental agencies which, whatever their alleged justification, repudiate and paralyze the principles of freedom.

SCIENCE, LEARNING, AND THE CLAIMS OF NATIONALISM

4
_____

We think of our own time as an age of enlightenment, but it flouts two essential principles of enlightenment: first, the priority of the claims of science and culture over those of politics, and second, the cosmopolitan and universal nature of science and culture. The *philosophes* of the eighteenth century—it is a word which embraces not only philosophers but scientists and statesmen, men of letters and critics—did not worship at the altar of nationalism; they were a fellowship bound together by common devotion to Reason in all of its manifestations, and they were sure that its primary and its most pervasive manifestation was in the realm of science and of learning. They believed, too, in the universality of knowledge as they believed in the universality of morals and of art. When they wrote history it was world history, as with Voltaire; when they studied religion it tended to be comparative religion, as with Christian Wolff; when they celebrated law it was the Spirit of the Laws, as with Montesquieu; when they contemplated art they sought the universal in art, as with Winckelmann or Sir Joshua Reynolds. Their scientists and men of learning were cosmopolitan, at home in every country, and moving easily from country to country and

Address at Lebanon Valley College, 1967.

236

from university to university—or, more often than not, from academy to academy, for the universities of that day were, many of them, in the doldrums. They knew that the commonwealth of learning was older than the commonwealth of political nations and that the learned academy and the university had flourished some centuries before the rise of the modern state. With most of them the claims of science and learning took precedence over the claims of the nation-state, for they equated science with truth, and, as truth was universal and could never conflict with other truth, they held that the sciences were never at war. Condorcet, himself a victim of ideological nationalism, spoke for all of his generation when he said that

. . . the philosophers of different nations who considered the interests of the whole of humanity without distinction of country, race or creed, formed a solid phalanx banded together against all forms of error, all manifestations of tyranny. Animated by feelings of universal philanthropy they fought injustice when it occurred in countries other than their own.

We have come a long way from this philosophy of the Enlightenment—the philosophy of Franklin and Jefferson and Tom Paine in America, of Joseph Banks and Edward Jenner and Joseph Priestley in England, of Rumford in Bavaria and Linnaeus in Sweden and Haller in Switzerland, and Buffon and Lavoisier and Diderot in France—and it is by no means clear that our shift in position represents an advance rather than a retreat.

Let us consider some of the characteristics of that world where the sciences were never at war, not even in time of war. It was an age when both the United States and the French governments could proclaim immunity, in time of war, for Captain Cook because he was "engaged in work beneficial to humanity"; when a Hessian officer, about to put to flame the house of Francis Hopkinson—one of the Signers—was so impressed by its library and scientific apparatus that he ordered the flames extinguished, writing on the fly leaf of a book: "This man is clearly a traitor but he is a man of learning and science and must be protected." Frederick the Great retained French as the language of his court while fighting France; Napoleon's mother put her money into British consols;

Goethe flaunted his French decorations when he received the re-
treating general of the allied armies, after Leipzig; the Royal
Society of London conferred its gold medal on Franklin, in
time of war; and the Institute in Paris voted a gold medal to Sir
Humphry Davy—likewise in time of war. The same Napoleon who
arranged that arranged, too, to spare the university city of Göttingen out of respect for the great classical scholar Heyne; it was
fitting that Sir Charles Blagden should recommend, in 1808, that
he be made a member of the Royal Society in London.

The world of art, like the world of science, was cosmopolitan,
and how fortunate that was for the rising Republic of the United
States. There is no more charming chapter in the history of American art than that which recounts how George III, even in time of
war, patronized young painters from America. A group of benefactors had sent Benjamin West to Rome to study painting, when he
was still but a boy; he served his apprenticeship there, and went on
to London, where one of his paintings caught the fancy of young
George III, and in 1772 he was appointed painter to the court, a
position he held—as he held George's friendship—throughout the
Revolution. What is more, it was during the years when the American Colonies were fighting for independence that West received in
his studio a series of American apprentices—among them Charles
Peale, John Trumbull, and Gilbert Stuart—who returned to America to paint a gallery of the Signers and the Founding Fathers.

Meantime other American artists were studying in France, all
through the turbulent years of the Revolution and the Napoleonic
Wars, and soon the current of artists flowed, ever swifter and
broader, to Rome and Florence, where, at one time, in the early
nineteenth century, over fifty American artists were living.

The new United States, in turn, drew upon European artists and
architects for her needs. Consider the creation of our own capital
city; was there ever a more cosmopolitan enterprise? The city's
name was American, but nearly all else was Latinate—"senate,"
"presidency," etc. As it turned out, the architecture was Roman,
too. The work of laying out the capital was originally entrusted to a
Frenchman, Major L'Enfant—he had come to America with Lafay-
ette and had made himself part of the New World even while re-

maining French. Soon L'Enfant was joined by James Hoban, who
had been born and trained in Ireland—and it was he who was
chiefly responsible for the White House. Next Stephen Hallet took
over—he had been born and raised in France and had come to
America in 1789 to set up a school of art in Richmond; it never
materialized, but some of his other plans did. Even more valuable
was William Thornton, born in the Dutch West Indies, educated in
Scotland, where he took a medical degree. Trained in architecture
in Paris, his designs for the national capitol, worked out while he
was in the West Indies on a honeymoon, won out over all rivals.
One of his co-workers on the capitol was George Hadfield from
England—he had actually been born in Italy, and he was brother-
in-law to that Maria Conway who had so charmed Thomas Jefferson. Most colorful of all was Benjamin Latrobe, a product of
Huguenot France and of Moravian Germany. Educated for the
ministry in Germany, he had happily turned to art; he practiced
briefly in England, then migrated to Virginia. Soon he was in
charge of building the national capitol; soon he was in charge of
almost everything, for he was a man of endless energy and resourcefulness. He brought in a small army of Italian artists to
finish the capitol building: Giuseppi Franzoni and his brother
Carlo; the sculptor Luigi Persica, who did the statues of Peace and
War and the Discovery in the Rotunda; Enrico Causici of Verona,
who did the panels of Daniel Boone and of the Landing of the
Pilgrims—how delightful that a Veronese artist should give us
Daniel Boone! And there was Antonia Capello, a pupil of the great
Canova, who had himself planned to come over and do a statue of
Washington, and the French sculptor Nicholas Gevelot, who carved
a panel of William Penn. What an international undertaking it
was, going on all through the Napoleonic Wars—and how much it
contributed to making good the devastations of war.

Or consider those two remarkable presidents of the Royal Soci-
ety, itself dedicated to the pursuit of science and learning for the
benefit of all mankind. The first president was Sir Hans Sloane.
Born in Ireland, he studied medicine under the German Nicolaus
Staphorst, then went to France for his formal training, at Paris and
Montpellier and the Jardin des Plantes, and, just to even things up,

at the Protestant University of Orange. He sailed for the West
Indies to botanize there, and the whole scientific world rejoiced
when he brought back a cargo of specimens from Jamaica. At his
handsome mansion in London he kept open house, just as did his
successor Sir Joseph Banks; the famous Haller came to see him—
not yet famous to be sure; Linnaeus came to see him, with a letter
from that greatest of medical professors, Boerhaave of Leyden;
and after him Linnaeus' pupil Peter Kalm, who was to write the
best botanical description of America; even Voltaire paid his respects, and that did not happen very often. Like Linnaeus at Uppsala, Banks corresponded with botanists everywhere in the Western world, not least with Americans, who sent over hundreds of
specimens to the royal gardens; with William Byrd, with Mark
Catesby, who wrote a natural history of Carolina, and with the
elder Bartram. It was during the presidency of Hans Sloane, too,
that was played out the curious and touching drama of the baby
elephant. A baby elephant had been sent to Réaumur of Paris—his
six-volume history of insects was one of the capital works of that
century—but had been captured by a British man-of-war and
brought to Portsmouth. Réaumur pled for his elephant, in vain it
seemed, until Abraham Trembley of the Royal Society intervened.
He appealed to Fox and eventually got permission to ship the
elephant on. Meantime the elephant had died; no matter; Trembley had him stuffed; the passports arrived; and in due time the
elephant was delivered to Réaumur. What a triumph for science,
what a triumph even for the baby elephant, who achieved immortality in the pages of Buffon's great *Natural History*.

Sir Joseph Banks continued the Sloane policies and enlarged
upon them: for forty years as head of the Royal Society he never
permitted war or revolution to interfere with the beneficent role of
science. As a youth he had sailed with Captain Cook; and he had
introduced the famous Tahitian Omai to England. He had botan-
ized in Iceland, too, and later when the British were at war with
Denmark, and Iceland was cut off from food and on the verge of
starvation, he intervened with William Pitt and saved the island. It
was Banks who had arranged that gold medal for Franklin; it was
Banks who intervened again and again, during the war with

France, to enable the work of science to go forward. Appealing to Grenville for permission for the French to ship a collection of specimens from Trinidad to Paris he wrote that "the very application offers, during the horrors of a war, unprecedented in mutual implacability . . . an unconditional armistice to Science." He intervened, too, to save for France the great collection which La Billardière had assembled in the East and which had been captured by a British naval vessel; he even persuaded George III and the exiled Queen of France to forgo it, and finally shipped it through the blockade to the Jardin des Plantes. "That the Science of two Nations may be at peace, while their Politics are at war," he wrote, "is an axiom we have learned from your protection to Captain Cook, and surely nothing is so likely to abate the Rancour that Politicians frequently entertain against each other as to see Harmony and Good prevail among Brethren who cultivate science." He enlisted the aid of Lord Nelson and Lady Hamilton, and, finally, even of Napoleon himself, to obtain the release of Déodat de Dolomieu—the Dolomites bear his name—from the dungeon to which the Neapolitans had consigned him. At a time when Napoleon was threatening to invade England he saw to it that the nautical almanacs, upon which depended safety at sea, got shipped to France as usual.

Edward Jenner, he who had discovered inoculation against smallpox, was no less cosmopolitan than his colleague Banks. So great was his fame that he was almost a sovereign: a letter from him was more valuable than a passport; monarchs everywhere respected it. And it was Jenner who, in appealing for the release of the young Lord Yarmouth from captivity, penned the memorable statement: "The sciences are never at war. Peace must always preside in those bosoms whose object is the augmentation of human happiness."

We have no more illuminating example of the operation of the community of learning than that which records the acquisition by Harvard University of the Ebeling collection of Americana. How neatly all the parts, so miscellaneous and disparate, fit together once we apply this principle of the sovereignty of learning. Let us begin with Ebeling himself, one of those prodigious scholars who

seem to have been the specialty of eighteenth-century Germany.
He had been educated at the new university at Göttingen; he had
planned to go into the ministry but was diverted to the classics and
to history—two of the Göttingen specialties. When we first meet
him he is director of the commercial school at Hamburg, professor
of Greek and Latin at the *Gymnasium* and, for good measure,
librarian of the city library. Somehow he found time to edit and to
write, as well. He was fascinated by geography and by freedom:
these interests pointed inescapably to America, and he set himself
to write a multi-volume history and geography of the American
states, one volume, at least, for each state. He wrote other things,
to be sure: thirty-four volumes altogether, on history, on geography, even on music, for though he was deaf music was his passion.
But how write thirteen volumes on America without books or documents? He called upon the community of learning and all difficulties vanished. He applied to the members of America's learned
societies, to David Ramsey in South Carolina, to Matthew Carey
and Dr. Barton in Philadelphia, to Noah Webster and Dr. Mitchill
in New York, to Jedidiah Morse the geographer, and the Rev. Dr.
Belknap the historian, and President Willard of Harvard College;
above all to the Reverend William Bentley in Salem—and all of
them responded. All through the years of the French revolutionary
war, and the Napoleonic Wars, the American *philosophes* sent
boxes of books, journals, newspapers, maps across the beleaguered
Atlantic, through the blockade. A stream of documents flowed into
the library at Hamburg, until in the end Christoph Ebeling had the
greatest collection of Americana to be found in the Western world.

Turn now to Madame de Staël, Necker's daughter and Benjamin
Constant's mistress, and Napoleon's bête noire, not the most beautiful woman in Europe, but with certainly the most dazzling mind.
She had written *Corinne, or Italia,* the first novel to deal with the
problem of national character, its hero, Lord Nevil, based on the
young Charlestonian John Izard Middleton, who lived in Rome and
wrote upon Grecian antiquities. She had been banished from Paris
by Napoleon for her radicalism, and had taken refuge in the family
villa at Coppet where she looked across Lac Leman toward the
Alps and bewailed her desolate position. There she settled down to

write what was to be her most famous book, *De l'Allemagne,* an analysis of Germany, and a paean of praise, too. The three volumes were ready in 1810, and Madame de Staël was allowed to return to Paris to supervise their publication. Ten thousand copies had been printed when the superintendent of police descended on her, and on the printer, to destroy all the books and banish her once again from France.

Madame de Staël fled from country to country, finding refuge, finally, in St. Petersburg, where, as Georg Brandes sardonically observed, she was at last able to breathe the air of freedom! Meantime she had managed to smuggle out one copy of her book, and it was published in London in 1813, and the next year—the United States was at war with Britain but no matter—in Boston.

Boston was not yet the Athens of America, but it was rapidly supplanting the previous claimant to that title, Philadelphia. Its merchant ships sailed the Baltic and the Mediterranean, the China Seas and the Indian Ocean; its clergymen were turning from Puritanism to an enlightened Unitarianism; its men of letters had set up the Anthology Society, which in turn sponsored the Athenaeum Library, and that most impressive of quarterlies, the *North American Review;* and Harvard College was rapidly becoming the leading institution of learning in the nation. But it was not good enough, and some of its graduates—and those of other New England colleges—thirsted for more knowledge than Harvard could teach. In 1814 they read Charles Viller's *Coup d'Oeil sur les Universités,* which sang the praises of the German universities and especially of Viller's own university, Göttingen; and the next year came Madame de Staël's *De l'Allemagne.* In these books they could read that German universities began where all others left off, and that the new university—new certainly by European standards— at Göttingen was the queen of them all, Göttingen which was already supplanting Leyden and Padua as the most cosmopolitan of institutions of learning.

What remarkable young men they were. There was George Ticknor, who became the first Smith Professor at Harvard University, wrote the great *History of Spanish Literature,* founded the Boston Public Library, and presided over Boston's most distinguished literary salon. There was Edward Everett, later to be president of Harvard and governor of Massachusetts, only to be remembered, alas, as the man who also spoke at Gettysburg on that famous day. There was George Bancroft, destined to be the first of American historians, and a politician, a cabinet member, a diplomat and a venerable first citizen. There was Joseph Cogswell, the least known of the four; he was somewhat older and was going abroad as tutor to young Augustus Thorndike; eventually he was to arrange and preside over the Astor-Lenox library in New York.

Off they went to the lovely town nestling on the banks of the Lahn. They carried with them letters from Dr. Bentley and Dr. Prince; and they corresponded with the venerable Ebeling, and in 1817 visited him and saw for themselves the famous library. A few months later Ebeling died. Everett and Cogswell moved swiftly to save it from dispersion at the auction block. Cogswell turned to his protégé's father, Israel Thorndike, who boasted one of the great fortunes of New England, and Thorndike put up the money to bring the library back to America: some thirty-five hundred books, eight thousand maps, several hundred volumes of newspapers—all in all, the greatest library of Americana in existence, and the foundation of what is doubtless still the greatest collection in existence.

By this time the community of learning was already under pressure: a good many of the shipments of books between Bentley and Ebeling seem to have been the victims of war. The change was dramatized by a minor incident of the nineties. In 1792 the Copley medal of the Royal Society went to the American who was then prime minister of Bavaria, Count Rumford; in 1794 it went to Alessandro Volta of Italy; 1793 is a blank. That year the medal was destined for the great Lavoisier, but the members of the society knew that Lavoisier was in peril and feared that an award from England would exacerbate that peril, and held their hand. Even that self-restraint did not save the great chemist. The story is familiar and prophetic. He was arrested, tried, and condemned; he asked for time to complete some chemical experiments; "the Republic has no need for savants," said Coffinhal, and Lavoisier's head rolled beneath the guillotine.

Nationalism, and national ideologies, now threatened the integrity of the community of learning. For nationalism, like romanticism, emphasized all that was provincial and particular in culture rather than what was catholic and universal. It celebrated national origins, the national language and even the provincial idiom, national literature, art, and culture. It repudiated the world of the Enlightenment, where scholars and scientists—and aristocrats, too, of course—had been able to ignore national barriers and move freely from country to country, even in time of war; where all men of learning shared a common language—French—and a common education in the traditions of the ancient world and a common loyalty to science. It emphasized separation rather than unity, fostered dissension rather than harmony, and encouraged parochialism rather than cosmopolitanism. It not only set nation against nation, but introduced what we have come to call total war—not as total as ours, to be sure, for we have made some progress over the years, but war involving a whole people and an entire nation. And in between wars it erected barriers to the free movement of men, goods, and ideas. Finally, it largely invented the notion of national character—for the Enlightenment had sought what was universal rather than what was local about a people—a discovery that in some providential way one's own country boasted the best of all characters, the most advanced culture, the most civilized society. From this it followed that even if one might raise awkward questions about the validity of military or political hegemony one could not question the validity of cultural hegemony, for that, surely, was beneficent!

The United States escaped, in part at least, the worst ravages of the new nationalism. To explore the explanations for this, and the manifestations, would take us far afield; we must content ourselves with a brief statement of some of the factors which mitigated chauvinistic nationalism in the early Republic.

First, the new United States was itself a creature of the Enlightenment, and almost all of its leaders—Franklin, Jefferson, Adams, Tom Paine, Benjamin Rush, to name but a few—were children of the Enlightenment.

Second, the new nation came into existence not as a highly centralized state, but as a federal nation, and, as such, had provisions for individual differences and experiments. There was no danger, therefore, of statism, and little of chauvinism. Nationalism was itself a thing of slow nurture; not for over half a century did it begin to take on chauvinistic characteristics—with Manifest Destiny, with the Mexican War in the 1840's.

Third, the United States started without a national church, or even state churches; at no time, therefore, was the new nation exposed to the temptation to identify religion with the nation-state, or the nation with religious faith. We have only to consider the role that religion has played, and still does play, in the nurture and exacerbation of nationalism elsewhere to realize what Americans escaped—in the nationalism of Ireland, for example, or of Spain, Israel, and the Arab states today.

Fourth, the new nation did not have—and did not develop for well over a century—a military establishment, or even a militaristic psychology. It is a commonplace that the military has almost always, whether from conviction or interest, or from an identification of the two, nourished chauvinistic nationalism. We need merely recall the role of the military in, let us say, Swedish nationalism, in the new nationalism of Germany, in the nationalism of many of the peoples of Latin America, to realize what we missed.

Fifth—closely related to the fourth—the American people started and long continued without a real "national enemy." The British might have played this role, but did not, chiefly because we emerged from our two wars victorious, and thereafter considered the British friends rather than enemies. Neither the Canadians nor the Mexicans qualified for the role; with both it was the other way around, and *we* were the national enemy. Only the Indians, really, played this role, and they played it in a manner calculated not to inflame but to assuage chauvinistic nationalism, for the Providence that presided over the destinies of the new nation arranged that the Indian threat should be sufficiently dramatic to provide a common denominator, but not sufficiently serious to provide a threat. This innocence, needless to say, has changed and—again needless to say—not for the better: we seem as determined now to embrace a national enemy as ever did the French, the Irish, the Swedes, the Italians, in the nineteenth century.

Sixth, the American people was, from the beginning, heterogeneous; the new nation did not put up bars against the most miscellaneous immigration, and the population grew increasingly heterogeneous throughout the nineteenth century. There were some pressures for chauvinistic nationalism here, to be sure—the passionate desire of newcomers to identify with their adopted nation, to be accepted by that nation, to justify their shift in allegiance; all this tended to exaggerate public manifestations of patriotism. But it was hard, in the circumstances, to exalt such things as racial superiority (except that of whites!), or cultural, and American nationalism escaped these, as it escaped religious and military affiliations.

Seventh, though American society of the eighteenth century was probably the most literate in the world, education was not a national institution, but particular and local. There was not and has never been a national educational establishment, and it has never heretofore been possible for the national government to use the school system (or nonsystem) for national or partisan purposes. Almost every Old World nation had—and for that matter still has—a national system of education, and in some, France for example, it has been and is highly centralized. Eighteenth-century Europe, and perhaps nineteenth- as well, took for granted that education was an instrument of the state, and that teachers, and even professors at universities, were servants of the state: even the much-vaunted "academic freedom" of the Germans did not reject this principle. As early as 1774 the Austrian government provided that "nothing must be taught the youth which they would use rarely, or not at all, for the benefit of the state"; Napoleon set up a highly centralized school system designed to produce good Napoleonic citizens; in the early nineteenth century Prussia went so far as to close up Froebel's *Kindergartens* on the ground that they were potentially subversive. None of this was possible in the United States, where chaos rather than regulation was the presiding spirit of schools; only now is there some danger of a reversal of this traditional safeguard against the misuse of education.

Finally, the new nation did not develop cultural chauvinism because she had as yet no culture to be chauvinistic about. Her language, literature, law, art and architecture, even her religious faiths, were inherited. It would have been ridiculous—as perhaps it still is—for Americans to insist either on the unique character of American culture, or on its superiority to other cultures. All through the nineteenth century the United States was dependent on the Old World for most of her cultural inspiration and much of her cultural activity. The story of American artists in Rome, Florence, Düsseldorf, and Paris; American musicians in Munich; American doctors in Edinburgh, Leyden, and Vienna; American theologians in Tübingen and Marburg; American educators in Germany, France, and England; the story, in short, of the cultural lend-lease which the Old World carried on with the New for over a century is familiar enough. One of the most significant things about it is that it made it extraordinarily difficult for Americans to exploit culture for nationalist purposes.

The dominant elements of American culture are still cosmopolitan. With its mingled and blended population and its miscellaneous inheritance from every Old World country, the United States represents the nearest thing there is to a European union and European culture. If—as the sociologists assure us—the racial melting pot has been somewhat exaggerated, the cultural has not: witness the architecture of almost any city or even of any college campus, the gastronomy of urban restaurants, the variety of churches and of faiths. The United States is proof that the peoples of Europe can, in fact, live and work together, and even pray together under one government—something which many Europeans deny as far as their own continent is concerned. It is scarcely necessary to observe that this observation provides no justification for complacency; after all we have not yet worked out a way in which whites and Negroes can live and work together: the greatest failure, this, in our history.

Here then was a heritage of cosmopolitanism, from the Enlightenment, a heritage on which we built and from which we progressed. Yet who can doubt now, as we enter the final third of the twentieth century, that we have in part succumbed to the temptations of chauvinistic nationalism? Who can doubt that now the sciences *are* at war, and that it is our own government which is a participant in this war?

There are, to be sure, counter-trends. As no other nation is so rich as the United States, no other has given so generously of its richness for the support of science and education in other countries. The story is familiar—the Fulbright program, which has now involved a hundred thousand or more scholars; the Peace Corps; contributions to UNESCO, the World Health Organization, the International Geophysical Year, and similar activities; the work of universities, one building a medical school in Indonesia, another establishing an agricultural college in Pakistan, others sponsoring technological institutes in India or Latin America. No one will say that we have done all that we ought to have done, but we have done as much as any other nation in this area of international scientific cooperation.

Our contributions to this area, official and private, are counterbalanced, and in part negated, by other practices and malpractices. Most of these are painfully familiar, and it is not necessary to elaborate upon them. There are the nefarious activities of the CIA at home and throughout the globe, corrupting the very bloodstream of international scientific and intellectual commerce by using universities and scholars for non-scholarly purposes. There are the still vigorous restrictions on travel to places thought to be hostile to the United States, and formal limitations on all travel by passport supervision—the kind of thing reduced to absurdity in the notorious case of the diplomatic "shadowing" of the distinguished Professor Stuart Hughes of Harvard because he was supposed to entertain ideas that seemed heterodox to the Bourbon minds in the Passport Office. There are restrictions on the entry into the United States of scientists and men of letters from countries which someone in the State Department regards as unfriendly to the United States. This policy, so injurious to the interests of science all through the fifties, has been relaxed, but it has not been abandoned. There are restrictions on our access to knowledge—on where reporters may go and what they may report, on mail deliveries from Communist countries or from countries whose ideological teachings might be thought to corrupt unwary American scholars. There are security controls on scientific research under government auspices, even when conducted by universities—a control against which our institutions of learning have protested and from which the academic community will no doubt emancipate itself in the near future. There is—more serious this—the use, perhaps the exploitation, of universities and research institutions for ends that have little to do with scientific advancement or the welfare of mankind, and much to do with the waging of war. It is probable—it is one of those things which cannot in the nature of things be demonstrated—that most of the money which the national government now devotes to research goes not to projects which scientists have, quite independently, thought to be beneficial to humanity, but to those which governmental officials think useful to government and, more specifically, to the conduct of war. Doubtless these things may overlap, and doubtless, too, the by-products of applied science will have important consequences for pure, but the principle is both potentially and actually pernicious.

What all this means is that officially, at least, we still reject the principle of a Joseph Banks, a Lavoisier, a Jenner, that "the sciences are never at war." We are, in fact, enlisting the sciences in war, even during time of peace, even at the risk of deflecting them from their rightful purposes. Nor is this the whole story. The circumstances of modern life, not just in Germany or Russia or China, but in the United States, too, have encouraged the notion that the scientist, as well as science, may be conscripted for war. Doubtless there is some justification for this: science may be said to have won the Second World War. But there is little justification for the extension of the original principle—that all of science must be enlisted in war, and that the scientist may not claim exemption from the claims of nationalism.

This was the principle behind the attack on one of the greatest of scientists, Dr. Robert Oppenheimer, a principle which found classic expression in the statement by the Gray Commission that Dr. Oppenheimer had "exercised the arrogance of private judgment," surely one of the most deeply immoral statements of American history. It is the principle which was used to rationalize the Dulles notion that science was an instrument of national policy. He did not mean by that that national policy should be illuminated by, or guided by, science; he meant that science should be guided by, and exploited by, national policy.

The danger is growing, in the United States as elsewhere in this world of competing ideologies, that the cosmopolitan world of science and learning may be permanently subordinated to the claims of chauvinistic nationalism.

No more difficult problem confronts the American scholar and scientist than that of educating their own—and other—societies and governments to the logic of exempting science from these claims. Since science must not and indeed cannot divorce itself from its own society, or from government, whose contributions have enriched it in the past and promise to prosper it in the future, scholars must somehow make clear to those in authority—eventually the American people—that to exploit science for narrow nationalist purposes will be fatal both to the achievement of those purposes and to the integrity of science.

Rarely before has the academy had so great an opportunity to influence the course of history as it has today. If it is to do this, it must be clear about its own character and make that character clear to society. It is to the modern world what the church was to the medieval—more nearly universal, and more free, and it should enjoy the same immunity from political or national control that the church came to enjoy. Its purpose is to search out truth and to serve mankind, the future as well as the present; it must do these things on its own terms, not on terms fixed by government.

TELEVISION: FAILURE
AND POTENTIALITY

5

Television is a new invention and a new medium, and it is, perhaps, no wonder that we have not yet come to terms with it; no
wonder that we do not understand its functions or exhaust its
potentialities; no wonder that it has not yet found its true character. That was the experience of two earlier—and greater—
contributions to communication: the university and the printing
press. The university was a twelfth-century invention, but it was
some two hundred years before it took on a firm and permanent
character, and we are still debating, eight hundred years after its
birth, just what are its proper functions. The printing press appeared to find its true character at once—that of making books
available in large quantities at low cost—but who that is familiar
with the long and painful history of censorship can suppose that
that character and function were acceptable to all and everywhere? The films, to be sure, did find their character almost at
once, and did achieve a kind of maturity with remarkable rapidity,
only to be reduced to a state of servitude by television. We have
had television for only twenty years now, a very short time in the
history of communications, and we have still not gone very far on

Address at Seminar on Television, Asilomar, California, May, 1967.

the road to understanding the nature and purpose of this new medium. Those who sit in the seats of power—theoretical power such as the Congress and the Federal Communications Commission, or actual power, the heads of the networks and the spokesmen for "sponsors"—do not know whether television is public or private; whether its center of gravity is entertainment or information and education; or whether its contributions should be judged by quantitative or by qualitative standards.

We are speaking, to be sure, of television as we know it in America. We must be on guard against two pervasive but fallacious assumptions. First, that the United States pattern of private ownership and control is normal, and, second, that change and development will be chiefly in the technological realm, e.g., the triumph of color, or the use of satellite broadcasting or of the multiband broadcasts, rather than in the cultural. Even in the technical realm American preconceptions are sometimes permitted to color our judgment: in the spring of 1967 the president of one of the major networks, Julian Goodman, expressed reservations about the propriety of satellite broadcasting from abroad. "It might be possible," he said, "for foreign countries to broadcast to American homes. I am not sure that would be very desirable. . . ." It is as if the president of a university should question the desirability of foreign books in American libraries.

One might suppose that the issue of private or public enterprise was clear enough, but it is not. The airwaves, after all, belong to the public, just as the skies belong to the public. The original FCC act of 1934 specifically required that television serve the public interest. Everywhere else in the world television is regarded as a public-service institution, and in almost every nation is run by the government itself, directly or indirectly. One might suppose, too, that the choice, if really open, was clear enough. There are, after all, enough private enterprises, enough ways for corporations to make money, and it is doubtful that we really need more of these. Even television concedes that it is public interest that must be served. And surely, too, the most exciting opportunities today are in the realm of public rather than of private enterprise, and the most significant contributions to the commonwealth rather than to private or corporate wealth. But, as it has turned out, television is controlled by men trained in the most competitive of private industries and by corporations which have had little experience in public service and lack therefore the standards and disciplines gradually built up in publishing, the theatre, the medical and legal professions, or the universities, and lack, too, the imagination commonly found in these enterprises.

There are, to be sure, gestures toward the public interest and the public service in commercial television, and sometimes these are more than gestures; sometimes they are almost historic events. Every so often television shows what it can really do when it tries: the coronation of Queen Elizabeth, the Kennedy and the Churchill funerals, documentaries on the McCarthy hearings, or on civil-rights demonstrations in the South, programs like Ed Murrow's *See It Now* or *The Valiant Years,* some news commentary—Eric Sevareid or the annual Walter Lippmann. The inevitable observation here is, if television can do this well when its masters wish, why does it not habitually do this well? We do not, after all, single out a few issues of the *New York Times* or the *Manchester Guardian,* a few great performances by the Boston Symphony or the Vienna Philharmonic, a few research activities at Harvard or Berkeley, a few operations at the Massachusetts General Hospital, a few decisions of the United States Supreme Court, to justify these institutions. We expect them to perform up to their highest capacity all the time—and for the most part they do. Why should not television maintain the same high standards of performance that we take for granted in these and similar institutions devoted to the public interest?

On the whole, however, notwithstanding its legal position, television is run as a private enterprise. It is private-enterprise psychology that obtains among those who administer it; and among the public, too. Americans tend to assume that their standards are normal, and even universal, and that if they march to a different tune from others it is the others who are out of step. Thus we take for granted, for example, a two-party system although only the English-speaking peoples have ever made one work; we take for granted the payment of tuition in colleges and universities though

rarely elsewhere are students expected to pay for education. So perhaps it is not surprising that we should take for granted that private enterprise controls television, and that where advertisers
(euphemistically called sponsors, just as advertisements are euphemistically called messages—we take the euphemism for granted,
too!) pay the piper, it is proper that they should call the tune. And,
after all, if the networks and industry control the FCC why should
not the sponsors control the networks?

This is not the result of a conspiracy, or of political or business
skulduggery. It is a product of popular psychology shared by industry and the public. A realization of this must moderate the
enthusiasm of those who would like to see the American system
approximate the British. Americans *do* trust private enterprise:
they *do* feel—mistakenly, I think—that governmental activities
should be reduced to a minimum; they *do* admire businessmen and
business methods inordinately. For reasons deeply rooted in history, private business occupied from the beginning a special and
specially favored position in American life. Where in the Old
World business was a late comer, and had to accommodate itself to
all the pre-existing institutions—the crown, the aristocracy, the
church, the guilds, and so forth—in the New World these were
absent, and business enterprise was in command. It could, and did,
pretty much fix its own terms, and it encouraged, if it did not
develop, the popular belief that business was somehow exalted,
and government somehow pernicious, and that the ideal was to
have more business in government and less government in business. This psychology still lingers on, long after whatever logic it
might once have had has evaporated.

If history explains, in part, the special position of business in the
American scene, it admonishes us, too, that change has been under
way for a long time, and that both special position and privilege
are fast giving way to doctrines of public interest. Ever since *Munn
v. Illinois,* in 1877, there has been a trend toward implementing
the constitutional doctrine laid down by Chief Justice Waite, that
when property is affected with a public interest the public has an
interest in the use of that property and may control it for public
purposes. In one area after another which entrepreneurs thought

sacred to private enterprise, government has successfully asserted its interest, and its right to regulate or control. Nowhere, not even with the railroads, or aviation, or education, is public interest more obvious and more pervasive than in television, and there is no reason to suppose that television will be immune to pressures that have operated elsewhere. It took a long time for the public to assert its interest and authority in such matters as health and medicine, but once that assertion had been made the regulation came swiftly. Television will not be an exception to a rule that almost has the force of a historical law: the steady and irresistible growth of governmental authority. It is already regulated—in principle: it will increasingly be regulated in fact. It is likely to find itself, in the near future, confronted by a well-financed public system in competition with existing private systems. What is happening here fits into and illustrates what we may call the Galbraith Law—that the private section of the economy is giving way to the public, and that the public will continue to grow at the expense of the private. That shift in the center of gravity from private to public, which we have seen in such varied areas as public lands, water, forests, cities, race relations, medicine, and education, will inevitably embrace television. It would be folly if television leadership did not recognize this and cooperate with it.

Actually we should not conjure up two distinct and opposing theories and policies in television: private and public. What has emerged out of the long contest for control of all those businesses affected with a public interest is not a governmental take-over, as in Britain, nor is it the defeat of government by private enterprise. It is a blending and a merging of the two, and with this a gradual evaporation of the importance of the issue. It is a mistake to suppose that in the realm of the economy, politics, education, and culture the people make a clear-cut choice between opposing systems. The railroads are both public and private; the private interest now clamors for public subsidies and the public interest tries to impose on the railroads some of those policies it once rejected, and in fact the public cares very little what label is attached to the whole enterprise, just so it works. So with hydroelectric power, banking, education, and health. Not only do the private and public interests merge, but the issue itself loses significance, for actually an enlightened public control does not imperil profits, initiative, enterprise, or freedom.

Many television owners and sponsors view more stringent public regulation of television with apprehension, and some fear the shape and thrust which the proposed public television corporation will take. I see no ground for this apprehension. Government-controlled television in this country presents no threat to freedom or to private enterprise. It should be and let us hope will be more adventurous, more experimental, more sensitive to the larger public interest than privately controlled. This is true of public television in Britain and in the Scandinavian countries and perhaps in Japan, and there is no reason to suppose that the American government cannot observe the same self-imposed restraints and discover the same talent for experimentation that Britain and European countries observe and discover. Nor do we need to go abroad for analogies. The federal government has controlled the Library of Congress, the military and naval academies, the National Archives, the Geological Survey, the Smithsonian Institution, and scores of similar activities for over a century without serious interference in their freedom, just as states have established, financed, and administered state universities without more greatly interfering with their freedom than is recorded in the history of private institutions. There is no reason to suppose that the federal government is not just as concerned with things like intellectual freedom, inventiveness, and comprehensiveness as are the private networks, or that the Congress is not capable of setting up mechanisms—like the BBC perhaps, or like the Parliamentary Grants Commission—to protect television from improper governmental intervention.

Governmental regulation and governmental competition will come—are indeed coming—because television seems unable or unwilling to set its house in order. What is it that needs to be set in order? Here, no doubt, you will differ sharply among yourselves. I submit that television has allowed itself to fall victim to one great, pervasive, and intolerable evil—but one that is not ineradicable. It is the evil of surrendering effective control of the medium to sponsors.

This it is which distinguishes American television from almost all otherwise comparable enterprises: newspapers, publishing houses, films, museums, libraries, higher education. Many of these are business enterprises—certainly newspapers, magazines, book publishers, film, and theatre are. So too are some hospitals, some art museums and music schools. And if colleges and universities are not engaged in making money they are certainly engaged in the parallel enterprise of raising money. Alone of all these, television permits the donor to control not the business but the product itself. No other public enterprise of a comparable or an analogous character permits the advertisers or the donors a comparable control. Advertisers do not have anything to say about the content or the editorial policy of newspapers, magazines, or books; donors do not have anything to say about the choice of programs for a symphony orchestra, of the senior doctors in hospitals, of faculty and curriculum in a university, or of what is done professionally in these institutions.

It is from this original sin that all subsequent failings and inadequacies flow—a sin as congenital as that of Adam's. For it is at this point that outside business interests take over the crucial and professional functions. Let me submit to you what appear to be the major failings and inadequacies of television:

There is first the sin of timidity—timidity in the face of the fears of sponsors; timidity when confronted by pressure groups from the far right—the Red Channel's paranoia of the 1950's for example; timidity too about experiments and ideas. The most notorious chapter of this melancholy history is that written during the era of McCarthy, the era of the blacklists and of loyalty oaths (those required by government were not enough), the era when the networks got rid of dangerous actresses like Jean Muir, dropped the William Shirer program, and abandoned *I Can See It Now*. Never was a great and powerful organization so easily frightened and intimidated, never so pusillanimous. And the explanation? It has been elaborately set forth in John Cogley's report on blacklisting, and in Fred Friendly's *Due To Circumstances Beyond Our Control*—which is of course nonsense, for none of the matters were beyond the control of the networks, but precisely

under their control. The explanation is that power had passed from
the networks to the sponsors. It was not the radio and television
people who were timid, not the broadcasters, the directors, the
script writers, the educators; it was not even the presidents and
vice-presidents. No, it was the sponsors who trembled lest an unpopular idea or a controversial individual might cost them some
sales. But it was the networks that caved in to these fears and
pressures. Imagine a great university, a great newspaper, a great
museum or library or hospital, caving in to comparable pressures!
And what is sobering is that the networks have not, to this day,
made amends for their cowardice and injustice; have not apolo-
gized for their violation of due process and their contempt for the
spirit of freedom. As they have not attempted to make amends,
they have not reassured us that they would not act in precisely the
same way in another era of tension—perhaps that in which we
even now find ourselves.

Can anyone now take seriously the argument from some of television's spokesmen that government control of television would
threaten that freedom of speech or of press so precious to the
television industry? As television does not come into court with
clean hands, it is estopped from making this plea.

A second major charge against commercial television is its
failure to develop professional standards. Compare television with
other public interests of a comparable nature: the academic, the
legal, the medical, the military—even the journalistic—professions.
All of these have built up, over the years, their own sets of standards, and those standards are designed, on the whole, to maintain
the integrity of the professions and to serve the public interest.

Why has television not developed anything comparable to the
concept of academic freedom—that concept which has done so
much to make the university the center of light and learning and
progress in the modern world? The great networks are wealthier,
stronger, and more privileged than the academy. As a public utility
they are in a position to invoke the constitutional protections of the
First and Fifth Amendments. Had they had a sense of professional
standards, and courage, they would have said to Red Channels and
Counter Attack and the American Legion, and to the sponsors as

well: "You are asking us to violate the spirit and even the letter of the First Amendment, for television is licensed; you are asking us therefore to subvert the constitutional system of our country."

They did not invoke this concept of academic freedom nor did they invoke other professional concepts. Over the years the legal profession has built up a great body of professional standards: the duty of every lawyer to take on the protection of anyone who is accused, the obligation of professional secrecy, and so forth. The medical profession has developed a body of standards that commands respect everywhere. So too the academic profession: academic tenure, academic freedom, academic self-government, the obligation to engage in research, the obligation to build up libraries and laboratories for the use of future generations, loyalty to the highest interests of truth, rewards not to popularity but to solid achievements. Almost all professions, indeed, have something comparable—the journalistic, the publishing, the architectural, the military. Why has television been so laggard, so lacking in enterprise and courage? The university, the foundations, the professions, are engaged in something more than competition for sponsors or for popularity as indicated by Nielsen ratings: they are engaged in a competition for the advancement of knowledge, justice, and truth. These are things worth competing for. We can hardly expect television to develop professional standards, principles, loyalties, until it dedicates itself to something more important than popularity ratings or increased earnings to shareholders.

A third criticism of television is its failure to develop leadership: the kind of leadership developed, again, in other professions. Where are the Eliots, the Gilmans, the Whites, the Harpers and Butlers, the Hutchinses and Deweys whom the educational world developed in the past half century or so? Where are the Pulitzers and the Cobbses, the Adolph Ochses and the Eugene Myerses and the Walter Lippmanns and Robert Lasches of television? Television is a business but it has not even developed a body of business leadership comparable to the leadership in railroads three quarters of a century ago, or in banking. Why has leadership been timid, unimaginative, unoriginal, and for the most part anonymous?

Compare television here even with the motion-picture industry.

Why is television so largely a parasite on the older and declining industry? Why has it not, with all its immense resources, developed its own directors, its own script writers, its own actors even? Television depends heavily on films, but where are the Fords, the John Hustons and Cecil De Milles, where, for that matter, the Renoirs and Fellinis, the Bergmans and Dreyers, the Antonionis and René Clairs? Where are the great actors and actresses which the films somehow permitted or encouraged to emerge: W. C. Fields and Laurel and Hardy, Harold Lloyd, Charlie Chaplin and Charles Laughton, Marlene Dietrich and Greta Garbo and the Marx Brothers. The sterility of television in this, its own medium, and one on which it increasingly depends, cannot be an accident; it is the natural result of conditions which discourage originality, cannot tolerate experimentation, and reward those who are prepared to play safe. Certainly in this realm it is an industry which is wedded to mediocrity.

The explanation of this, again, can be laid at the door of sponsors. For sponsors are interested in the largest possible number of viewers, and that means the lowest common denominator. President Goodman of the National Broadcasting Company has recently endorsed this position in a statement of impressive opacity. "Some people," he said, "argue that television should meet more specialized interests, but it is not that sort of medium: since it serves everybody it must serve all tastes." But, if television serves all tastes, then it must serve specialized tastes as well.

This should not be difficult, and would not be difficult if it were not for the shadow of the sponsor brooding over the networks, the breath of the sponsor hot on the necks of television presidents. Serving specialized interests on television should not be more difficult than serving them in newspapers, magazines, books, films, and schools. We are after all a nation of two hundred million people, and with something like seventy or seventy-five million television sets. The term "specialized interests" conjures up some small esoteric group: actually it may include millions of interested men and women and children, an audience whose standard of attention is probably higher than that of the casual viewer of a baseball game.

Once again it is the sponsor who insists on an audience of many millions rather than of one million and who does this for business reasons. Suppose other public-service institutions in our society adopted this adulation of numbers, this contempt for standards? Suppose Harvard and Chicago, Amherst and Swarthmore took numbers of students for their standard of success: what would happen to education and to research? They have not suffered in popularity or in public support because they maintain standards higher than those of Oklahoma State or Kent State in Ohio. Suppose libraries stocked only books which were to be in great popular demand: what would happen to literature, to scholarship, to the individual character of society? The great libraries have not suffered. Suppose art museums bought only pictures which were guaranteed to be popular: what would be the impact not only on the artistic tastes of the community but on artists themselves? Has any society ever achieved greatness by deliberately aiming to level down rather than to level up? And is not television, whether regarded as a private or a public enterprise, as deeply concerned in the character and the prosperity (I mean, of course, moral and intellectual prosperity, not unrelated to economic) of our society as any other institution? Somehow great universities like Harvard and Chicago and Berkeley, great newspapers like the *New York Times* and the *Post-Dispatch,* great symphonies like the Boston and Cleveland, have not only survived the kind of pressures to which television has yielded, but have managed to create a public prepared to support them in their concept of excellence. Why has not television created such a public?

Doubtless what television does best is photography: the photography of the football and baseball game, of the documentary, of news coverage and political campaigns and war. It provides us, it has provided the historian, with the most ample, most comprehensive, and most authentic record of a civilization that has ever been assembled. What would we not give for a comparable record of the Constitutional Convention, the Jacksonian campaign, the Civil War—or for that matter the Peloponnesian War or the Crusades! It is hoped that somewhere the industry is preserving a comprehensive archive of all documentary films and all news broadcasts. The film industry failed to provide such an archive and we have lost thousands of films of inestimable value, and must go abroad for many of those which have been, somehow, preserved.

Yet here, in the achievements of the documentaries and the reports and the newscasts, we are confronted again with that curious gap between technological achievement and intellectual that strikes us in so many other fields. We have hitherto believed (it has been an article of faith since Jefferson) that if only the people were informed democracy would work, that all that was really needed was to enlighten the people; they would do the rest. No other people in the past, or elsewhere on the globe (unless the British) have been and are so elaborately informed by documentaries, news commentary, panel discussions, and so forth. In all of this, television is at its best. Out of all this should have come the most mature body politic in history, the highest level of political discussion, the widest grasp of the complex issues of domestic and foreign relations. Television should have speeded up social reform, and it probably has, but only (as far as we can see) where the inclination was there before. It has not, for example, notably educated the whites of Alabama to the realities of race relations. It should have added new dimensions to education, but so far it has added new techniques rather than new dimensions. It is not even clear that this generation is better informed on the most elementary levels about politics or international relations than the pre-television generation. It should have given the whole people a much deeper feeling for the beauty and the value of our natural resources: forest and soil, river and lake; but there is little evidence that it has in fact achieved anything here. The generation of television is also the generation when the ruin of the landscape, the pollution of the air, and the decay of the city reached a terrifying climax.

Even in the educational arena, where television has things all its own way, as it were, where it *has* contrived new techniques, where it has a receptive and cooperative audience, its achievements have been disappointing. And if we look away from formal educational television, the kind intended purely for classroom instruction, the failure is even more unmistakable.

If we compare television with the university or with an institu-

tion almost as new as television itself, the great foundation, we see
at once the nature of the failure. Even those departments of television devoted to information have greater resources than most
universities or foundations, but what do they have to show for
their resources? There is educational television, to be sure, now at
long last changing from a stepchild to a legitimate child. Now and
then commercial television gives us a brief interlude of culture, and
does it very well indeed: *The Glory That Was Greece,* perhaps, or
The Story of Columbus, or a Gielgud *Hamlet.* But these are exceptions. Frequently highbrow productions turn out to be as mere-
tricious as the usual fare. On the whole the contribution of this
new and potentially powerful medium to education or to enlargement of intellectual horizons is meager, and more than counterbalanced by its contributions to noneducation, to the narrowing of
intellectual horizons. Television has so far performed none of the
central functions of the academy except, perhaps, fortuitously. It
neither transmits knowledge of the past to the next generation, nor
contributes to professional training, nor expands the boundaries
of knowledge.

Unquestionably the primary function of television is entertainment. We cannot doubt that television does this task reasonably
well; whether it could, in fact, do it better or not is another matter.
But relevant here is the observation of Lord Reith of the BBC: "It
will be admitted by all that to have exploited so great a scientific
invention for the purpose and pursuit of entertainment alone,
would have been a prostitution of its powers and an insult to the
character and intelligence of the people."

Nor can the masters of television escape responsibility for the
low level of much that passes for entertainment by insisting, as
they do, that they are merely giving the public what it wants. It is
not at all clear that it is the audience that has imposed its standards
on television, not television which has imposed its own standards
and its notions about how to make money on the audience. Nor is
it clear that the good done by bringing some pleasure to the old,
the infirm, and the housebound outweighs the harm done to a
whole society by debasing the public taste or pandering to a taste
already debased, and discrediting or making obsolete the habits of

self-entertainment which, after all, kept most people happy for a good many centuries. To prove by statistics that so many million people watch a professional football game is not to prove that they would not be better and happier if their tastes had not been so corrupted that they were incapable of doing anything else.

All of these failings: timidity, unoriginality, lack of professional standards, lack of leadership, the passion for the lowest common denominator, can be laid at the door of the sponsor system. And if we ask why television, alone of respectable media, has allowed itself to get into this fix, the answer again is fairly easy. Television needs the support of sponsors so desperately that it thinks it has to take it on terms the sponsors lay down. And the reason for this is that television has allowed itself to get caught up in a spiral of rising costs that has deprived it of independence. An analogy here is big-time college football, which forfeits amateur status and therefore its purpose. Is it not clear that television is in the process of corrupting itself and its audience and perhaps much of the business and academic community by following this *ignis fatuus* of high costs? Is it not on the face of it absurd that any actor should earn ten times what we pay the President of the United States and twenty-five times what we pay a justice of the Supreme Court? The scandal of the decline of original and brilliant programs in favor of series, the scandal of interruptions for "messages" from sponsors so frequent that they all but ruin interest in a film or a football game, these can be laid squarely at the door of spiraling costs. Why should there not be an agreement to eliminate costs which are on the face of it absurd? Why should there not be limits on what television will pay to film a football game, a Broadway play, a popular novel? If television cannot itself work out some method of limiting these costs, why should not the FCC, or some other agency of the government (let us say the Treasury Department) intervene in this matter. Television is, after all, a public utility and its expenses should be scrutinized just as are the expenses of telephone or electrical utility companies. Suppose the Treasury were to rule that any amount over X dollars (let us say over one thousand dollars a week or ten thousand dollars for a sporting event) was illegitimate and could not be charged to expenses; that might be painful to some people now making large fortunes, but it would immensely benefit the American public.

Why is it that almost alone of public utilities the television permits itself these exorbitant expenses? No university pays a million dollars a year for even the greatest scholar; no symphony orchestra for the most talented of conductors; no hospital for the most skillful of surgeons. Television itself should welcome regulation here which might save it, and the American society, from even further corruption.

The pervasive evil, then, is loss of control. We will never have a strong, independent television unless we change this most fundamental of all factors. Let advertisers take their chances in television as they do in the *New York Times* or *Life* Magazine, as they do even on ITV in England. If newspapers and journals can command a large and affluent audience by special features (let us say *Peanuts*, or good sports coverage, or Walter Lippmann), advertisers choose them for their purposes. The advertiser in newspapers and magazines is not in fact very much interested in editorial opinion because he has learned that editorial policy makes little difference in the effectiveness of advertising. If *The New Republic* should somehow achieve a two-million circulation we might be reasonably sure that its advertising would boom, just as the advertising of *Playboy* boomed with a three-million circulation. Let the advertisers learn this lesson in television.

What will the historian say of television when, a quarter of a century from now, he comes to assess its meaning and evaluate its significance? What difference will he conclude it made in the life of the nation, or in the progress of civilization? That it made a quantitative contribution in entertainment, and therefore the use of time, will at once be conceded. But what qualitative contribution did it make?

Alas, that is difficult to answer, far more difficult than with other media: the printing press, the university, even the film. Television has not connected itself with the great issues of American, or of modern life. It has made little or no contribution to the solution of those problems which glare upon us ceaselessly from every quarter of the horizon—to urban rehabilitation, to saving the natural resources of the nation: soil, water, forest, air; to education (here it should have made its greatest impact but has not); to civil rights and civil liberties; to population control; to healing the friction of the cold war and making for international understanding—with China, for example; to advancing the cause of world peace.

There are, in television and out, ample resources to illuminate these and other problems. The task is to enlist them on behalf of society rather than on behalf of private industry, profit, or enterprise. Who can doubt that in time the opportunity to use this great medium of enlightenment for public welfare and the progress of society and civilization will prove irresistible to the men and women of good will?

STUDENT RECRUITMENT

AND

UNIVERSITY RESPONSIBILITY

6

All across the country, from Harvard Yard to Madison and Berkeley, students are taking into their own hands, and hearts, what university administrators have so heedlessly failed to take into their hands or their minds: the problem of the obligation of the university to private corporations and to government. Students are protesting and, where protests are ineffective, demonstrating against the practice of lending the facilities of the university to recruitment of students by corporations and the military. Sometimes their protest takes the form of forcibly banning recruiters from university facilities, thus exposing them to the wrath of deans and presidents who, unwilling to face the central issue of on-campus recruitment, embrace with enthusiasm the marginal issue of bad manners.

For the explosion of this controversy on campus, the university authorities have only themselves to blame. The crisis developed because the academy failed to anticipate it, failed to think about it, and failed therefore to formulate any policy which could stand the test of logical scrutiny. Nor are universities now formulating any policy. Instead they are, most of them, sullenly taking refuge in precedent or invoking irrelevant arguments of "freedom of infor-

The New Republic, February 24, 1968.

mation." Student demonstrations against recruitment are, then, a monument to the absence of foresight and of imagination in university administrators and an excess of imagination in students. All who are concerned with the academic enterprise will agree that an excess of imagination, and of moral passion, in the young is to be preferred to the absence of either.

University spokesmen everywhere have spread a fog of confusion over what should be a relatively simple issue.

The basic principle which should govern the relations of the university to recruiters is that which should govern all other activities of the academy. The university is an educational institution. It is not an employment agency; it is not an adjunct of corporations; it is not an instrument of government. Wherever feasible the university should make available its facilities to legitimate educational enterprises. It is under no obligation whatsoever to make its facilities available to what is not educational.

Now guided by this simple principle the university can deal with this awkward problem of recruiting with reasonable consistency and fairness. As in all situations there are, and will be, exceptions and borderline cases. This need not disturb us overmuch; there are—as Supreme Court opinions testify daily—exceptions and borderline cases in the interpretation of the Constitution and the Bill of Rights. So far, however, none of these borderline cases has caused any difficulties: students have not protested against recruitment by the Peace Corps, or Head Start, or the United Nations, and it is unlikely that they will. The organizations whose recruiting has precipitated the crisis throughout the academic world are not borderline cases. By no stretch of the imagination can it be alleged that Dow Chemical Company, the Marines, and the CIA are educational enterprises, or that they contribute anything to education. Dow Chemical is a business corporation; its business is to make money, and it recruits students at universities because that is one of the ways it hopes to make money. That is no doubt a laudable activity, but no university is under any obligation whatever to help Dow Chemical make money. The Marines and the Navy, admirable as they are, are not educational enterprises. Their business is to fight. The university is, no doubt, an interested party in this enterprise, just as it is an interested party in tax collecting or in the maintenance of law and order, but it is under no more obligation to lend its facilities to the Marines and the Navy than it is to lend them to the Treasury or the Justice Departments.

But, it is asserted, every student has a right to hear what these, and other, organizations have to say. So they have, and a university which sought to deny them this right would be derelict in its duty to its students and to its own character. The argument is, however, wholly irrelevant to the situation which confronts us. Every student has a right to a great many things that the university is not obliged to provide. He has a right to read all newspapers, all magazines, and all books, but the university is not obliged to provide him with all newspapers, magazines, and books. It subscribes to the *New York Times* and *Foreign Affairs,* not to the racing *Morning Telegraph* or to *Playboy.* Any student who wants to read these can buy them at the local newsstand, but anyone who argued that the principle of free access to information required the university library to subscribe to these would be regarded as bereft of his senses. So any student who wants to hear what Dow Chemical or the CIA wants to say can, without serious inconvenience, visit them off campus. Dow Chemical, like all corporations, can rent space in local office buildings just as it buys space in local newspapers. The Marines and the CIA can use the local post office to conduct interviews. Except at a very few colleges, so remote from civilization that there are neither stores nor offices nor post offices available, no student (and no recruiter) will be seriously inconvenienced if universities adopt the common-sense rule of confining the use of their facilities to purposes that are incontrovertibly educational.

Balanced against what is merely ingrained habit or, at the most, the inconvenience to a few students of walking a few blocks to office building or post office, are two considerations of considerable importance. First is the principle (if it rises to the dignity of that) that the college should not throw its facilities open indiscriminately to all comers—business, religious, fraternal, political, military—for if it did it would find those facilities swamped. It must, and in fact it does, even now, discriminate. Even those who defend most ardently the "right" of students to interview Dow Chemical are not prepared to provide facilities for the Rotary, the Lions, and the Kiwanis, the Elks and the Masons and the Woodmen of the World, the Baptists, the Mormons and the Jehovah's Witnesses, and so on *ad infinitum*. The only sound basis for discrimination is educational. The second principle is more fundamental. When the university is called upon to weigh the conflicting claims of those who plead habit, or convenience, against those who plead deep moral convictions—moral convictions which are shared by a large segment of our society and are therefore neither eccentric nor perverse—it should not hesitate to tip the balance on the side of moral convictions. Certainly it is unworthy of the academy to drift —or to allow itself to be maneuvered—into a position where out of stubbornness, out of thoughtlessness, out of inertia, it flouts the legitimate moral sentiments of its students and its faculty. To argue that some students may entertain moral convictions about seeing recruiters on campus rather than off campus is frivolous, for it ascribes moral significance to what is a mere matter of personal convenience.

Some institutions—prepared to concede that they are not, in fact, under any obligation to provide facilities for recruiting to private corporations—do insist, or at least assert, that they have some kind of moral obligation to cooperate with government, especially at a time of crisis and war. Therefore, they add, even though government has ample facilities already available to it in federal, state, and local governmental buildings, the university should stand ready to lend its premises to government recruiters.

This is a plausible argument when used selectively, but not persuasive when applied indiscriminately. It has, for example, been defiantly asserted that even the CIA has a legitimate claim on the university, and may demand access to its facilities under any circumstances. Quite aside from the implication—which is of course absurd—that a student who wishes to see a CIA representative can do so only in some college office, what is ominous here is the readiness to extend hospitality to the CIA.

Time and again in the past, the university has acknowledged an obligation to cooperate with state and national government—and keep in mind that what we are considering here is not an obligation to obey the law, but a voluntary cooperation which is beyond the obligation of the law. Does it follow from past and current practice that the university has an obligation to cooperate with every branch, every department, every bureau of government for any and all purposes?

Such a conclusion is clearly untenable, and universities have already rejected it. Few universities are prepared to make available to snooping committees of legislatures, or even to the FBI, the names of members of all student organizations. Many have refused to provide draft boards with records of student grades. No self-respecting university now would cooperate with un-American activities committees, state or national, in investigating professors. Nor are universities under obligation to lend their facilities indiscriminately to the enforcement of laws. The laws of Massachusetts (and until recently of Connecticut) made the use of contraceptives by anyone, single or married, a misdemeanor; it is scarcely conceivable that any university in that state, public or private, would entertain a request from state law enforcement agencies to help discover and bring to justice members of faculty or student body who violate these laws. Nor do universities yield, generally, to the plea of convenience. If students want information on taxes, they expect to go to the local tax authorities, or perhaps to a bank; if they want information on voting they go to the town hall; if they want to take out a driver's license, they go to the local police. The universities are not expected to provide these services, or even to provide facilities where these government agencies can give out "information."

Even when it comes to carrying out programs of scientific research, which are clearly educational in character, universities do not casually or indiscriminately make available their offices and laboratories or libraries, but select what is valuable to *them,* and then draw up contracts which carefully safeguard the right of the university to supervise the research, protect scholars, and avoid secrecy, and which provide, too, for compensation for the use of academic facilities.

Does the university then have the right—the moral right, for the legal is clear beyond dispute—to decide with which governmental activities it will cooperate? Does it have the right to say yes to the Peace Corps, but no to the Marines, yes to the Smithsonian Institution, but no to the CIA?

Let us consider—because it is the most controversial of them all—the obligation of the university to the CIA.

The readiness of the university to lend its facilities and its good name to the CIA is clearly the most notorious example of the fix in which it finds itself when it blindly follows the principle of the open door to all governmental agencies.

For the CIA is, by definition, subversive of the academy. Its business is subversion at home as well as abroad, and by giving it a free hand and ample money, the Congress has endorsed this function. It has, by its own admission, subverted universities, scholars, student organizations, research, publications, even churches and philanthropic institutions. Its whole character is at war with what the university stands for. It loves secrecy, but the university flourishes only in the light. It takes refuge in anonymity, but the university must know the credentials of those to whom it gives its confidence. It is chauvinistic, but the university is by its nature cosmopolitan and international and does not acknowledge national boundaries to knowledge. It works not to find and certainly not to proclaim truth, but the major purpose of the university is to extend the frontiers of truth.

Clearly the university is under no obligation to collaborate with the CIA simply because it is a government agency. This conclusion has not only the sanction of centuries of the history of universities; it has legal sanction as well. For to the argument that the university should not look beyond the official credentials of an agency of the government—an argument advanced with considerable earnestness by those who wish to avoid the moral issue—we must consider the counter-argument of the legal principle adopted by the United States at the time of the Nuremberg war-crimes trials. The official American position, submitted by no other than Supreme Court Justice Robert Jackson, was quite simply that no citizen is bound to accept as legal and valid every act of his government, nor can he avoid responsibility for his conduct by placing responsibility on the government. This position was accepted by the tribunal, and under it men like Albert Speer, Minister of Munitions, were found guilty. It is not necessary to argue that the CIA is violating international law; it is enough to recognize the validity of the principle that institutions such as universities are not precluded from inquiring into the credentials of such branches of the government as make demands upon them.

Whatever we may think about the larger place of the CIA in the general scheme of national defense, we can scarcely avoid the conclusion that it is degrading for the university to lend its facilities, and a reputation painfully won over a period of eight hundred years, to cooperate in its own subversion. It is degrading for it to extend the hand of fellowship to those who are engaged in perverting its character.

Even those who are prepared to concede in principle the right of students to oppose corporate or military recruiting on campus deplore the manner in which they have asserted, or demonstrated, that right. Almost everywhere student demonstrations have been accompanied by bad manners, and in some places by force and violence. Now it is clearly very wrong for the young to display discourtesy in these situations, and quite intolerable for them to resort to violence, even the somewhat negative violence of refusing access to a recruiting-office room. Clearly the young should model themselves here on those who are older and wiser, model themselves on the spokesmen and representatives of our nation, on whom rests ultimate responsibility for the maintenance of an orderly society. What a pity that they do not follow the example, in their protests, of distinguished statesmen like Senators Long and Stennis, who think all dissenters should be failed; of Presidential candidate George Wallace, who thinks they should be shot; or of Congressman Rivers of South Carolina, who thinks the proper response to flag burning is burning the Bill of Rights. What a pity that they do not model themselves on official defenders of law and order like the police of Watts, Cleveland, Detroit, Newark, and Philadelphia, or the U.S. marshals in Washington. How distressing that they do not conform to the models of the military who try so hard to enlist them, General "Bomb-Them-Back-to-the-Stone-Age" Le May, for example, or the Air Force officers who habitually fly over Communist China in violation of international law. How much wiser they would be if they studied the conduct of the CIA, whose interests their deans so sedulously protect, which has never been known to resort to violence, and which conducts its operations in some sixty countries around the globe with the nicest regard to the legal amenities. How it would improve their characters if instead of milling about the campus in futile demonstrations they resorted to their libraries and read how their government eschewed violence and championed law at the time of the Bay of Pigs invasion of Cuba, or of the intervention by Marines in Guatemala and Santo Domingo. How much wiser they would be if they had studied the Kellogg-Briand Peace Pact, or the Charter of the United Nations, and reflected on their own government's faithfulness in its commitment to these renunciations of war. But we should remember that students are very young, and that they have not had the training and experience which have made their leaders such models of moderation and of reason.

On this whole matter of the discourtesy and the violence that so often accompany demonstrations it is relevant to recall what the Rev. Samuel Jo. May—he was uncle to the Little Women—wrote to his friend the Rev. William Ellery Channing about the demonstrations of abolitionists against slavery:

You must not expect those who have left to take up this great cause [of abolition] that they will plead it in all that seemliness of phrase which the scholars . . . might use. But the scholars and the clergy and the statesmen had done nothing. We abolitionists are what we are— babes, sucklings, obscure men, silly women, publicans, sinners, and we shall manage the matter we have taken in hand just as might be expected of such persons as we are. It is becoming in abler men who stood by, and would do nothing, to complain of us because we manage this matter no better.

To this Dr. Channing answered in words that apply to the demonstrators against the Vietnam War as to the abolitionists: "The great interests of humanity do not lose their claims on us because sometimes injudiciously maintained."

Indeed they do not. Yet more and more those in authority, in the academy as in government, are avoiding moral issues and taking refuge in questions of conduct or of manners. Instead of falling back on the familiar principle, "I disagree with what you say but shall defend to the death your right to say it," they substitute, "I may agree with you, but I disapprove profoundly of the manner in which you say it."

What is this silence that has fallen on the leadership of the university in America—presidents, deans, boards of trustees and regents alike? The leaders of the religious community have spoken out boldly enough—heads of great theological seminaries, distinguished theologians, and clergymen. The scientific community— Nobel Prize winners, and heads of scientific organizations—has taken a strong stand on the moral issues of the war and of nuclear weapons. The rank and file of the academic community, teachers, scholars, students, have seen clearly enough that here were moral issues that must be faced, and have wrestled with them. But from Cambridge to Berkeley, from Madison to Baton Rouge, not a single president of a great university has taken a public stand on what is the greatest moral issue of our time.

Why stand they silent? Is it because they are bemused by the notion that with their position they take a vow of moral continence? They did not reason so in the past—not at the time of the two World Wars, not during discussions of the League of Nations or of Communism. Is it because they fear that if they spoke out like independent men they would somehow "commit" their institutions? If so they are mistaken in fact and in logic. No president can commit his university, which consists of faculty and students, to a moral position or a political one. No one supposes that a senator who speaks out somehow commits the United States Senate, or that a judge who speaks his mind commits the Supreme Court, or even that a business executive can commit his corporation and his stockholders to political positions. Why should presidents or deans indulge in the vanity of supposing that they can somehow commit great universities? Yet here they stand numbed by timidity, palsied by indecision, taking refuge from the obligation to confront great moral questions by escaping instead into the easy activity of applying petty disciplinary measures to students who embarrass them.

If presidents, deans, trustees, and regents are unwilling or unable to protect and exalt the dignity of the university, they should be grateful to students who have remembered it and exalted it. If universities have refused to face the major moral issues of our day they should rejoice that they have, somehow, helped to produce students who are neither paralyzed nor timid, who are sensitive to moral issues and prepared to respond to them, however convulsively.

On this matter of recruitment, as on the larger issues of the relation of the academy to the moral problems which confront us from every quarter of the horizon, this generation of university presidents, so respectable, so cautious, may yet hear from their own students that immortal taunt of Henry IV: "Go hang yourself, brave Crillon; we fought at Arques and you were not there."